COMPLETE
SEA KAYAK
TOURING

COMPLETE
SEA KAYAK
TOURING

JONATHAN HANSON

RAGGED MOUNTAIN PRESS • CAMDEN, MAINE

NEW YORK • SAN FRANCISCO • WASHINGTON, D.C.
AUCKLAND • BOGOTÁ • CARACAS • LISBON • LONDON
MADRID • MEXICO CITY • MILAN • MONTREAL • NEW DELHI
SAN JUAN • SINGAPORE • SYDNEY • TOKYO • TORONTO

International Marine/
Ragged Mountain Press

A Division of The McGraw·Hill Companies

10 9 8 7 6 5 4 3 2 1

Library of Congress Cataloging-in-Publication Data
Hanson, Jonathan
       Complete sea kayak touring / by Jonathan Hanson.
              p.   cm.
       Includes index.
       ISBN 0-07-026204-7
       1. Sea kayaking   I. Title.

GV788.5H36   1998
797.1′244—dc21   97-48590
                                            CIP

Questions regarding the content of this book should be addressed to:
Ragged Mountain Press
P.O. Box 220
Camden, ME 04843
207-236-4837

Questions regarding the ordering of this book should be addressed to:
The McGraw-Hill Companies
Customer Service Department
P.O. Box 547
Blacklick, OH 43004
Retail customers: (800) 262-4729
Bookstores: (800) 722-4726

Visit us on the World Wide Web
www.books.mcgraw-hill.com

Printed by Quebecor Printing Company, Fairfield, PA
Design by Daniel Kirchoff
Project management by Janet Robbins
Production assistance by Mary Ann Hensel and Shannon Thomas
Page layout by Publishers' Design and Production Services, Inc.
Edited by Pamela J. Benner, Tom McCarthy

All illustrations by the author, unless otherwise noted.

To Roseann

Warning: This book is not intended to replace instruction by a qualified teacher nor to substitute for good personal judgment. In using this book, the reader releases the author, publisher, and distributor from liability for any injury, including death, that might result.

CONTENTS

PART FOUR

TRANSPORT, MAINTENANCE, AND REPAIR   182

12. Traveling with a Kayak   183

13. Maintenance, Repair, and Modification   191

Appendix A: Resources   201

Appendix B: Provisioning Lists   211

Appendix C: English and Metric Conversions   213

Index   214

ACKNOWLEDGMENTS

I'd like to thank Tommy Thompson, who not only sold me my first sea kayak, but sent it home with me on the basis of a handshake agreement that I would make payments. Although we went on to become friends, it was his friendship to a stranger I remember most.

To other good paddling partners: John Gentile and Katie Iverson, who taught me just how much food and gear an average sea kayak can hold and still float; Michael Cox, always willing to push the envelope of rough-weather landing technique; and my wife, Roseann, as delightful a partner on land as on water.

Many thanks to Tom Derrer of Eddyline Kayaks, for building fine boats, and Rich Wilson of Snap Dragon Design, for excellent spray skirts. Thanks also to Chris Cunningham and Karen Matthee of *Sea Kayaker* magazine, who originally recommended Roseann and me to Ragged Mountain Press.

I extend much respect—and many lighthearted jabs throughout this book—to Derek Hutchinson, Britain's ambassador of sea kayaking. His vast experience, good humor, and often infuriating imperialism have informed and entertained his readers on both sides of the Atlantic for years. If he is sentenced to purgatory for any time, it will be in a 28-inch-wide American sea kayak with an enormous rudder, giant square cargo hatches secured with rubber bands, and a fully upholstered, reclining seat with vibro-massage, riding out a Force 10 storm off Fastnet Rock.

Finally, thanks very much once again to everyone at Ragged Mountain Press. The enthusiasm, support, and unflaggingly cheerful moods of Jeff Serena, Jonathan Eaton, Tom McCarthy, Katie McGarry, and April Emery continue to make me deeply suspicious of all of them.

INTRODUCTION

A HORIZON FILLED WITH ADVENTURE

The memory of most events in our lives fades with time. Some, though, because of a particular impact they create, retain perfect clarity—a first kiss, the first glimpse of a foreign land from an airplane window, a transcendent passage in a book. One of those events for me was the sight of my first sea kayak.

Ironically, I was 200 miles from the nearest body of salt water, looking through the dusty window of an outdoor shop in Tucson, Arizona. The shop was closed and the lights off, but by the late afternoon sun angling through the glass I could see it, hung in nylon slings from a wooden rafter. Its long ivory hull was elemental in shape, the distillation of *boat* to its simplest form. The forest green deck was peaked to shrug off waves, its businesslike appearance reinforced by the mounted compass, strapped-down cargo hatches, and sturdy rudder. I thought it was the most romantic-looking craft I had ever seen, and the next day I convinced the shop owner—who would later become a friend and mentor—to take payments out of my meager part-time-student income.

The promise of that first impression was not only fulfilled, but exceeded again and again in journeys to the Sea of Cortez, the Pacific Northwest, and the Arctic Ocean. The magic of exploring the sea in a craft reduced to pure, graceful function has never dimmed.

There are those who say the great age of exploration is over, that even real adventure travel is dead. Those people have never been in a sea kayak.

Certainly all the continents have been mapped, all the big peaks climbed, and all the oceans crossed—but a new dimension of discovery still awaits us, on a more intimate level. I think of it as fractal exploration: you take smaller bites of the world, but examine them more closely. It may seem a presumptuous example, but a sea kayaker who traverses a 100-mile stretch of the Arctic coast of Canada will see more of that stretch than Amundsen did when he steamed by in *Gjöa* on his way to conquering the Northwest Passage.

The continents were first explored on foot, and subsequently traversed by train, motorcar, and bicycle, which trampled into obscurity the footprints of the first adventurers. But the opposite sequence is occurring in the ocean. Having crossed the seas and charted the coasts with sailing ship and steamer, now are we returning to explore the same waters in small human-powered boats. Indeed, within this century kayaks have even crossed oceans. First Franz Romer, and then Hannes Lindemann used Klepper folding kayaks to cross the Atlantic; more recently Ed Gillette used a modified fiberglass double kayak on a 60-day voyage from San Diego to Hawaii. While each of these men utilized sail power to augment paddling, their feats nevertheless represent the outer envelope of kayak journeys.

The spirit of exploration still burns in the human heart, but our perception of the world as having already *been done* often warps our quests for adventure into mere stunts. Children flying light aircraft across the country, people rollerblading coast to coast, Range Rovers retracing the route of Hannibal—these undertakings might be technically difficult or physically challenging, but they push no frontiers beyond those of absurdity. Not so with sea kayaking—the simple grace of a small boat powered by a single person resists any taint of outlandishness. When Howard Rice paddled a folding kayak alone around Cape Horn, one of the most difficult tests of seamanship in the world, he established his name with the likes of Sir Francis Chichester—not with those who jump semitrucks over school buses.

Very few of us are capable of paddling around Cape Horn—but we can all challenge our personal frontiers with a sea kayak. The first zigzag paddle across a sheltered harbor is like a first wobbly bicycle ride: excitement and pride at a new accomplishment, and a sense of vast potential for adventure. This book is intended to help realize that potential.

I've written *Complete Sea Kayak Touring* around what, for me at least, is the raison d'être of the modern sea kayak: exploring remote coastlines, with the ability to be not only self-sufficient but comfortable, for days or weeks at a time. The goal is to give you the information needed to plan and realize your own adventures. Some of the contents will be lighthearted, some will be downright morbid, but the aim is the same: a safe and enjoyable journey. And, although this book covers some essential ground (water?) regarding technique and equipment, it was not intended as a beginner's guide to sea kayaking. *Complete Sea Kayak Touring* offers those already familiar with the basics a guide to expanding their explorations with multiday trips—from weekend getaways to full-on expeditions. Keep in mind that all the information herein, whether it be rescue techniques or equipment selection, is oriented to the goal of traveling safely with a loaded kayak.

The book is divided into four parts:

- *Part One: Touring Equipment*

  Chapter 1, "The Kayak," discusses kayak selection—how to pick the right boat for your needs, desirable characteristics of touring kayaks, and comparative discussions of different built-in accessories and features.

Chapter 2, "Necessary Gear," covers ancillaries such as paddles, spray skirts, and PFDs, in addition to dry bags and dry boxes.

Chapter 3, "Safety Gear," is an in-depth look at safety equipment, from paddle floats to flares, with some recommendations on what to carry for different trips.

Chapter 4, "Clothing," starts with some admonishments about the "T-shirts in Glacier Bay" phenomenon in kayak clothing, then suggests several alternative strategies for comfortable and safe paddling.

- *Part Two: Techniques for Touring*

  Chapter 5, "Paddling Techniques," might be remedial for some readers, but it discusses paddling technique from the perspective of a kayak loaded with gear.

  Chapter 6, "Rescues and Recoveries," is a pragmatic approach to handling trouble. Every situation covered assumes you'll be paddling a kayak that is full of gear. I've simplified a few techniques, and debunked a couple others.

  Chapter 7, "Seamanship," introduces the reader to the moods and currents of the sea—the part-scientific, part-instinctual, approach to understanding the ocean; an understanding we call seamanship.

  Chapter 8, "Navigation and Piloting," combines the general information given in Chapter 7 with some essential chart-and-compass work to help you plot your own coastal journeys, with tips on handling currents, shipping traffic, and other navigation issues.

- *Part Three: Camping Equipment and Techniques*

  Chapter 9, "Camping Gear," covers—you guessed it—tents, sleeping bags, stoves, and many other items, from the perspective of a paddler. Basic equipment coverage is interspersed with tips on a few luxuries.

  Chapter 10, "Planning, Provisioning, and Packing," talks about how to plan for a trip, how to shop for food, how to fit it all in the boat, and what to add for extended expeditions.

Chapter 11, "Camping," offers much about how to choose good campsites, how to be comfortable in the wilderness, and how to enjoy related activities such as hiking and beachcombing.

• *Part Four: Transport, Maintenance, and Repair*

Chapter 12, "Traveling with a Kayak," deals with safely transporting your kayak by car, truck, airplane, and ferry. Finally . . .

Chapter 13, "Maintenance, Repair, and Modification," is a nuts-and-bolts introduction to field and at-home repairs, proper gear care and storage, and customizing.

Throughout the book, I have kept several major goals in mind: first, to orient everything, whether rescues or paddle selection, toward the touring paddler interested in multiday kayaking trips. Second, I've tried to organize rescue and recovery techniques into a simple, logical strategy, and eliminate techniques that are dubious, redundant, or even dangerous for someone in a loaded kayak. And finally, I have hammered on areas that are neglected by too many paddlers—proper clothing and safety equipment, for instance—while keeping the tone light. I've tried to convey that safe kayaking is fun kayaking.

I'd like to add one more thing. Sea kayaking is the most rewarding and least-invasive means of traveling through some of the best places left on earth. It's not enough, any more, just to visit those places and store them away in our memory. We need to fight to preserve them. This fight isn't a difference of political philosophy like taxes or welfare or gun control, issues that can reverse course with each election. Once our last miles of virgin coastline are gone, they are gone forever. The tree farm that is replanted when an old-growth forest is logged bears no relation to the entity that preceded it.

The good news is, it has never been easier to fire effective volleys for this cause than it is now. Letters and petitions are wonderful, but all it takes is a toll-free call or e-mail to let yourself be heard. A list of conservation organizations and e-mail addresses at the end of Appendix A, "Resources," will get you started.

Enjoy the book, and happy paddling.

PART

ONE

T O U R I N G
E Q U I P M E N T

1
THE KAYAK

Choosing the Right Kind of Sea Kayak

A sea kayak is the most intimate oceangoing craft the world has ever known. It is also one of the most capable—but its seaworthiness depends in equal parts on boat and paddler. This vital fusion between the craft and its pilot is frequently neglected by both the stores that sell kayaks, as well as the people who buy them.

To exploit the kayak's inherent strengths, you must ensure a proper fit, which enables you to efficiently use *your* abilities to control the boat. The best way to shop for a sea kayak, then, is first to decide on the general type that suits your needs—single or double, rigid-hull or folding, and so on—and then try as many kayaks as you can until you find the one that feels right. With that in mind, we'll look first at the different classes of sea kayaks, then discuss design characteristics, dimensions, and details.

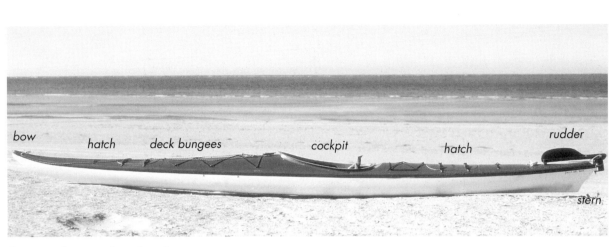

Features of a typical sea kayak.

SINGLE OR DOUBLE?

When I was leading sea kayaking trips, my fleet included both single and double kayaks, so couples could experiment paddling together or separately. Their preferences were invariably clear-cut regarding tandem kayaking: they either loved it or hated it. This decision had nothing to do with how the couple got along

on land—the most compatible pair in the group could transform into sniping, whining shrews when confined to the same boat.

If you are a couple contemplating sea kayaking, make sure you try a double kayak before buying one.

Double kayaks have several advantages over singles. First, a double kayak costs less than two singles (although two singles cost much less than a typical

Before buying a double kayak, test your ability to paddle in peace with a partner; sometimes two singles are better.

divorce). Doubles are more confidence-inspiring to novices, both because of their wider beam and the security—real or perceived—of having a companion in the same boat. Virtually any double kayak is faster than any single. Under certain circumstances, doubles are easier than singles to reenter in the event of a capsize, since the paddlers can assist each other directly. And double kayaks are great equalizers; that is, if one person is a weak paddler, and the other very strong, their efforts will complement each other. If they were in two singles, the weaker paddler would tend to lag behind.

But double kayaks have disadvantages as well. Gear space in a double is usually less than in two singles. The weight of a double—often close to 100 pounds—is harder to manage than that of two 60-pound singles, particularly when loading and unloading from a vehicle. Also, even if you get along fine in a double, it's often fun to separate a bit to explore different coves, or sing off-key without disturbing your partner.

The other factor that will enter into your decision is fit. If one of you is 5'1" and 100 pounds, and the other is 6'2" and 250, it will be hard to find a double with cockpits that will suit you both. With singles you can each get a boat that fits (see page 20, on proper kayak fit).

An important design factor on a double is the distance between the cockpits. If it is short, the paddlers have to synchronize their strokes, or their paddles will clash together. Doubles with a center storage compartment, or a third cockpit, don't force the paddlers to coordinate so closely.

TRADITIONAL OR SIT-ON-TOP?

Sit-on-top kayaks, with their open, self-draining cockpits, are great fun for putzing about harbors and coastlines. Technique is reduced to a minimum—there's no need for fancy rescue skills; if you fall over, you can just climb right back on. This makes sit-on-tops especially useful for snorkeling and scuba diving. Several models even have special recesses to strap in a scuba tank.

Sit-on-tops, however, have significant disadvantages for serious touring and expedition use. First, you are constantly exposed to the weather and water, which can be uncomfortable or dangerous in cold and stormy parts of the earth. Second, the storage space in most sit-on-tops is meager compared with traditional kayaks. Finally, at present virtually all sit-on-tops are *designed* as daytrippers—fairly short and broad, and thus not very efficient for long distances. I see signs that this is changing—Ocean Kayak now produces a model called the Scupper Pro, which is equipped with a rudder and has pretty decent storage. A few fringe designs are made for extreme surf kayaking and exploring exposed coasts; these are awesomely seaworthy, but still intended mostly for daytrips. For the paddler attracted to longer trips, who wants a craft that provides a combination of seaworthiness, storage, and weather protection, the extra investment in skill required by a traditional kayak is well worth it.

RIGID HULL OR FOLDING?

Although they now occupy but a corner of the market, folding kayaks such as the wood-framed Klepper and Nautiraid have been around much longer than rigid-hulled fiberglass and plastic kayaks. More recent folding designs, such as the Feathercraft, substitute aluminum and polyethylene in the frame, and use Cordura nylon instead of cotton canvas in the deck. Just about everyone uses heavy-duty Hypalon rubber in the hull.

The single outstanding advantage to a folding kayak is—it folds. If your kayaking plans include far-flung destinations such as the fjords of Chile or the Scottish lochs, a folding kayak can be checked on an international airline as excess baggage, then assembled into a seaworthy craft in less than 30 minutes. Transporting a rigid kayak to the same places would involve considerably more complex logistics—and considerably more money. Also, if your address is a one-bedroom apartment on the ninth floor, a folding kayak can be stored in a closet.

Many fans of folding kayaks are nearly religious in their devotion. Particularly in the case of the traditional wood-framed models, this attraction is understandable. After assembling a sturdy, capable craft from elegant substructures of gleaming, varnished ash and birch, even the most graceful fiberglass kayak looks like a soulless appliance.

No one can reasonably argue, however, that folding kayaks don't have certain drawbacks. Aficionados claim that the slightly flexible frame of a folder makes

Folding kayaks offer ultimate freedom: just pack it up, check it in, and fly anywhere in the world. In half an hour your craft is ready to take you on an adventure.

it more seaworthy, as the boat can follow the contours of the water to a degree. Possibly. That same flexibility, however, inevitably absorbs some of the paddler's energy as well, reducing efficiency. Likewise, some folding kayak manufacturers like to draw analogies between their hulls and the flexible, rubbery skin of dolphins and orcas, among the swiftest creatures in the sea. Suffice it to say that Hypalon stretched over an angular wood or aluminum frame has little in common with the organic fuselage of any marine mammal.

Because folding kayaks have no internal bulkheads, you must rely on the flotation in your dry bags if the boat is overturned and swamped. Most folders have inflatable *sponsons*—bladders that run along the

outside of the hull—that serve both to tighten the structure of the boat and provide some flotation, but they must be augmented for complete safety.

Another disadvantage of folding kayaks is their high initial cost, often nearly double that of a quality fiberglass equivalent. Supporters rightly point out the tremendous life span of a well-kept folder—many 25-year-old Kleppers are still in service. And when the skin of a folder finally meets its last patch, it can be replaced without having to buy a whole new boat. Keep in mind, though, that the price of just a new skin can be the same as that of an entire new fiberglass kayak. The many frame pieces of folders are subject to breakage as well, although they too can be replaced individually—or even fabricated from local materials in remote locations.

I think supporters of folding kayaks miss the point when they attempt to imbue their boats with spurious advantages over rigid kayaks. The simple fact is, a folding kayak can easily be transported to places practically inaccessible to fiberglass or plastic models, and will perform admirably in almost any conditions. Enough said.

If your kayaking is likely to be closer to home, or at least within driving range, and you have the storage space, a hard-shell sea kayak will probably be your first choice. In addition to the price advantage, a rigid kayak will have a stiff, hydrodynamically efficient hull, with greater storage space than an equivalent-size folding boat, since it has no internal frame. Built-in bulkheads will provide flotation at both ends, with convenient access to gear through hatches.

Another option for the traveling kayaker is the sectional hard-shell design. This is a fiberglass kayak made in (usually) three sections that bolt together. Each section has its own bulkhead, so that when the boat is assembled, each joint comprises a double thickness of fiberglass. It is an immensely strong system, possibly

DIY Kayak

Undoubtedly the most rewarding sea kayak to paddle is one you have built yourself. Several manufacturers offer plans or complete kits that anyone with some hand tools and minimal carpentry skills can construct.

Most kit kayaks are made from thin but strong marine plywood and are constructed using the "stitch-and-glue" technique. After the components of the boat are cut out, using a template, they are joined along the edges by drilling a series of holes through both pieces, then threading a length of wire through each hole and twisting it tightly to draw the sections together. The joint is then fiberglassed, creating a very rigid structure that is nevertheless astonishingly light in weight—often no more than 40 pounds, compared with 50 or 60 for a fiberglass or plastic boat.

More labor-intensive in construction is the fabric-covered, wood-framed kayak, barely a generation removed from the original Inuit designs. Using longitudinal stringers lashed to steam-bent frames, and covered with cotton duck or aircraft Dacron, these represent the ultimate in craftsmanship and authenticity.

Although they are perfectly efficient, plywood or fabric-covered kayaks would be prone to damage on an expedition, with a hundred or more pounds of gear inside. A moderately rough landing on a rocky shore could gouge the plywood or snap a frame member. When I build my own wood-framed kayak, I will reserve it for lightly loaded daytrips, in between which it will hang from the living-room ceiling as an objet d'art.

For a good primer, read *The Kayak Shop: Three Elegant Wooden Kayaks Anyone Can Build* by Chris Kulczycki (Camden, ME: Ragged Mountain Press, 1993), and consult *The Whole Paddler's Catalog,* edited by Zip Kellogg (Camden, ME: Ragged Mountain Press, 1997) for a wonderful compendium of historic references and do-it-yourself texts for building kayaks and more.

The Seal Landing

It was a very stormy morning off a rocky Baja coast, and my friend Michael and I were ready for a break. Instead of looking for a better stopping point, Michael decided to try an arcane British technique called a "seal landing," which involves surfing the crest of a wave as it washes over a large flat boulder on shore, theoretically depositing the kayak gently on the rock, after which the paddler nimbly hops out and drags the boat beyond the reach of the following wave.

Michael set up beautifully for a promising-looking rock—but at the last second the kayak broached just a tiny bit, and the wave dumped it with a nasty crunch *between* two large flat boulders. Mike hopped out and heaved on the bow toggle, but the boat was well and truly wedged, in addition to which the next wave dumped about 300 pounds of ocean into his cockpit.

I immediately performed an arcane American technique known as a "chicken landing"—I paddled down the coast for a half-mile until I found a sandy spot. It took us 30 minutes to get Mike's kayak unstuck and above the surf, only to find a foot-long split clear through the fiberglass on each side of the cockpit. Out came the duct tape, and two-thirds of the roll later, the kayak was once again seaworthy.

We portaged Michael's boat to a safer launching spot. As we paddled back past the ill-fated shore, Michael called to me, "Do you notice anything significant about that stretch?" When I said I didn't, he yelled, *"There aren't any seals there!"*

The author's companion attempted an ill-fated "seal landing" on this rocky Baja beach.

even stronger than a one-piece boat, although heavier by several pounds.

Sectional kayaks retain all the advantages of hard-shell kayaks but are significantly more portable—and storable—when disassembled. They still do not approach the portability of a folding kayak, however, which might take up no more space in its duffel bag than the center (cockpit) section of a sectional. You can transport your life jacket, spray skirt, and other items inside the sections, thereby saving some other luggage space.

I owned a sectional kayak for many years and found that in some ways it lived up to its promise, but in others didn't. While researching airline fares for a planned trip to the Canadian Arctic, I found that the sectional would be considerably cheaper to transport than a one-piece kayak, but still more than a folder. On another Arctic trip, when we hired a floatplane to return us to our vehicle, we discovered that the pilot preferred tying the assembled boat to a float, rather than putting it in the plane disassembled.

Choosing the Right Kayak Material

The question of what material your kayak will be made from will probably be answered by your budget. Kayak materials follow a nicely linear progression in both price and, in my opinion, performance. By performance I imply durability, strength, hydrodynamic efficiency, and appearance.

PLASTIC

Plastic—that is, rotomolded polyethylene—kayaks take a lot of grief from "purists," including myself. How we purists decided that a molded plastic boat is an aesthetic abomination, whereas fiberglass, which is technically known as FRP (fiber-reinforced plastic), represents "olde-worlde" craftsmanship, is beyond me. But there it is.

Rotomolded kayaks are formed in gigantic heated molds. Beads of plastic are poured in, and the whole mold spins slowly to distribute the material evenly across the kayak-shaped interior. The result is a strong, very resilient structure that is highly resistant to impacts from rocks and dropping—which is why virtually all whitewater kayaks are plastic. Plastic boats will take a lot of abuse on the ocean as well, but they are not invincible.

Plastic sea kayaks can be dragged over sharp-edged rocks with seeming impunity. But such treatment will abrade the hull, raising a fuzz on the surface and increasing hydrodynamic drag measurably. If a plastic boat is cinched down too tightly on a roof rack, or stored improperly, the hull can take a "set," warping the keel line out of true and drastically affecting the handling, until the material slowly resumes its proper shape (see Chapter 13, page 200, for recommended storage tips). Finally, polyethylene is subject to ultraviolet deterioration, to a greater or lesser degree depending on the boat's degree of exposure. In any case, plastic has a definite lifespan. The material eventually turns brittle and can shatter on impact without warning—although this condition often reveals itself by the appearance of little stress cracks around the through-hull fittings.

If the boat is made from linear polyethylene, it can at least be recycled at the end of its life. But if it's cross-linked polyethylene, often touted as a tougher material, it's just garbage. Because of its structure, cross-linked polyethylene cannot be remolded. Several manufacturers of linear polyethylene kayaks will pay freight charges if you send back the boat at the end of its life, so it can be reused—an admirable policy. The companies that make cross-linked boats don't want to see them again. Ask which material you're looking at, and let your conscience be your guide.

Another type of polyethylene is produced by the German company Prijon (pronounced Preeyon). Called HTP, it is blow-molded rather than roto-molded, and is said to be much stiffer than conventional polyethylene. It is also 100 percent recyclable, meaning it can be used to make new boats. Linear polyethylene can be recycled only into secondary products such as hatch covers.

To keep all the above comments in perspective, remember that a polyethylene kayak will go anywhere a fiberglass model can; so if your budget so dictates, don't hesitate to choose one. It might not be the last sea kayak you own, but it should be easy to sell to an aspiring paddler when you're ready to upgrade to . . .

FIBERGLASS

The first fiberglass sailboats were built a half-century ago. Many of those boats are still around, the hull material showing virtually no sign of degradation—in fact, it was discovered that fiberglass actually gets stronger after curing for a number of years.

Fiberglass is a nearly ideal material for sea kayaks as well. Besides being durable, it is lightweight, very rigid, and resistant to impact damage. While it can't match plastic in the latter regard, fiberglass is much easier to repair in the field—you can fix virtually any split in a fiberglass boat with duct tape, and keep right on paddling. And fiberglass, thanks to the glossy outer finish layer called *gelcoat,* is not only handsome but hydrodynamically slick too. The gelcoat is fairly easily scratched if the boat is dragged over rocks, but overall performance suffers little.

Fiberglass kayaks are laid up in two pieces—hull and deck—and joined together. Thus the hull can be a different color from the deck, avoiding the squeezed-from-a-tube look of rotomolded boats.

It's difficult to abuse a fiberglass kayak. Storing it in the sun will cause the gelcoat to fade and will rot webbing and bungees, but that's about it. After one trip in Baja I had to leave my kayak with a Mexican family for several months. It sat outside the entire time and had 4 inches of moldy water in it when I returned, but after a bath and a wax job it was just fine. A polyethylene boat treated that way would probably disintegrate into a large pile of plastic cornflakes, and imagine leaving a wood-and-canvas folding kayak in the same situation (of course, if I'd had a folding kayak I could have hitchhiked home with it in the first place!).

All fiberglass kayaks are not equal. Some manufacturers use a finer weave cloth in their layup, which improves the strength-to-weight ratio slightly. You can see the difference in cloth by examining the interior of the boat; the texture of the weave is apparent. However, standards in general among U.S., Canadian, and, increasingly, British makers are very high—it's hard to find a poorly built sea kayak. It is the details that vary most.

KEVLAR

Kevlar is the DuPont proprietary name for an extremely strong synthetic fiber called aramid (*aromatic polyamide*). The material comes in a cloth that is laid up in layers of resin, just like fiberglass. Kevlar is even stiffer than fiberglass, and thus boats made from it can be lighter while retaining similar or superior rigidity. Many manufacturers use strips of Kevlar to reinforce high-stress areas of their fiberglass kayaks, particularly along the keel line. Kevlar cloth can be identified by its golden color—many Kevlar kayaks are finished with a clear gelcoat to show off the material. An interesting characteristic of Kevlar is that it darkens with exposure to the sun, so don't be alarmed if your boat changes shades gradually.

Kevlar's only major disadvantage is its fiendishly high cost. A Kevlar kayak can cost $400 to $500 more than the same model in fiberglass, and the weight savings is rarely spectacular: a boat made of Kevlar might weigh 5 to 8 pounds less than a 55 pound boat made of fiberglass. Once you've loaded the boat with yourself and 200 pounds of gear, that hundred-dollar-a-pound difference seems pretty insignificant. Its real benefit comes when carrying the kayak, or lifting it onto a roof rack. If you commonly travel alone, own a tall sport-utility vehicle, or live where the tidal range often results in a 300-yard portage between vehicle and beach, Kevlar might be worth the cost. Otherwise, I usually advise people to put the money into lighter *paddles*, which will gain you more real performance than a light boat.

POLYCARBONATE

In another few years, this discussion of polycarbonate will probably appear right between polyethylene and fiberglass in the revised text, but since it's pretty new, I've tacked it on at the end. Tom Derrer at Eddyline Kayaks was the first to introduce a sea kayak made from a polycarbonate alloy, similar to the stuff in the lenses of ski goggles. The alloy is stiffer and more abrasion-resistant than polyethylene, and has the appearance of well-polished fiberglass—in fact, when Tom intro-

Kayak Terminology

- Beam: the measurement of the kayak across its widest point.
- Overall length: the distance from the bow to the stern.
- Waterline length: the length of the kayak at the waterline (because the bow and stern usually overhang somewhat, waterline length is less than overall length); waterline length increases as the boat settles in the water with a load.
- Wetted surface: the area of the kayak's hull that is under water, usually measured in square inches or square feet; wetted surface determines how much friction against the water the kayak produces, and it also increases with a load.
- Keel: the line along the very bottom of the kayak, from bow to stern.
- Rocker: the amount of upward curvature in the keel at bow and stern.

duced the new boats at a trade show, several competitors never realized they *weren't* fiberglass.

The polycarbonate comes in sheets, which are vacuum-molded into separate hulls and decks, just like a fiberglass boat, then joined along a seam, just like a fiberglass boat. This means the hull and deck can be different colors—just like a fiberglass boat. Eddyline says the material is more resistant to ultraviolet deterioration than polyethylene and is recyclable to boot. The cost slots in neatly between polyethylene and fiberglass. Although the company ran many accelerated-wear tests on the boats, their real-world durability has yet to be proven; but indications are very promising. It surely won't be long before other companies have climbed on this bus.

FOLDING KAYAKS

Wood-framed folding kayaks are the most esthetically delightful mass-produced sea kayaks in the world. Two veterans of the industry, the German company Klepper and the French Nautiraid, are still producing models similar to those they made decades ago, in both style and quality. Seavivor, a more recent American company, also makes very high-quality wood-framed boats.

Feathercraft, a Canadian manufacturer, has taken a decidedly more technological approach to their boats. The frames are made from high-density poly-

ethylene and anodized aluminum; the decks are Cordura nylon.

Both approaches work just fine; the differences are more in hull design. The Feathercraft K1 single and K2 double have dimensions and handling characteristics very similar to most hard-shell kayaks, whereas the Klepper Aerius I and II and Nautiraid boats are shorter and wider, making them astoundingly stable in small to medium seas, if slower and less responsive to body English. The Seavivor Greenland Solo and the Feathercraft Khatsalano are narrow high-performance craft more suited to advanced paddlers. (Whoops—I just found out Feathercraft is introducing a wide double, similar to but longer than the Klepper Aerius II. This is getting confusing.)

The wood-framed boats obviously require more maintenance, although, depending on your attitude, the yearly sanding and varnishing can be a pleasant task. The aluminum frame of the Feathercraft is virtually maintenance-free; on the other hand, the numerous pieces and very fine tolerances result in a longer assembly time, and occasional problems when wind-blown sand gets into the works. Still, the choice between high- and low-tech is largely personal preference rather than a distinct superiority of one style over the other.

One distinct advantage of Feathercraft boats is that they have access hatches front and rear, significantly easing gear loading, because you can reach in and pull or push gear into the ends of the boat. The Klepper has no hatches; furthermore, the Klepper expedition spray skirt tucks up under the cockpit rim and can be removed only by deflating the sponsons. Loading through the spray skirt is a pain (see Chapter 10, page 154, for an effective, if expensive, solution).

On the other hand, the Klepper can be equipped with an effective sail rig (see Chapter 5, page 77). You pays your money. . . .

For a listing of boat and accessories manufacturers and suppliers, see Appendix A, page 201.

INFLATABLES

High-quality inflatable kayaks, such as the Aire Sea Tiger, are the most portable of all kayaks, rolling up into a very small package. As long as the hull remains sound, they are unsinkable and can carry a lot of gear. As with sit-on-tops, however, you have no protection from weather and water, and furthermore your gear is all out in the open too, because there are no compartments. Inflatables also have more windage than do traditional kayaks; that is, they get blown around more.

Of course, the ever-present worry with an inflatable is that it might become a deflatable. But the material in a quality inflatable is amazingly tough, and can take a tremendous amount of abrasion on reefs and sand. In fact, I've seen an inflatable bounce bumper-car-like off a rock that surely would have holed a fiberglass kayak. The chief danger is from sharp punctures, and the material can easily be patched—as long as you're not in the middle of a 20-mile crossing when you stop to slice some cheese and stick your Swiss Army knife through a tube. Even then, the multiple chambers of the boat would prevent it from sinking, but you'd be clinging to nothing more than a glorified life jacket with only part of the hull inflated.

For exploring in tropical regions—say, island-hopping in the South Pacific—an inflatable would be an attractive option. Be prepared if you decide to consider one, though. The good ones approach the cost of a fiberglass kayak.

Design, Dimensions, and Performance

"Long, narrow kayaks are fast but tippy."
"Short, wide kayaks are stable but slow."
"Narrow kayaks are better in rough water."
"*Wide* kayaks are better in rough water."

These are but a few of the axioms you'll hear or read when shopping for a new sea kayak. Like most dogma, there is enough truth in each statement to, shall we say, hold water. But reality is more complex. There are so many variables in hull design, human anatomy, sea conditions, and intended usage that *any* blanket statement should be treated with suspicion. Let's look at a few of the parameters.

There are essentially four elements to a sea kayak's performance. In no particular order of importance, they are:

- Stability
- Speed
- Maneuverability
- Tracking—the ability to hold a course without wandering from side to side

Into this mix must be designed adequate storage space, a comfortable cockpit, and many other details. The perfect sea kayak would be utterly stable in any conditions, would turn on a dime, cruise effortlessly at 5 knots, hold a true course no matter what wind or waves or currents were doing, and be able to carry 300 pounds of gear. Of course, such a mix is impossible—it would be like having a pickup truck with the handling of a Porsche that got 50 miles to the gallon. So a designer must carefully balance all these desirable, but to some extent mutually exclusive, properties. The result is always a unique mix—you could assemble a group of 4, 5, even 10 kayaks from different makers, with apparently identical measurements, and each one would behave differently.

Although it's risky to separate each aspect of hull design and relate it to overall performance, while ignoring the effects of other aspects, it's the only way to get some sort of a handle on boat design—and how it affects the paddler.

LENGTH

Most single sea kayaks are between 15 and 19 feet long; doubles go from around 17 to 22½ feet. Varying the length affects the boat's performance in a couple of ways. All else being equal, a shorter hull will be more maneuverable, while a longer hull will track better. The best analogy I've heard to demonstrate this is sliding a ruler edge-down along a carpet and trying to turn it, then doing the same with a quarter. Obviously the quarter is easier to turn, while the ruler "holds a course" better. Whitewater kayaks essentially dispense with tracking ability to gain turn-on-a-dime maneuverability; a must in turbulent, boulder-strewn rapids. Sea kayaks, on the other hand, need to track well to avoid constant course corrections on long crossings, yet they must be reasonably maneuverable for exploring rocky coastlines and negotiating rough seas.

In theory, a longer hull also has a higher top speed than does a short hull. As any boat moves through the water, it creates both a bow wave and a stern wave. About 60 percent of the energy needed to propel the boat at top speed is used in creating and pushing these waves, and the farther apart they are, the easier they are to push. At a certain point, the boat essentially gets sucked down into the trough of its own waves, and paddling harder will result in little or no increase in speed. This "wall" is known as the *hull speed* of the craft, and is figured in knots by multiplying the square root of the waterline length by 1.34. For example, a kayak with a 16-foot waterline length has a hull speed of 5.36 knots, or about 6.2 miles per hour (a knot equals 1.15 miles per hour). This theoretical hull speed *can* be exceeded under certain circumstances, but it provides a clear point of reference for boats of different length. Of course, one way to far exceed it is with

a hull designed to plane on top of the water, but that takes far more power than a paddler can muster, and brings to mind the old joke about the slavemaster addressing the wretches chained to the oars on the Roman ship. "Well, boys, I've got good news and bad news. The good news is, double rations today. The bad news is, the captain wants to go waterskiing."

Okay, so a longer kayak is faster. The problem is, the higher hull speed of a longer boat is attainable only when you are paddling at maximum effort—which is rarely the case when touring. At lower speeds, another factor plays an increasingly important part: the wetted surface of the hull. This is the actual area that is under water when you and your gear are in the boat. The larger the wetted surface, the more friction against the water. Overcoming this friction takes about 40 percent of the paddler's effort at hull speed, but the proportion rises at slower speeds—at 3.5 knots, a normal touring pace, fully 85 percent of the resistance is friction, because the bow and stern waves are very small.

This means that, at average cruising speeds, a long kayak might actually take more energy to move than would a shorter boat with less wetted surface. An analogy—to go back to cars—would be a Porsche Carrera with a top speed of 150 miles per hour versus a Toyota Corolla that can do only 100—but when they both go 65 on the highway, the Toyota gets better gas mileage. So if someone tries to talk you into a long kayak just because "it's faster," use caution, and factor in your other needs first.

A characteristic closely related to length is the rocker designed into the hull. *Rocker* refers to how much higher the ends of the boat are than the middle when you view the boat from the side while it sits on a flat surface. A boat with a lot of rocker will turn faster than one with little rocker, at the expense of some tracking ability, because with the ends of the boat out of the water the craft functions as if it were shorter. This

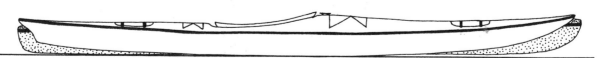

The hull of the kayak in front has considerable rocker; the hull of the kayak behind has very little.

The War of 1812 Revisited

For many years, a minor feud has been waged across the Atlantic Ocean, regarding the respective merits of American and British sea kayaks (or canoes, as they're sometimes called across the pond). A well-known British writer and designer once characterized American sea kayaks as suitable for "sheltered North American waters." Indeed, the slender British designs of the 70s and early 80s did seem ahead of the curve in seaworthiness, whereas American boats tended toward the large and comfortable. That disparity, real or imagined, has vanished, however. Modern American sea kayak designs span an enormous range of talent, while British designs have been influenced significantly by our market. Today it's possible to buy a seaworthy *and* comfortable kayak from either side of the Atlantic.

Nordkapp Kayak from Great River Outfitters.
(Courtesy Great River Outfitters)

One prejudice for which the British still make a strong case is their general disdain for rudders. They have a point—many Americans rely entirely on their rudder for boat control and are hard-pressed if a cable breaks in bad conditions. If your kayak has a rudder, you should practice without it as often as possible, so you won't be caught off-guard in the event of a failure. American designers have begun to adopt worthy British features such as perimeter lines around the deck, recessed deck fittings, and truly watertight rubber hatch covers, while British builders have improved the quality of their fiberglass layups, at which American builders have long excelled, and have even begun offering such hideously bourgeois fittings as backrests.

changes, however, when a load lowers the boat in the water, submerging more of the bow and stern.

Rocker figures into wetted surface as well. On paper, a boat with the least wetted surface for its volume would be shaped like half of a sphere. Look at a half a sphere from the "side," and it obviously has a great deal of rocker. So a kayak with a fair amount of rocker theoretically should have a bit less wetted surface, and thus be more efficient to paddle, than a similar boat with little or no rocker.

Here's the moral of the whole story: Tests have proved the differences in speed and efficiency among most touring kayaks to be very small at the pace most paddlers travel. So unless you're considering open-water races, pay more attention to your own size, to how the boat feels, and to your storage requirements than to what someone tries to tell you is fast or slow.

BEAM AND HULL SHAPE

Variation in the *beam,* or width, of a sea kayak, produces the most immediately noticeable difference in how the boat feels to a person sitting in the cockpit. A novice who tries both a 21-inch and a 24-inch beam will invariably prefer the wider craft, because of the greater apparent stability. On the other hand, many experienced kayakers feel that a kayak *has* to be narrow to be seaworthy. Neither perception is entirely true.

Kayakers refer to two kinds of stability: initial and final. *Initial stability* refers to the amount of side-to-side rocking motion you experience just sitting in the boat. *Final stability* is the big one, when you lean and lean and suddenly you're watching fish instead of birds. The two are not necessarily related—a boat can feel very stable at first, but capsize with little warning; another might feel very tippy initially but "firm up" as you lean it farther and farther.

A very wide kayak with a lot of initial stability is confidence inspiring at first. But when the waves begin kicking up—especially those coming broadside to the boat—the paddler needs to be able to lean the boat into the waves with body English, the goal being to keep the craft essentially level with the horizon. Otherwise the kayak will tip more and more as the waves steepen, until a capsize occurs. A too-wide kayak is like a multihull sailboat: it's stable in small to moderate seas, but once capsized, it's just as stable *upside down.*

A narrow kayak is usually easier to lean than a wide one. But a too-narrow boat will require constant vigilance, lest even a small wave catch you unaware and cause a capsize.

The cross-sectional shape of the hull has a strong influence on stability as well as feel. A hull with a shallow V bottom and sharp chines (a noticeable "corner" where the bottom of the hull meets the sides) usually displays a lot of initial stability, while a more rounded hull without chines rocks noticeably.

The ideal touring kayak strikes a balance between stability and responsiveness. The kayak should be easy to rock back and forth with body English, while displaying enough reserve stability that you can look around through binoculars, or take photographs, without feeling like you're walking a tightrope. Among all the kayaks I have paddled, this combination seems to occur most frequently in boats between 22 and 24 inches in beam. The one that works for you will depend on the specific hull shape, as well as your own

What About Capsizing?

Newcomers to kayaking tend to worry about capsizing. In a way, that's good—you should be aware of the possibility, and should practice the techniques in Chapter 6 so you'll know what to do if it happens. Once you practice a few controlled capsizes, you'll no longer be afraid of capsizing.

That said, modern sea kayaks are, for the most part, incredibly stable, and the chances of capsizing are low in anything but really rough conditions. Many, many sea kayakers never experience an unintentional capsize. So the rule is, prepare for it, then you won't have to worry about it.

size and proportions. One of the most seaworthy kayaks I've ever owned was quite wide—24¼ inches—with a very rounded hull that felt tippy at first, but got stiffer and stiffer the farther you leaned it. Despite its width, which many purists would have scoffed at, the boat was astonishingly self-sufficient in truly frightening conditions. Ever since, I have shunned the dogma that narrow kayaks are necessarily more seaworthy. On the other hand, I recently reviewed a boat that felt so stable I thought it must have been at least 24 inches wide. Not until I read the specs did I find out it was only 22 inches across.

VOLUME

It's easy to think of the volume enclosed by a sea kayak as simply the measure of how much gear it will hold. But both the amount and distribution of volume affect the boat's performance in other ways.

Some kayaks concentrate most of their volume near the cockpit, and have very narrow ("fine") ends. Others carry their volume well forward and back, tapering only right at the bow and stern. A fine bow usually tracks better, and will tend to cut through very small waves, so the kayak doesn't "hobbyhorse" over them. Such a bow, however, will also cut through *big* waves, sending water over the deck. The worst (though unlikely) scenario in this case is that the kayak pitchpoles, driving right through the base of a big wave and submerging the whole boat. A kayak with fuller ends, while a bit bouncier in small stuff, will carry you over larger waves. Also, a boat that carries its beam well forward and back will tend to have better secondary stability than a boat with the same maximum beam, but which is narrower toward the ends. Finally, the fuller ends carry more cargo. I've seen 18-foot kayaks with ends so constricted that they functioned more as 15-footers when it came time to pack.

Note the volume differences between the Eddyline Raven (left) and Wind Dancer. The Wind Dancer has more lateral volume toward the stern, and more height volume toward the bow.

Gear space is something you should consider carefully. For example, on typical trips to the Sea of Cortez, which is surrounded by desert, we will load 100 pounds of water in our boats before any other gear goes in. A different problem arises on expeditions to Arctic regions, where we need a lot of warm clothing, bulky sleeping bags, and sturdy tents. Although lighter, such items take up more room than water. Both situations demand a kayak with a lot of volume. If you're mostly interested in weekend trips in moderate climates, you won't need as much space.

COLOR AND SAFETY

Some people are happy with any color kayak that is in stock. To others, getting just the right shade is of vital importance. Although it might be the last thing on your mind in the store, consider that, someday, you might want someone to be able to see your kayak from a long way off—such as, for example, from a rescue helicopter.

While you might be tempted by a pleasing pastel, or an organic green or sea blue deck, keep in mind that such colors disappear at an alarmingly close distance. Rescuers less than 200 feet away have missed dark kayaks in storm-tossed seas.

Experiments have shown that red and yellow show up best in a variety of conditions. Semibright alternatives such as purple and mint green stand out in some conditions, but fade in others. Remember, however, that even the most brightly colored kayak is visible only from a few hundred yards away; to attract help from a greater distance, you need flares or mirrors (see Chapter 3).

One good tip to make your kayak more visible at night: apply strips of reflective tape on the top and sides of the deck. These show up in a searchlight beam from much farther away than the boat itself will.

A couple of final notes on color: if you're buying a fiberglass boat, order a bright deck color, but stick with a white or off-white hull, which hides scratches better and is easier to match if you decide to touch up the gelcoat. If you're a warm-weather kayaker shopping for a plastic boat, stay away from white (on a polyethylene boat, of course, the deck and hull will be the same color). I've found that white plastic seems to collect more of the sun's heat inside than a slightly darker color.

Bulkhead Materials

Bulkheads in fiberglass kayaks can also be made from fiberglass, or they can be cut from high-density foam panels secured to the hull with adhesive. I strongly prefer fiberglass bulkheads, which are bonded to the boat with resin and are part of the structure. Unfortunately, the trend seems to be toward the foam, which are easier to install, but significantly more inclined to leak or even come loose. Newer boats utilize better adhesives, but I still don't trust them. The only argument I've heard against fiberglass bulkheads is that they create a hard spot on the outside of the hull, where it can't flex as much to ride over rocks. Personally I've never run into a problem with this; on the other hand I've spent hours stuffed upside down in cockpits, recaulking loose foam. Besides, kayak makers could do what sailboat builders do with hard bulkheads, and glass in a small wedge of foam around the perimeter of the fiberglass panel to provide some give. If you can't talk your boatbuilder into installing fiberglass bulkheads, keep a very close eye on those foam substitutes. (See Chapter 13 for more on boat maintenance and repair.)

A loose or leaking bulkhead is not just an annoyance—it's a direct threat to the safety of the boat. If a bulkhead can come loose from the normal stresses of packing and paddling, imagine what could happen if several hundred pounds of seawater were sloshing back and forth in the cockpit after a capsize.

Most polyethylene kayaks also use foam bulkheads, with the added complication of how poorly many adhesives bond to plastic. A few manufacturers are using polyethylene for the bulkheads instead, and plastic-welding them in place—much better. Dagger has switched to a very stout molded bulkhead of this type on its plastic boats, and Valley Canoe Products even provides a lifetime warranty on its polyethylene bulkheads. Three cheers.

OTHER FEATURES

- Bulkheads. Never buy a sea kayak that does not have front and rear bulkheads. Period. Some older kayaks, and a few bottom-of-the-line new ones, have only a rear bulkhead, forcing you to use dry bags for front flotation. It's just not worth the risk. Front and rear compartments help ensure that the kayak will stay afloat and level if capsized, even if the cockpit is completely filled with water. Of course, there is no way to equip folding kayaks with bulkheads, so you have to rely on dry bags in that case.

- Cargo hatches. There are nearly as many designs of cargo hatches as there are kayak makers. If the hatches are held down with straps, make sure they're stout. I like having more than two if possible, for redundancy in case one breaks. Hatches held on with only bungee cord are inadequate. On the other hand, the all-rubber hatch covers that secure with a lip seal, with no straps at all, work very well. Examples of these include the oval VCP (Valley Canoe Products) and Kajak Sport hatch covers, both of which are bombproof and very watertight.

  Big hatches are easier to load gear through, *as long as they are stout and well secured.* Some of the really big rear hatches I've seen, with thin molded plastic covers and only two straps, would make me nervous in rough water. As long as the hatch is big enough to take a medium-size dry bag, it's big enough. On the other hand, the odious little 7-inch round VCP hatches are maddening to get anything through (the 10-inch size is better).

  Recessed hatch covers are nicer than ones that protrude above the line of the deck. They look better and don't throw as much spray. The covers should be leashed to prevent loss.

- Rudders and skegs. If the boat has a rudder, inspect the hardware for quality and sturdiness. A rudder that flips up over the rear deck is a good feature; when the kayak is beached it helps prevent damage

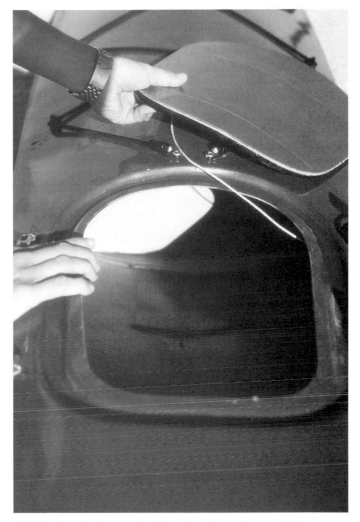

Bulkheads—the forward bulkhead is shown here—divide your kayak into three compartments, two of which provide dry storage and vital flotation in the event of a capsize.

to both the rudder and passing shins. Check to make sure you can easily operate the line that raises and lowers the blade.

Some kayaks, particularly British designs, come with a skeg, a retractable fin like the centerboard on a sailboat. The skeg is lowered to aid tracking, and raised when more maneuverability is needed. Since they have fewer moving parts, skegs are generally more trouble-free than rudders. The housing for the blade, though, does intrude significantly into cargo space.

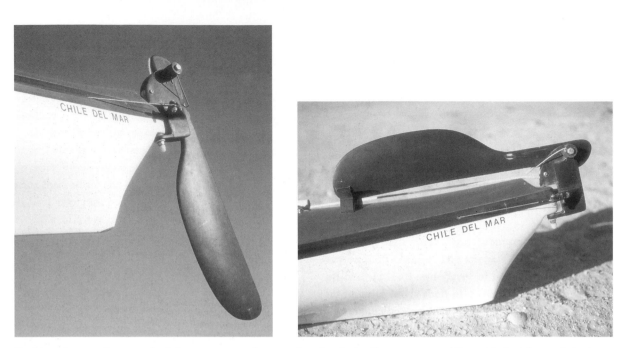

Rudders that can be turned all the way up and secured to the deck allow you to paddle rudderless for surf-playing, launching, or landing, but quickly deployed for tracking control while touring. (A flip-up rudder also reduces the chance of whacking your shin on it while beached.)

• Perimeter lines. Another useful British innovation is a nonelastic line running through recessed fittings around the perimeter of the deck. This is designed as a rescue hold, either for another kayaker, or yourself, if you are out of the boat. More American companies are now incorporating perimeter lines into their kayaks, an admirable addition.

• Paddle-float rigging. Another welcome feature appearing on increasing numbers of boats is a rigging system on the rear deck to secure a paddle for a paddle-float rescue. For too long the rear bungees were supposed to do double duty for this purpose, and bungees are utterly worthless for properly anchoring the paddle. Straps, or at least nonelastic cords, work much better. (See Chapter 3, page 35, for more on paddle floats.)

Skeg or Rudder?

The two most mutually exclusive characteristics a sea kayak is expected to possess are the ability to track straight through waves and wind and yet maintain sharp turning capabilities. But a kayak designed to track well rarely turns with alacrity, and vice versa. So most sea kayaks employ a movable device—either a skeg or a rudder—to bridge the gap.

(continued on page 19)

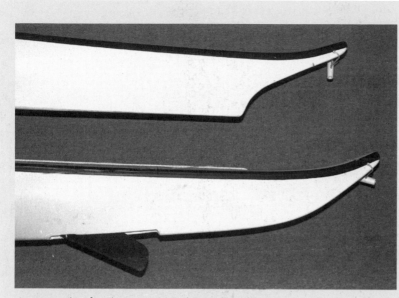

An example of a skeg on a British Nordkapp boat.

The foot-controlled rudder is prevalent among American kayaks. It's a very user-friendly accessory, especially for beginners, since it minimizes the number of specialized strokes you need to get started. A rudder can be used to help both turning and tracking. Its chief drawback is its relative complexity—at least compared to the rest of a sea kayak—and the risk of breakage of cables and fittings.

A skeg is like the centerboard on a sailboat; it retracts into a slot built in to the rear cargo compartment of the kayak (thus reducing gear space), and can be dropped fully or partway, depending on conditions. Since the skeg does not pivot, it is designed purely as a tracking aid; thus most boats designed for skegs show a good deal of rocker in the hull, to enhance turning when the skeg is up.

There's not much to go wrong with a skeg (although rocks can occasionally jam in the slot upon launching, preventing deployment). A skeg-equipped boat will usually track well in nearly any conditions; however, the boat's turning ability is solely dependent on hull design and the skill of the paddler.

Feelings run high on the relative merits of these devices. I'm agnostic. The rudder is probably the more versatile, at the expense of complexity and the crutch factor mentioned on page 13 in the "War of 1812" sidebar.

Fit to Be Tried

Don't buy a sea kayak because it conforms to some preconceived set of measurements; buy it because it works for you.

Above all, look for a kayak that fits. The cockpit and seat should be comfortable, but snug enough that you can use body English to control the attitude of the boat. You should be able to brace your knees against the underside of the deck while working the rudder pedals, if the boat is so equipped. Paddle the boat for as long as possible, and remember: if it's uncomfortable after 15 minutes, it will *not* get better during a three-hour crossing.

Keep in mind your own size when comparing different-size boats. If you're large or tall, you'll prob-ably feel most comfortable in a kayak with a 23- to 24-inch beam; if you're small, you might feel just as secure with a 22-inch beam. Again, give the boat a chance with a test-paddle. A kayak that feels just a little insecure at first might simply take some getting used to.

Choose the length by your own height as well. If you stand 5'1" you wouldn't enjoy wrestling with a 19-foot-long kayak—look for something in the 16-foot range. If in doubt, stay in the 17-foot region; it's probably the most versatile length, and is available in more hull designs than any other length.

Lastly, there will always be an element of emotion involved in choosing a sea kayak. The measurements might all be perfect, yet the boat in question just doesn't stir your soul. Don't ignore that inner voice, for one of the chief pleasures to be derived from sea kayaking is the grace intrinsic to the sport.

2
N E C E S S A R Y   G E A R

Don't Buy Retreads
for the Porsche

It's a common malady—you've just dropped over $2,000 on a sleek sculpture in fiberglass, and the Visa card is groaning. No problem, you think, you can economize on the extras.

Don't do it. Your sea kayak is only part of a system, and the proverbial weak-link metaphor holds true: break a cheap paddle in rough conditions, and your expensive kayak is going nowhere; scrimp on the spray skirt, and your seaworthy craft will collect bilgewater like a tramp steamer; trust your life to a $14.99 PFD and, well. . . .

Remember: in the long run, the best, more expensive gear will cost you less, because it will outlast cheap equipment by many times over, and will function much better as well.

The Paddle

If someone told me he had $1,000, and not a penny more, to spend between his kayak and paddles, I'd tell him to buy a good used rotomolded sea kayak for $500, and spend the other $500 on two of the best paddles available. Nothing, perhaps not even the boat, has as much influence on efficiency, comfort, and safety as a paddle.

WEIGHT AND MATERIALS

Hikers know that every ounce on their feet means weight they must lift at every step. Yet support and protection are vital. The same holds true for a kayak paddle. When you are constantly lifting and swinging weight, every ounce counts. Yet the blades and shaft are subject to immense stress when bracing or rolling. During a paddle-float rescue the paddle must support nearly your entire weight. So strength cannot be compromised. Fortunately, modern construction methods, whether in wood or synthetics, can produce paddles that are both light and strong.

A well-made sea kayak paddle shouldn't weigh more than about 40 ounces. Thirty-five is better, 30 better still. And kayaking with a 25-ounce all-carbon-fiber paddle is delightful, although somewhere around this point you begin to compromise strength—or at least durability—for weight savings. While many superlight paddles are strong enough for bracing and rolling, you definitely don't want to use them for pushing off rocky beaches or as makeshift awning poles.

The question of materials is largely a matter of personal preference. Laminated wood paddles are very strong and aesthetically pleasing. They are often less expensive than synthetic models, although usually a bit heavier. But many are well under 40 ounces.

The bane of wood paddles is, ironically, water. When new, they are protected by the finish, but if subsequent scratches or gouges penetrate through to the wood, water can soak in and eventually break down the wood fibers. Because abuse tends to be concentrated at the tips of the blades, many wood paddle manufacturers laminate solid fiberglass ends on their wood blades. As long as you keep an eye on your paddles, and revarnish when necessary, you shouldn't have a problem.

Synthetic paddles, whether fiberglass, carbon fiber, or graphite (which is a form of carbon), undoubtedly have less soul than any wood counterpart. But the nature of the synthetic material allows the manufacturer to precisely balance strength, weight, and durability to reach a specific goal. A reasonably priced fiberglass paddle will weigh about 35 ounces and put up with tremendous abuse. At the extreme is the all-carbon version that feels lighter than air, and will lighten your wallet in an alarmingly parallel fashion.

A good compromise, if you want a lightweight paddle but don't have unlimited funds, is to order carbon or graphite blades with a standard fiberglass shaft. This combination reduces what's known as "swing weight" out at the ends of the paddle, where it's most important, but saves $50 or so over an all-graphite paddle.

ONE-PIECE OR TWO?

Most paddles are made with a joint in the middle, so they come apart in two pieces. You can save a little money, as well as add (at least theoretically) a bit of strength, by ordering a one-piece model instead. But beware—one-piece paddles are astonishingly awkward to store and transport. My first paddle was jointless, but every successor has been two-piece. I've never had a joint fail. I have, though, had them fuse together, so I keep a light coating of dry graphite lubricant on the mating parts.

BLADE WIDTH

One of the biggest, and most contentious, variables in sea kayak paddle design is blade width, which determines the surface area of the blade. A wide (7- or 8-inch) blade offers more power per stroke, and more surface area for firmer bracing and rolling. A narrow (4- or 5-inch) blade is less stressful to use for long periods, reducing the chance of strain injuries to wrists and elbows, and also offers less area for wind to grab. This latter attribute is what landed me firmly in the narrow-blade camp, after having a wide paddle repeatedly nearly torn from my grasp during one of my first

Paddles widths range from skinny to wide, and depending on your mood or the water conditions, each might find a place.

very windy expeditions. I have never had trouble producing enough power with a narrow blade, nor any trouble bracing or even rolling—though I will grant that rolling is noticeably easier with a fat blade. I have also never, knock on wood, experienced any wrist or elbow problems; whether this is happy coincidence or the result of my paddle choice is hard to prove.

Some people buy one wide and one narrow paddle, and use either as conditions or mood warrant. Others compromise with a medium-width blade of 5 to 6 inches. Those who do much rough-water or surf kayaking might find that the power advantage of a wide blade outweighs the wind resistance. But I stick with my skinny paddles all the time.

PADDLE LENGTH

The overall length of a paddle is important, too, although the effect it often not immediately apparent. A friend with whom I paddled on several trips experienced persistent elbow pain. I wasn't sure of the cause at first; she was using a narrow-blade paddle, and there was nothing wrong with her stroke. Finally I checked the length of her paddle against my own—hers was at least 4 inches longer, and this for someone 6 inches shorter than I. We switched her from that

Good Paddles

My favorite all-around paddle is the Little Dipper, by Werner Paddles. In two-piece fiberglass it weighs a reasonable 34 ounces, and is stout enough to tolerate my habit of snaking through offshore rock gardens, using the paddle as a boathook to fend off barnacle-encrusted boulders. My first Little Dipper is more than 10 years old, and while the blade ends are severely chewed up, it's still perfectly serviceable.

I have an example of the same model, in graphite, that weighs barely a pound and a half. It's a treat to use, but I'm loathe to subject it to the same abuse as the heavier version. So my preferred combination for trips is one of each. On long crossings I use the graphite paddle; for poking around along the coast I switch to the heavy-duty alternative.

Lest I come across as the Werner poster boy, I should note that several other manufacturers make similar models of equivalent quality. See Appendix A for a list of sea kayaking accessories manufacturers.

The paddle on the left is unfeathered, while the paddle on the right is feathered.

with their extrawide beams, typically need fairly long paddles to avoid banging against the hull with each stroke. Keep in mind, though, that a paddle longer than necessary will increase *yawing*—the back-and-forth waggling of the bow—as you stroke on either side of the kayak; it's exacerbated the farther away from the centerline of the keel your power stroke reaches.

FEATHERING

To feather, or not to feather? This is yet another much-discussed issue, with good arguments for either approach. With a *feathered* paddle (that is, one with the blades at right angles, or nearly so, to each other), the blade that is out of the water is parallel to the surface, which helps it to slice through headwinds and not get pushed by stern winds. An unfeathered blade must be pushed broadside through the air. On the other hand, a feathered paddle catches wind coming from the side if it is lifted too high.

An unfeathered paddle is much easier to learn with because the blades are in line and there is no confusion as to which is angled where. This is especially important when learning to brace, because the flat of the blade supports you noticeably better than an edge mistakenly plunged into the water. An unfeathered paddle, if it is torn from your grasp by wind, is less likely to "helicopter"—spinning in the wind and sometimes flying an impressive distance before disappearing into the waves. Also, since you do not have to rotate one wrist with each stroke to orient the blade properly, an unfeathered paddle is much less likely to cause tendinitis.

The question was moot for me because my first paddle was a used one-piece model that was permanently feathered. After learning a feathered stroke, I wouldn't switch, but I'm not prejudiced toward either

260-centimeter flagpole to a 230, and her pain disappeared. She had simply been working on the wrong end of a long lever.

Paddle lengths are typically listed in centimeters, and can range from 210 to 260 centimeters. Average is around 230 to 240. If you're small, and/or paddling a narrow kayak, you might want something shorter. Very strong or large paddlers can utilize the extra power available with a longer model. Double kayaks,

Your spare paddle should be secure enough to stay put in rough water, but accessible enough that you don't have to struggle to extract it.

camp. I suspect some people adopt feathered paddles simply because they think it makes them look more experienced.

SPARES

Never be tempted to scrimp on your spare paddle—and never, ever be tempted to paddle without one. The hazards of doing so on a major expedition should be obvious, but the embarrassment of dog-paddling your kayak back to shore in front of camera-toting tourists and the Hobie sailing club shouldn't be ignored, in case you decide on a quick tour of the harbor and think you'll *never* need a spare paddle *here*.

Regarding quality—perhaps you shouldn't think of it as a *spare* paddle, a term that excuses lower specification, but simply as your second paddle. If you ever lose the first one, it's likely to be in high winds and rough seas—exactly the situation when you don't want inferior equipment. So grit your teeth and order two comparable paddles.

For a listing of kayak equipment and accessories manufacturers and suppliers, see Appendix A, pages 201–205.

Spray Skirt

A spray skirt fits around the cockpit rim and around your chest, to keep both paddle drips and dumping waves out of your lap. A release loop at the front allows you to quickly pop it off the boat in the event of a capsize.

In the past, spray skirts were made either from coated nylon fabric or neoprene. Nylon is lightweight and comfortable, but saggy—the deck tends to let water collect and pool. Neoprene is warmer and more waterproof, but very constricting and a pain to get on and off. The best setup for most touring is a combination—a taut neoprene deck sewn and bonded to a comfortable nylon chest tube (or chimney). This has

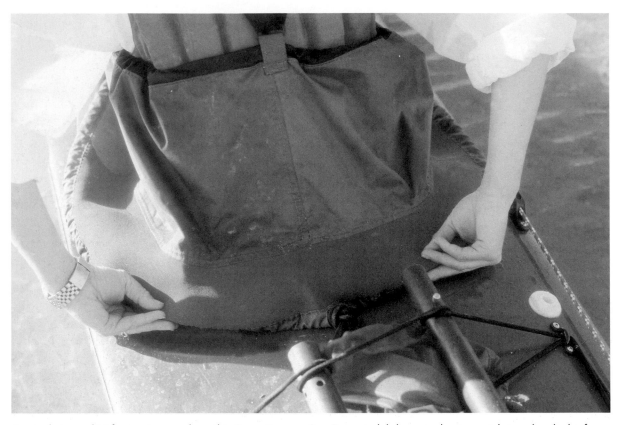

A good spray skirt for touring, such as this Snap Dragon Sea Tour model, has a nylon torso tube and a deck of neoprene, with adjustable, elastic shoulder straps. A front pocket for sunscreen and lip balm is a nice addition.

remained my only choice of spray skirt for years. I have a Sea Tour model from Snap Dragon Design, expensive but durable and worth every penny. Rich Wilson at Snap Dragon also makes, for less money, very nice all-nylon skirts, with heavy Cordura decks that resist sagging. See Appendix A for other sources as well.

If you're paddling in cold conditions, you might consider an all-neoprene skirt, which fits very snugly around your torso, adding a bit of insulation and helping to retain your body heat in the cockpit.

Beware of inexpensive nylon skirts with no separate chest tube; they are adequate to fend off minor splashes, but when conditions deteriorate they sag, leak, and can even pop off the cockpit rim, instantly transformed from merely annoying to dangerous. Make sure the skirt you buy has a taut deck and a

cylindrical chest tube both sewn and bonded to the deck. Shoulder straps or elastic prevent the chest tube from falling down, and a pocket is handy for sunscreen.

Buy a skirt that is sized properly to your cockpit. A spray skirt, to be effective and safe, has to ride a line between being firmly attached to the cockpit rim, so that the heaviest waves cannot dislodge it, yet easy and quick to yank off by an upside-down paddler. The larger the cockpit opening, the harder this balance is to achieve, because a big wave can dump a *lot* of water on a large spray deck. A useful accessory for the upside-down eventuality is called the Kayak Safe, a stout nylon webbing loop that attaches to the underside of the deck in front of the cockpit and extends out under the spray skirt. It acts as both a powerful skirt release and a handle to maintain a grip on the kayak after a capsize and wet exit.

A very worthwhile traveling accessory to the spray skirt is a separate, nylon cockpit cover. During transport, the cover keeps dust and rain out of the cockpit. Camped on the beach, it keeps out windblown sand, and your spray skirt and PFD can be stored in the cockpit, safe from UV rays or being blown away or from mischievous rodents.

Personal Flotation Device (PFD)

Very few people buy a kayak without purchasing a PFD as well. But it's surprising how many of them seem to think PFD stands for "Perception Flotation Device," or "Prijon Flotation Device," judging from how many life jackets I see strapped to the rear deck of the kayak while the owner paddles unencumbered. Certainly nothing I can say will convince every single sea kayaker in the world to wear a PFD all the time—in fact, if pressed, I'd have to admit to a few past violations myself, on those warm, calm Baja days. The fact remains, however, that it's just plain stupid to paddle without a life jacket.

My self-discipline is now pretty good, and it's become better because I wear a PFD that fits, one that is comfortable and designed for sea kayaking. The first PFD I owned was a discount water-skier's model, slab-sided and stiff. It was a revelation to switch to a flexible, Airex foam model with large arm holes and a body short enough to clear the spray skirt. Its color is anathema to my normal khaki sartorial preferences: an uncompromisingly loud and visible yellow.

PFD FIT AND FEATURES

Make sure your PFD fits properly. It should allow completely free arm-swinging movement, yet not be so loose that it winds up around your ears if you have to swim. It should have *at least* one pocket for flares,

Your PFD should fit snug but not tight; check the arm-hole for possible chafing. When seated, your PFD should not ride up to your ears. Pockets and D-rings for attaching a knife or other safety items are good additions.

and a D-ring or plastic lash tab is a good place to clip a rescue knife or personal strobe.

Palm Equipment, in England, makes some of the best ocean PFDs I've seen. One model has two large pockets on the front plus a small key pocket, and a useful lash tab. On the back is an even bigger pocket, which could hold an anorak or several items of survival gear. It's expensive but worth it. It's also not (currently) U.S. Coast Guard approved, so if you were stopped by a patrol boat and someone checked the brand, you could, theoretically, be cited. Hmm. Wild-Water, another English company, makes a similar model that is Coast Guard approved, lacking only the back pocket.

Another nice PFD is the Strait Jacket (get it?) by Lotus Designs. It lacks the back pocket of the Palm, but has two on the front plus a lash tab, as well as reflective tape on the shoulders, and an elastic pocket on the back for a strobe. It is American-made as well as Coast Guard approved. And Stohlquist offers a very similar vest called the Omni.

For significantly less money than the Palm and Wild-Water products, and a bit less than those of Lotus and Stohlquist, Seda and Extrasport in the United States make decent PFDs. The Extrasport Shadow Plus has two pockets and a lash tab in front. A new model, the Mona Lisa, uses stamped and molded foam for a very comfortable fit, but it has only two pockets and a low-mounted lash tab.

INFLATABLE PFDS

A tempting alternative to a foam PFD is an inflatable model with a CO_2 cartridge. These lie flat and unobtrusive until you pull a ring, instantly inflating the vest. Most also include an oral inflation valve.

Besides avoiding the Michelin Man look, a PFD with a somewhat lower R-value than a house is seductive to a hot-weather kayaker such as myself. However, I have reluctantly avoided the inflatable approach to PFDs.

My reasoning is that if I ever *need* my PFD to save my life, the last thing I want to worry about is the chance, however minute, of a technological failure— yanking that cord and hearing an asthmatic wheeze instead of a reassuring whoosh. In another scenario I

imagine myself, vest successfully inflated, still upside down, tangled in my paddle leash or deck lines or something, slashing wildly with my serrated knife and hearing an unpleasant reverse whoosh.

These might be statistically unlikely situations, but there are other good reasons to wear permanent flotation. If you capsize, the buoyancy of a foam PFD will significantly assist the first part of an Eskimo roll. In fact, combined with a strong brace a PFD might help circumvent a capsize in progress.

Bilge Pump

Rest assured, water *will* get into your boat. The amount can vary, from a few ounces sloshed in during a bouncy crossing to a cockpit full of several hundred pounds of ocean after a rough-weather capsize. The former is merely an annoyance, but the latter is a serious threat to safety. Even though the flotation in the front and rear compartments will keep the kayak from sinking, a flooded cockpit is enough to reduce the inherent stability of the boat, and must be emptied as quickly and efficiently as possible.

The old axiom among sailors is "The best bilge pump is a scared man with a bucket." The same holds true for kayakers: a plastic half-gallon drink pitcher with a handle is the fastest way I've ever tried to empty a full cockpit—at least on the beach. But several problems arise using the bucket approach while afloat.

If you're sitting in the boat and using a container to bail, the spray skirt must be off the cockpit rim. Assuming your need to bail was caused by rough weather, perhaps a capsize and reentry, with an open cockpit you

Electric bilge pump.

chin is marginal. One suggested modification is to fabricate a T-fitting on the bottom of the pump, to lock it under your thighs, although this increases the awkwardness of storing the unit. These pumps, by the way, will sink without a foam float collar, and really should be leashed to prevent loss overboard.

I believe the best bilge pumps for use in anger are the built-in type, standard for years on British kayaks. These units actually bolt to the kayak and operate by means of a lever instead of a plunger. They are designed to be operated with one hand, and because the pump itself is firmly attached to the boat, a great deal less coordination is needed. After a dumping, especially in cold water, your fine motor skills vanish, making any manipulation of tools difficult. A built-in pump has a distinct advantage here because all you have to do is move a lever back and forth. And of course a built-in pump cannot be lost overboard. A cylindrical pump will work quite a bit faster if you can manipulate it with both hands, but in rough conditions, operating one-handed, I think the disparity is small. The only other advantage to a handheld pump is that it can be used in

could find yourself working at a deficit, waves dumping in water faster than you can remove it (although the reswamping effect can be minimized if you can keep the bow of the kayak pointed into oncoming waves, either with a tow from another kayaker or by using a sea anchor—see Chapter 3, page 39, for a description of a sea anchor). Some sea kayaks have cockpit openings small enough that using an effective-size container while sitting in the boat would be nearly impossible.

Most American kayakers rely on the ubiquitous cylindrical plastic bilge pump. These pumps are simple and reliable, and move a lot of water. They can also be used —albeit awkwardly—while the spray skirt is attached, if you stuff the body of the pump down the chest tube of the skirt. By gripping the pump with your thighs, you can operate it one-handed, though the appearance of this operation to an on-looker is comical, and the leverage available with the thing tucked under your

Built-in bilge pump.
(Courtesy Great River Outfitters)

different boats—but each boat should have its own pump anyway.

The most common built-in pump is the Henderson Chimp, which is mounted on the rear deck just behind the cockpit. It is ready to work at all times; you simply reach behind you and work the lever. It can empty a swamped cockpit in a few minutes. By carrying an extra length of suction tube and a connector, you can even use it to pump out your front and rear compartments—sort of like a central vacuuming system for your boat. The Chimp pump can be retrofitted to almost any fiberglass kayak. Its only weak point is the possibility of freezing up in extremely cold conditions.

Another built-in pump is the Compac 50, which works by means of a removable lever that fits into a socket in the deck in front of the cockpit. It's not as instantly usable as the Chimp, and you need to keep the lever leashed to avoid losing it, but you don't have to twist around behind you to pump; in high seas, with a sea anchor out, you can lean forward into the wind while pumping. The Compac 50, though, is more difficult to retrofit because a fiberglass recess kit must be installed in the foredeck to accept the pump. Some boats that come with a Compac pump as standard even have a cunning little recess in the deck where the lever rides. It's speculation on my part, but I think the more concealed design of the Compac (the socket is nor-mally covered by a little hinged flap) should make it more resistant to freezing than the Chimp.

If your kayak lacks a rudder, you can install a foot-operated pump behind the front bulkhead. The advantage to this is that your hands are both free, so you can brace effectively or even continue paddling while you are pumping. But a foot pump must be very carefully fitted to suit your leg length. The only ones presently available are also very slow, much slower even than deck pumps, and thus not really suited for use as a primary pump.

Theoretically, a further advance in built-in pumps is one you don't have to pump at all. Electric pumps have been around, off and on (so to speak), for many years, and I had one for some time. Paddling with it gave me a mixture of confidence and doubt—confidence that, in an emergency, all I had to do was flip a switch and the boat would pump itself dry in two to three minutes, while I was yet reentering, fastening the spray skirt, and bracing with both hands free; doubt that, at the crucial moment, the rechargeable battery would die and the thing would squirt once and quit. This paranoia gained substance on one trip when I let someone else try my boat. A couple of hours later I went to get something out of it and heard the pump wheezing fitfully inside. The person had inadvertently hit the on switch, and the battery was nearly dead, and I had no way to recharge it.

Adventures with a Bailer

Several years ago my friend John, who is an expert on orca behavior, along with his marine biologist wife, Katie, guided my wife and me on a trip through the Johnstone Strait area off Vancouver Island. In the middle of one long, calm crossing, John spotted a beautiful jellyfish drifting next to his kayak and scooped it up in the plastic pitcher he used for a bailer, so we could all take a look. The diaphanous creature was eventually returned to its element, and we paddled on, until John announced that he absolutely had to answer a call of nature. The rest of us stroked off to a polite distance while John turned his bailing pitcher to multiple use.

He rejoined us—but very soon began showing signs of acute distress. A short inquiry led to the obvious conclusion: the jellyfish had left a few dozen of its nematocysts, or stinging cells, stuck to the lip of the pitcher, which were subsequently transferred to a very delicate portion of John's anatomy.

The most intense pain passed fairly quickly, but it was still lucky that John had already been married several years, because, for this trip at least, the honeymoon was definitely over.

Finally the paranoia won out, and I reverted to a manual pump. I might consider another, preferably using standard D-cell batteries, but I'd always have a manual pump as a backup.

It's nearly impossible to install a built-in pump on a folding kayak. I say nearly because I've seen a Chimp pump mounted to the floorboard of a military Klepper, and suppose it could be fitted to a civilian model as well. But the paddlers of most folders rely on a portable pump.

By the way, in a double kayak each cockpit should be equipped with its own pump, whether built-in or portable.

Compass

I wouldn't think of paddling the most familiar stretch of coast without a compass. Compasses are essential for orienteering, but many people fail to realize how useful they are for just plain *orienting*.

If you've ever tried to point out a distant object to other paddlers in other kayaks, you know how difficult it is to translate your subjective direction to theirs. The clock-face system is useless unless their boats are pointed the exact same direction as yours. Gesturing toward a boulder-strewn shore and saying, "Right between the really big dome-shaped rock and the sort-of-big dome-shaped rock," is also worthless. But with a deck-mounted compass you just point your own boat at the object or animal and say "240 degrees." They point their boats the same direction and there it is. Of course this usefulness increases logarithmically when you actually have to find your way somewhere. (See Chapter 8 for more on kayak navigation.)

Any kayak can be equipped with a deck-mounted compass. Several models are available with little bungees that hook to your existing deck fittings. But mounts that are molded right into the deck's surface are cleaner.

I prefer a dome-type compass mounted fairly far forward on deck—right behind the front cargo hatch or on top of it. I've found it much less disorienting on a rough crossing to be able to glance just below the horizon line to get a fix. The flatter, recessed compasses are very sleek and won't throw spray, but they

A good-quality deck-mounted compass is essential gear on your kayak. Make sure you don't pack any ferrous metals near it, or it will be "confused" and show a false bearing.

must be mounted close to the cockpit so you can see the face properly. Not only does this force you to lower your line of sight, but the compass often is installed right where your deck bag should be.

If you ever plan to do any night paddling (even if you don't), consider a lighted compass. Some use a bulb and a small battery pack; other, simpler, designs use a disposable light stick to shed a glow on the instrument.

For chart navigation you'll need an orienteering-type compass as well. See Chapter 8, page 110 for more information.

Waterproof Storage

DRY BAGS

"Watertight compartments." "Leakproof hatches." "Waterproof bulkheads." These are all optimistic terms. Water will get into the tightest cargo holds. It's best to anticipate it.

Dry bags not only keep your stuff dry, they also function as reserve buoyancy in the event of a holed hull, loose bulkhead, or even a lost hatch. In addition they help organize your gear.

Acrylic-lidded dry boxes can provide excellent storage for sharp items such as screwdrivers and knives. Options for dry storage in your kayak include: Heavy-duty PVC dry bags in medium sizes; lightweight clear PVC dry bags in small sizes; plastic dry boxes.

I buy the heaviest-duty PVC-coated bags I can find. They are stiffer and thus a little harder to seal, but I find them more resistant to pinhole leaks than lighter-weight PVC or coated nylon bags. Since they are opaque, it's easy to locate leaks that do occur by holding the bags up to the sun and looking inside for pinpricks of light. I also buy as many colors as I can find, which is a great help for organizing, although it tends to make your camp look sort of, uh, perky. Even in kayaks with large hatches, I find the medium or small bags more versatile and easier to fit in nooks and crannies then really big ones. Buy several different configurations too—some short and fat, some long and skinny. We'll talk more about packing in Chapter 10.

DRY BOXES

Hard-edged storage boxes are problematic for storing in a kayak; nevertheless, small ones can be useful for storing things that might puncture a dry bag, or for which you need a little extra organization and accessibility.

I carry a Pelican Mini D Case—about 7 by 9 by 10 inches—for my first-aid kit. It's immediately recognizable, permits excellent organization of the contents, and is utterly bulletproof. I also have two smaller dry boxes from Underwater Kinetics, with transparent lids. One serves as my tool and spare-parts kit, safely carrying screwdrivers, wire cutters, cable, and other things that would be hard on a dry bag; the other carries spare flashlights and batteries, a small pocket microscope, a little Grundig short-wave radio, and my wallet, car keys, and money.

Another good hard case is the cylindrical BDH Safe Pack, which comes in several sizes and uses a latex collar to provide a watertight seal. The medium size (5 inches in diameter by 10 inches long) would work well for tools.

3

S A F E T Y   G E A R

Getting Serious About Safety

Is it coincidence that the people I see with no paddle floats or radios on deck, and no evidence of flares or mirrors elsewhere, are also most likely to be wearing T-shirts when the water temperature is 50°F (10°C)? I'd hate to think there's some sort of twisted machismo at work; more likely it's just the typical "won't happen to me" ignorance—nevertheless, very few kayakers bother to equip themselves with proper safety gear.

So far the equipment we've discussed is common to all sea kayaking. But the issue of safety gear begins to separate the serious kayaker from the amateur, or the just plain careless.

The equipment in this chapter is the cheapest of insurance. Statistically, you will never need most of it. But if the unlikely ever happens, you'll be glad you were prepared.

With that said, please note that this chapter is intended as an overview of available safety equipment, with some recommendations—not a comprehensive list

What to Take

Here are a few suggestions of what safety gear to have along for various outings. See Chapter 10 for ideas on where and how to pack your safety equipment.

- Daytrip: whistle, three meteor flares, signal mirror, personal strobe, paddle float, VHF radio, knife, first-aid kit.
- Overnight or weekend trip: all of the above, plus extra meteor flares, one parachute flare, one hand-held and one smoke flare, sea anchor, See/Rescue distress flag.
- Major coastal journey or remote expedition: all of the above, plus an additional parachute flare, additional handheld and smoke flares, EPIRB, extra first-aid items.
- For group expeditions: add Sea Wings float, tow lines for each boat.

of what to carry on every outing (you'd wind up looking like a demented Royal National Lifeboat captain).

Think of your safety gear (and procedures) in terms of two goals: first, to help *yourself*, then, if that fails, to attract outside assistance. If you organize both your equipment and your plans in a logical order, you'll stand a much greater chance of success. Above all, do not forget that you, not the Coast Guard or the Longshoremen or the Hobie sailing club, are the responsible party when you paddle. No one minds rescuing someone who has been caught out by circumstances, but carelessness that results in risk to others is unforgivable.

Safety gear should be organized according to what you carry on your person, and what goes in or on the kayak. What you carry on you should be signaling equipment—mirrors, meteor flares, and the like—designed to attract immediate help should you be injured, suffer a capsize or, at worst, become separated from the boat. Larger items—radios, parachute flares, EPIRBs, etc., can be stowed either well secured in the cockpit, or on deck in a deck bag. And gear for self-rescue—paddle float, sea anchor—should be kept secure, but ready for instantaneous use.

Paddle Float

Probably the most contentious piece of safety gear in the world of sea kayaking, the paddle float is viewed as a surefire get-out-of-jail-free rescue device by some,

A paddle float is stowed deflated with your most accessible safety gear, in a deck bag or lashed to the deck. You slide it over a paddle, inflate it by mouth, and use it as an outrigger to reenter your kayak.

and reviled as a worthless, even dangerous, placebo by others. As usual when opinions vary so widely, the extremist views at both ends are wrong.

Briefly, a paddle float is designed to turn your paddle into an outrigger to stabilize your kayak, just like the outrigger on a Tahitian dugout. If you capsize and have to exit the boat (what we call a *wet exit*), you fit the float over one blade of your paddle, brace the other end of the paddle over the rear deck behind the cockpit, and then climb back in. Some kayaks now have special rigging behind the cockpit to secure the paddle, creating a more stable platform.

Even if you are an accomplished Eskimo roller, any number of circumstances could prevent you from rolling up successfully in bad conditions. In at least some of those circumstances, a paddle float could mean the difference in regaining the cockpit quickly. Since they are both inexpensive and compact, there is little reason not to keep one tucked in the cockpit— just in case. See Chapter 6 for paddle-float rescue techniques.

Sea Wings and BackUp Floats

Recently several products have appeared on the market that attempt to improve on the paddle-float idea—that is, to give a capsized kayaker a rapid and stable reentry system.

The Sea Wings system consists of a pair of tube-shaped floats, which are inflated individually and strapped on each side of the cockpit, forming a double pontoon system. The resulting platform is extremely stable—you can stand up in the boat in calm water— but obviously more complex and time-consuming to employ than a paddle float. One promising use of the Sea Wings would be to stabilize a kayak with a weak or injured paddler inside.

The BackUp is a CO_2-inflated bag that stores in a small tube on the foredeck. If you are capsized, you remain in the cockpit, grasp the large D-ring that protrudes from the tube, and pull out the bag, which inflates automatically in a few seconds. You can then lean on the bag to right the kayak. It provides much more buoyancy than a paddle float, in addition to which there is no need to exit the cockpit. On the other hand, the instructions tell you to *drop your paddle* so you can use both hands to manipulate the bag. Bad idea, even with a paddle leash. Then, assuming you've been capsized by high winds and seas, there you are, trying to retain your precarious upright status, and you've got this bloody great whoopee cushion to deal with. It must be deflated and stowed before you can do anything else, and must have a new cartridge installed before it can be reused.

Sea Socks

A sea sock is designed to limit the amount of water that gets into your cockpit if you capsize and wet-exit. It comprises a simple, coated nylon sack that fits around the cockpit rim under your spray skirt and extends down into the cockpit. You sit in the sack, which, if you are capsized, holds much less water than your whole cockpit; in fact, it's generally possible to safely paddle a kayak with a sea sock full of water—a completely swamped cockpit often renders the boat very unstable. The downside is the extra impedimenta of all that fabric, and the hassle of getting anything out of the cockpit while underway. Sea socks are often used by people who seek out rough water to test their abilities, and who *expect* to capsize now and then. They are also very useful in folding kayaks, which have no bulkheads to provide built-in flotation and can hold much more water than a bulkheaded rigid kayak.

Signaling Devices

Even a Day-Glo yellow kayak disappears from sight just a short distance away in rough weather. The little bit of a bright PFD that sticks above the water disappears even quicker. And at night, neither is visible at all. To attract attention from a distance should you require help, you need active signaling devices, something you can use when you think someone might see or hear it.

Signaling devices in general can be divided into day use and night use, although some will function to a degree anytime. Daytime devices include mirrors, smoke signals, dye markers, flags, and noisemakers such as air horns and whistles; night signals include strobes, and handheld and aerial flares. Flares can sometimes be seen during the day as well, particularly if it is overcast.

Don't buy just one type of signal device. The more you have to employ, the better your chances of being seen. A good basic kit would comprise a mirror, a personal strobe, and several aerial flares, all of which can be comfortably carried on your person—in the pockets of your PFD or paddling jacket, or a spray skirt pocket. For extended trips you can add a couple of parachute and handheld flares strapped into the cockpit, and any other devices you think might be useful.

MIRRORS

A signal mirror is one of the most reliable and effective rescue tools you can own. Aircraft pilots have reported seeing the flash of a mirror from more than 25 miles away. Unlike a flare or dye marker, a mirror will continue to signal your location for as long as you need.

Of course, the only drawback to mirrors is that they need full sun, making them worthless to anyone who kayaks in the Seattle area. But for the rest of us they should be considered an essential item.

It's worth it to buy a real signal mirror; that is, one with a sighting hole or cross in the middle. These make it easy to aim the flash accurately. Most are also equipped with a lanyard hole to secure the mirror against loss. Acrylic mirrors, such as the Safe Signal, are harder to break than glass ones, but you need to treat the reflective surface with more care or it will dull.

A point to remember regarding the use of mirrors—once it is clear that you have been spotted and located, *stop flashing*. Pilots have reported being nearly blinded by overzealous mirror wielders during final approach. Smoke flares are much better for this application; see page 38.

STROBES

A battery-operated strobe is the night-time equivalent of a mirror. Although not as eye-catching as an aerial flare, a strobe can flash for hours on one or two batteries, constantly advertising your predicament and leading rescuers to your exact location.

There are waterproof strobes available for under $20; however, my favorite is the well-proven Firefly from ACR. The current model, which sells for about $60, uses two standard alkaline AA batteries, and will flash once every second for up to eight hours. The flash is visible for well over a mile at night.

A strobe shares the advantage with a mirror of being small enough to keep on your person. A strobe such as the Firefly can be strapped to the outside of a PFD, and activated with the flick of a switch.

For a listing of kayak equipment and accessories manufacturers and suppliers, see Appendix A, pages 204–205.

METEOR FLARES

Compact—about the size of a fat pen—and inexpensive, meteor flares are the best buy in personal night-time signaling equipment. They send a bright flare 350 to 450 feet high, highly visible at night and reasonably so in the daytime. Multiple flares are one of the best ways to first alert potential rescuers, and then lead them to your location.

For many years, the Skyblazer XLT meteor flares were the best low-cost flares available. Recently, the Orion company has released their own design, called the Star-Tracer, which supposedly go a little higher and burn a little brighter than the Skyblazers. Three of either model—about 15 bucks' worth—fit in the pocket of a PFD, and because they are waterproof you can leave them there all the time. With three flares and a signal mirror in a PFD pocket, and a strobe strapped to the opposite chest, you always have at hand several means to attract help—even if you become separated from the kayak.

PAINS-WESSEX PARACHUTE FLARE

This is the undisputed king of signaling devices. Fire off one of these, and there's no telling from which direction help will appear: "Houston, this is Columbia.

Personal safety gear, carried in secure pockets on your PFD, should include an unbreakable signal mirror and flares (pictured at right) as well as a strobe; the VHF radio should be stowed in your deck bag (see Chapter 10, page 155, for tips on packing and stowing your safety gear).

to 40 seconds. Due to both size and cost (about $40 each), one or two of these would be considered a full complement for a kayak, but in a tight spot nothing else will attract the same attention.

HANDHELD FLARES

Handheld flares aren't as much fun as aerial versions. Wait. I didn't mean to say that. What I meant was that handheld flares can't be seen from as far away as aerial flares, but their burn time is much longer—up to several minutes. So, while they're not as good at attracting initial attention, they are excellent for enabling rescuers to pinpoint your location. They are particularly effective if you become stranded on an island near a shipping lane.

SMOKE FLARES

Smoke flares—surprise—give off a stream of dense, brightly colored smoke. I think they are of less value in attracting initial attention than they are for guiding help to you on final approach. For example, after getting the attention of a helicopter pilot with a signal mirror, when it is clear the aircraft is headed toward you, stop flashing and pop a smoke flare. This will not only pinpoint your location, but indicate wind direction for the pilot.

We've spotted something odd off the coast of Alaska." Or: "Captain. Sensors detect an anomalous light source coming from the direction of Earth." ("Shields up! Red alert!")

A parachute flare comprises a fairly bulky handheld tube from which a powerful flare is launched. Nearly 1,000 feet up the flare deploys a parachute and floats slowly to earth, burning brightly the entire time—30

DYE MARKERS

A dye packet, when activated, releases a concentrated powder that spreads into the water around you, turning fluorescent green. It can be of value to rescuers in aircraft who are aware of your general location, but is of little use in attracting attention in the first place. Of course, the rougher the conditions, the quicker the dye disperses and fades.

DISTRESS FLAGS

A distress flag performs a similar function to a dye marker. The surface area of the attractant is smaller, but of course it doesn't disperse.

The most effective distress flag I've seen is called the See/Rescue. Instead of the usual rectangle of 2 by 3 feet or so, the See/Rescue is a bright orange banner 6 inches wide by 25 *feet* in length. A larger version is 12 inches by 40 feet. The banner is made of buoyant polyethylene, so the entire length floats. It would be helpful in many conditions, such as an overcast day when a mirror wouldn't work and a strobe might not show up well. The banner comes in either a tube or a soft pouch. Tests by the U.S. Navy indicate the See/Rescue can be seen from more than a mile away.

WHISTLES AND AIR HORNS

I put these last on the list because, frankly, in my experience their range is limited. I once tried an experiment with a very loud whistle, attempting to signal a group of friends as they paddled toward me from about a half-mile away, on an utterly calm and windless day in a protected bay. I kept blasting furiously, but it was clear they heard nothing until barely a couple of hundred yards separated us. By then my red face would have attracted more attention anyway. Apparently the ambient noise of their own paddles and conversation had prevented them from noticing the whistle from farther away. Had the day been windy, the results would have been even worse. I still keep a whistle attached to the zipper pull of my PFD, but I consider it a way of alerting nearby companions rather than attracting outside rescuers.

Air horns are significantly louder than whistles, but considerably bulkier too. Some big ones can reportedly be heard up to a mile away, but that is under ideal conditions—not when you are likely to need assistance. Compact, nonrechargeable models suitable for a kayak are available, with necessarily reduced output. Another recent full-size design utilizes a regular bicycle pump to recharge its tank.

If you kayak in areas prone to fog, an air horn is a vital piece of equipment. With visibility reduced to a few feet, noise could be your only means of attracting attention or warning off approaching boats.

Medical Kit

I used the term "medical kit" rather than "first-aid kit" on purpose. Often while kayaking you will be hours or even days away from medical help, so the typical first-aid kit, with its scant contents designed for only essential treatments, is inadequate. You need a real expedition kit, with enough instruments and supplies to stabilize a variety of conditions or wounds.

You can assemble your own kit, or buy one of the excellent ready-made kits from Atwater Carey or Adventure Medical Kits. The Fundamentals Aquatic Kit from Adventure Medical Kits contains a good basic selection, and comes in an organizer bag inside a roll-top dry bag, or in a Pelican dry box as an option. The Comprehensive Aquatic Kit is even better. For extended expeditions, their Expedition Kit has a full range of care modules, with room for prescription drugs. It comes in a standard folding pouch and must be protected further for paddling. Each of the above kits includes a guide to wilderness and travel medicine, and several components specifically designed for troubles associated with marine sports: motion sickness, muscle strain, coral scrapes, marine envenomation, and the like.

Once you have the basics, consult your doctor for prescription drugs to handle serious ailments, and add any items you need for personal conditions. See Appendix B for a checklist of recommended basics. See also Chapter 10, p. 158.

Sea Anchors

I'll go out on a limb here: I believe sea anchors are the most undervalued tool related to sea kayaking.

A *sea anchor*—also called a *drogue*—is just a small parachute on a long line, designed to be dragged through water rather than air. When deployed from the bow of a kayak, the anchor fills with water as wind and waves push the kayak. The resistance provided by the sea anchor drastically slows the downwind drift of the boat, and holds the kayak pointing into the wind, where waves more easily roll past. A sea anchor makes

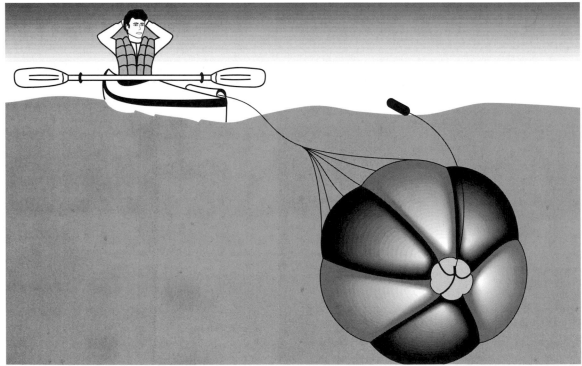

The sea anchor is one of the most undervalued safety items a kayaker can have. If you buy one, make sure you learn how to use it correctly.

a paddle-float rescue in rough conditions much more manageable, and will minimize the bracing needed after you reenter and are pumping out the cockpit. If you capsize off a rough lee shore (the shore toward which the wind is blowing), a sea anchor will give you extra time to reenter.

However, sea anchors aren't just for emergencies. They can also be used when you just need a break during a long upwind slog (or want to fish), and don't want to lose the last mile you fought for. While the anchor doesn't completely stop downwind drift, it significantly slows it.

The only sea anchor of which I'm aware that's designed specifically for sea kayaking is the Drift-stopper, by Boulter of Earth. It's an excellent piece of gear, designed to both deploy and retrieve easily. It stores on the foredeck, ready to use instantly.

Tow Line

Tow lines are almost unheard of in the United States, but they're more common in England. A tow line—actually it's a whole system—consists of a buoyant line about 50 feet long with a snap link at the end, which is clipped to the bow toggle of the towed boat. The other end is attached through a fairlead and jam cleat to the tower's rear deck. The bulk of the line is coiled in a nylon bag from which it can be quickly deployed, and there is a section of elastic to absorb shock between the boats.

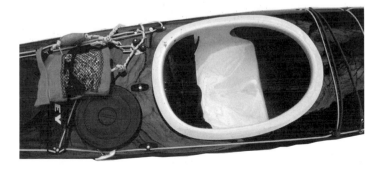

Great River Outfitters Towing system.

A tow line can be useful in many situations: towing a kayak with an injured or exhausted paddler (perhaps in conjunction with the Sea Wings floats), or keeping a capsized boat and paddler off a lee shore, and stabilizing the same boat into the wind once the paddler has reentered so he or she can pump out the cockpit.

Tow lines that fit into a waist-belt pack are available too. These can be deployed very quickly, but I feel the dangers of being attached directly to the tow line even with a quick-release buckle—outweigh the advantages. However, I must add that Roger Schumann, a kayaking instructor and writer whose experience and commonsense approach I admire greatly, makes a strong argument for the speed and accessibility of a properly constructed waist-belt tow system in certain circumstances.

Binoculars

Very few people think of binoculars as a safety item, but I wouldn't think of paddling without a pair. Binoculars are extremely useful for scouting the route ahead—either from a hill before the launch, or from the boat during a long crossing. They're also good for keeping an eye on ship traffic, and identifying distant buoys. They have many additional benefits, of course, chief among which is close-up views of birds and other animals.

For years I have carried a pair of Swarovski 10 × 50 binoculars, a fine, completely waterproof Austrian instrument. My confidence in these is high enough that they ride simply strapped to the deck (with a stout safety cable). My wife has a pair of 8 × 30 Swarovskis, which are much more compact and more suitable as all-around glasses. I've also used a Leica 8 × 42 Ultra, another superb waterproof instrument.

If you want a good pair of marine binoculars, look for those that are completely sealed and nitrogen-purged. Nitrogen purging prevents interior condensation from forming, and is the sign of a truly waterproof binocular. In fact, Swarovski and Leica both test their binoculars several *feet* underwater. Binoculars such as these are expensive, but they are the last ones you'll ever have to buy, and the image they project is unmatched.

VHF Radios

VHF (very high frequency) radios are designed for short-range two-way communication—because they work only within a line-of-sight, 5 to 10 miles is the maximum to expect from a handheld unit, and two kayakers will be out of range of each other within a couple of miles, due to the curvature of the earth. The range can be increased somewhat with an external antenna, or if you can climb something tall such as a lighthouse or hill, but VHF radios are obviously most useful where there is a reasonable density of boat traffic, or nearby monitoring stations on shore. Most powerboats and sailboats with VHF radios monitor Channel 16, the emergency channel, or Channel 9, the hailing channel.

There are exceptions to the close-range rule, however. For example, on the remote but frequently traveled Mackenzie River Delta in the Canadian Arctic, automatic repeater stations have been set up that can relay a signal for dozens of miles. On one trip, we were able to ask about the progress of a storm by radioing the Inuvik Coast Guard station from our location in the Beaufort Sea, more than 90 miles away.

The great advantage to VHF radios for emergency use is two-way communication. You can describe to rescuers your exact location and situation, and lead them right to you after you spot them coming. The psychological factor in just being able to talk to another human being should not be underestimated.

VHF isn't just for emergency communication. You can use alternate channels for talking with other boats, or other members of your own party if you decide to break up for the day. In many areas, up-to-date weather reports are available on a dedicated channel. You can even make telephone calls if you are within range of a marine operator.

In recent years both the cost and size of handheld VHF units have shrunk significantly. A couple I've

A VHF radio can be invaluable for summoning assistance or for staying safe—so you don't need to call for help. This kayaker is using a VHF to monitor Canadian Coast Guard weather reports about an approaching storm on the Beaufort Sea.

Force 8

"There is a Force 8 storm moving across the Gulf of Alaska toward the Tuktoyaktuk Peninsula," the radio operator said, "with gusts to 45 knots."

We were stopped on a little gravel spit on the coast of the Beaufort Sea, 200 miles north of the Arctic Circle. Bluffs rose above us; this was no place to camp. But the sky was blue, the air warm, and barely a breeze stirred the water. We launched again and paddled another couple of miles. Still the weather appeared benign. I checked the forecast again, and got the same report. Then Roseann said, "Wow, look west." I did, and saw a flat black line on the horizon that hadn't been there before.

We hit maximum warp, and found a high beach another mile down the coast, while the black line turned into a black mass of clouds hurtling toward us. We got the boats up the beach, locked everything down and pitched the tent above the storm tide line, well staked and guyed. An hour later the front hit, taking 10 minutes to go from dead calm to 50 mile-an-hour blasts (reminding us why they call it the Beaufort scale).

The view from the tent: a Beaufort Sea storm.

After wine and a supper of rice and vegetables cooked under the vestibule, we climbed in our bags and dropped off to sleep while the tent thrummed tautly in the gale.

About 2 A.M. Roseann had to brave the elements for a nature call (*"Eeeeeee! It's blowing sideways!"* I heard her shout). I looked out toward the beach in the Arctic dusk that is as dark as it gets in early August. The entire sky churned black and gray, while a steep surf pounded tons of logs and limbs—the outflow debris from the Mackenzie River—against the shore. Spume from the crests of the waves blew over the top of our tent. The forbidding Arctic landscape of nineteenth-century painter Frederic Church had come to life.

tried would, in my boat at least, stand more danger of being lost than of taking up too much room. Two years later I'd find the thing under the seat. Many models are now waterproof as well; waterproof pouches are available for others. I use a waterproof pouch anyway, just to be safe.

Most VHF radios use a rechargeable battery pack. Power draw is light when you are just listening to weather reports, but increases dramatically when you transmit—especially if you use the full 5-watt power of most handhelds. For any extended trips you should carry a spare, fully charged pack, or consider an alternate style that uses standard alkaline batteries, available as an option for many models.

UHF-FM Radios

The FCC recently designated what it calls "Family Radio Service" frequencies in the UHF range to license-free communication. These radios are intended for communication within a group, not for attracting help. The radio units, such as the Motorola TalkAbouts, are incredibly compact, and have a range of up to two miles. They would be a good choice for keeping everyone in a group in contact with each other.

The TalkAbouts have 14 channels, with 38 further "interference eliminator codes" that effectively function as separate channels. They are "splash-proof"— meaning you should buy the optional waterproof case. Retail is around $160 each.

EPIRB

An EPIRB (emergency position-indicating radio-beacon) is a one-way radio transmitter that sends a signal that can be received by an orbiting network of SARSAT satellites (certain rescue vessels and ground stations also listen for these signals). The satellites relay the signal to a ground monitoring station, which can determine the location of the unit.

EPIRBs are available in two classes. Class A models activate automatically when they get wet; Class B EPIRBs must be manually activated. Since everything in a kayak eventually gets wet, most kayakers use Class B.

Civilian EPIRBs use one of two frequencies: 121.5 MHz and 406 MHz. The 406 EPIRBs are more sophisticated, because the satellites that listen to this frequency can store the signal until they are over a ground station. The 121.5 signal is simply relayed instantly, and if no ground station is within range, the signal is not read. The 406 EPIRBs also are registered to the craft, so the station knows exactly who is sending the distress call.

However, 406 EPIRBs are bulkier and at least three times as expensive as the 121.5 models, and therefore more suited for larger vessels. Some 121.5 models are barely larger than a pack of cigarettes (isn't it about time someone thought up a new analogy here?), and store easily in a kayak.

EPIRBs can summon help from vastly greater distances than any radio, and should be seriously considered by anyone undertaking an expedition into an isolated area. But they aren't perfect. Chief among their disadvantages is the fact that you have no way of knowing if the signal has reached a ground station until someone shows up. The popularity of the inexpensive 121.5 EPIRBs has resulted in an alarming rate of false alarms—about 95 percent—from accidental or mischievous activation. And the fix computed by the satellites still has a margin of error. You should still have other signaling methods with you, along with a VHF radio.

Barometer

If you're planning trips to regions out of the range of VHF weather reports, you need to do your own weather forecasting—in fact, it's a good idea anyway. The more information you have at your fingertips, the better informed your choices will be regarding long crossings and exposed coasts. A barometer, which reads atmospheric pressure, is the most reliable means of predicting meteorological trends.

If you look for barometers at outdoor equipment store, you might not find them. What you'll be shown instead is an altimeter, which is nothing more than a barometer with elevation marked on it. Since atmospheric pressure drops as you gain elevation, a barometer can gauge elevation too, although it will still fluctuate according to weather changes.

I carry a Thommen barometer/altimeter, an exquisitely made mechanical instrument, but less expensive digital models work okay too. If I'm faced with a long crossing or a dangerous stretch of coast, I set the marker line on the current reading before I go to bed, then check it in the morning (after giving it a couple of light taps, essential with a mechanical model to allow the needle to stabilize). If the pressure has changed significantly—especially if it has dropped, indicating a storm might be on the way—I might think twice about heading out. See Chapter 7, page 106, for more on barometers, and information about weather forecasting and seamanship.

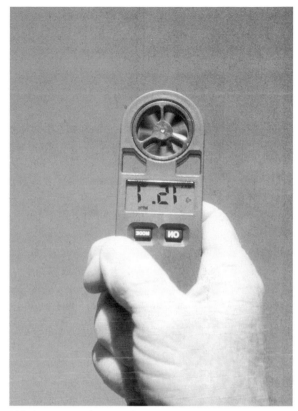

While not must-have safety equipment, an anemometer can be useful for judging windspeed.

A simple hand-held altimeter (from an outdoor shop) can be used as a barometer for monitoring pressure changes—and thus changes in weather—during your trip.

Anemometer

I hesitate to call a wind meter a safety item because I can think of very few situations when I would let such an instrument make a paddling decision for me. If sea conditions look dangerous, but my anemometer says the wind is blowing only 15 knots, should I go out anyway? Heck no. Nevertheless, anemometers are fun and interesting. If nothing else, *after* a killer crossing you can use it to determine how close to death you might have been.

The extra information could be useful at times. If your barometer is dropping, and the averaging function on the anemometer shows a steadily increasing breeze, you've got two excuses to make more coffee.

Cellular Telephones

Recently a national forest headquarters near where I live received a cellular call from a hiker requesting a helicopter evacuation. The dispatcher asked the nature of the emergency, to which the hiker replied, "I'm tired."

"I beg your pardon?"

"I said, I'm *tired*," the hiker repeated. Further interrogation revealed that, no, she wasn't injured or out of water or suffering any symptoms of heat exhaustion, she was just *tired* and wanted a ride the last 3 miles out of the canyon. When the dispatcher told her that $1,000-per-hour helicopters weren't normally wasted on such troubles, the woman became abusive, threatening to sue the dispatcher and the whole U.S. Forest Service.

That delightful incident, plus many similar ones of which I'm aware, is why I've listed cellular telephones last on the list of safety items. What could have been a valuable safety tool has instead come to be viewed by many as not just a free ticket out of trouble, but a cheap substitute for personal responsibility.

Remember the days when, if we screwed up, we looked around sheepishly to make sure no one was watching? Now the first reaction seems to be to blame it on someone else and then sue them.

Excuse me, I'm ranting. But I'd like to make a call to arms to keep sea kayaking free from such idiocy. Let's self-police our ranks. If you see someone paddling without the proper equipment or clothing, politely point out the error to them. If they become belligerent, become belligerent right back. If enough of us land on these people, with luck they'll decide that sea kayakers are a bunch of meddling jerks and take up another sport.

What was I talking about? Oh, yeah—cellular phones. Along coasts that are developed enough to have repeater stations, a cell phone could be a valuable safety tool. As yet, though, I'm unaware of any that are waterproof, so if you decide to carry one put it in a bag made for a VHF radio. Then program it to speed-dial the numbers you might need: the Coast Guard, the Harbor Patrol, and of course a reputable law firm such as Dewey, Cheatam, and Howe.

Paddle Leash

A paddle leash is something I've never used, but always thought I should, maybe. It's a simple line that tethers your paddle either to the boat or to your wrist, to avoid loss in the event of a tumultuous wet exit or a sudden fierce gust of wind. The concept is irreproachable—you should avoid losing your main paddle if at all possible, so anything that ties it down should be a good thing.

I've neglected to buy or make a paddle leash because of the simple inchoate fear of having too many lines in which I might become tangled in the event of an emergency. This might be nonsense, similar to not wearing a seat belt in a car because you might become trapped in a fire, but it's my only excuse.

Knives

Buy a top-quality rescue knife with a serrated blade that can be deployed with one hand, then never, *ever*, use it for anything but a life-and-death emergency. No slicing cheese, no cleaning fingernails. Use your Swiss Army knife for odd jobs.

Don't leave home without it: a razor-sharp boating knife—the kind that can be opened with one hand—could save your life if you become entangled in line or fishing netting. Use a lanyard to secure your knife to your PFD—and don't use it to cut bagels at lunch.

I like folding knives, such as the excellent Spyderco Clipits, for rescue work, but a fixed-blade knife with a clip-in sheath might be even better, since there is nothing to manipulate. Gerber's River Runner has a plastic sheath that attaches securely to a lash tab on your PFD; a simple yank puts the knife in your hand.

A serrated edge cuts through line like nothing else, and in addition would serve as a saw blade for hacking through fiberglass or polyethylene.

4
CLOTHING

Beyond Fashion

Sea Kayaker magazine publishes accounts of sea kayaking accidents—from the merely embarrassing to the fatal—as object lessons to the rest of us, particularly those who recognize our own carelessness mirrored in the experiences of the victims. The proximate causes of these accidents are many, from wind to waves to currents to rogue powerboats. But the factors that separate a subsequent interview with a sheepish rescuee from an obituary can nearly always be boiled down to one of two things: the deceased weren't wearing PFDs,

or they weren't wearing outerwear designed to prevent immersion hypothermia.

That's a distinctly somber note on which to start my only chapter on fashion, but I can't stress a simple fact bluntly enough—sea kayaking, which is already an incredibly safe sport, would be virtually free of tarnish if kayakers just dressed properly and wore their damned life jackets.

A one-sentence rule will keep you out of trouble: Dress For The Water Temperature (D.F.T.W.T.). Hmm, that doesn't work very well, does it. Let's see . . . how about C.O.R.P.S.E. (Clothing Offers Respite for Paddlers Suffering Ejection). That should stick a little better.

This kayaker is properly dressed for the cold-water conditions she's paddling in: synthetic long underwear, fleece stretch pants and top, waterproof anorak with hood, knit cap, waterproof pants with ankle seals, snug rubber boots, and neoprene articulated kayaking gloves with grippy palms.

To appreciate the importance of proper clothing for sea kayaking, try an experiment. Take off all your clothes and go outside on a 45°F (7°C) day. Sit somewhere for a half-hour. How you feel at the end of that half-hour is how you'd feel after floating for one *minute* in 45°F (7°C) water, even wearing street clothes. Water conducts heat away from your body about 25 times faster than does air. So efficient is this effect that the water doesn't even have to be cold to cause hypothermia—the U.S. Coast Guard considers it a danger in any water less than 70°F (21°C).

A more immediate danger to a capsizing kayaker is *cold shock*—an involuntary reaction to sudden, unprotected immersion in very cold water. The mildest symptoms of cold shock are immediate disorientation, panic, and hyperventilation; at worst the syndrome causes an uncontrollable gasping intake of breath—which, if the victim is upside down at the time, leads to drowning. And you thought this book was going to be entertaining.

Now, there are parts of the world where cold shock and immersion hypothermia pose scant danger. But many of the most popular areas for sea kayakers—the Pacific Northwest, Alaska, Maine, Great Britain—often combine a misleading mix of pleasant air temperature with dangerously cold water temperature. Even the Sea of Cortez, in sunny Mexico, can be tricky—upwelling from deep offshore trenches around the midriff islands results in very chilly water conditions there even in late spring.

Many books show charts correlating water temperature with survival time. I think these are misleading. There are just too many variables on the ocean—most of which will be working against you—to trust a chart to tell you anything. Besides, "survival time" has little to do with how long you'll be able to function to save yourself. One chart lists survival time

Lessons Well Learned

Sea Kayaker magazine recently worked with Ragged Mountain Press to produce *Deep Trouble,* a book of true kayak rescue stories and their lessons, compiled from reports published in the magazine. The 20 accounts provide better instruction than any nagging on my part could about the importance of good safety gear and techniques.

in 40°F (4°C) water as one hour for an unprotected swimmer. Could be. However, it's likely that for the last 50 minutes of that hour you would be utterly incapable of coherent movement—unless you were wearing a dry suit, an appropriate garment for such conditions.

It's virtually impossible to draw firm rules for clothing in different water temperatures. There are simply too many variables: sea state, speed of any currents, distance from shore the route will reach, distance from medical help, plus paddler physique, rolling and reentry skills, number of companions, how long ago you ate—you get the picture. What I'm going to offer, then, is a suggested list of clothing that follows a steadily ascending level of protection. Here's a sample "wardrobe," starting with merely chilly conditions, with water temperatures in the 60s, and progressing to really cold (seawater can reach temperatures under 30°F [–1°C]without freezing).

1. Synthetic underwear, coated nylon or Gore-Tex paddling jacket and pants.

2. Synthetic underwear, fleece midlayer, paddling jacket and pants. Fleece or neoprene gloves. Hat.

3. Thermal stretch-fabric farmer john (that covers your legs and torso while leaving yur arms free), fleece top, paddling jacket, neoprene gloves and booties. Hat.

4. Farmer john wet suit, fleece top, paddling jacket, neoprene gloves and booties. Hat.

5. Full wet suit, fleece top, paddling jacket, neoprene gloves and booties. Hat or wet-suit hood. Pogies on paddle shaft.

6. Synthetic underwear, fleece midlayer, dry suit, neoprene gloves and booties. Hat or hood. Pogies.

There are various combinations possible within these parameters; for example, you can wear synthetic underwear under a wet suit to add insulation.

Types of Clothing for Cool-to Cold-Water Paddling

MINIMALIST PROTECTION

For conditions where the water is merely chilly—say in the 60° to 65°F (15° to 18°C) range—and you might be dealing with warm air temperatures, versatility is the key to both comfort and safety. This can be accomplished with an underlayer of lightweight synthetic underwear and a shell of water-repellent or waterproof/breathable fabric. The shell can be opened for ventilation while paddling, keeping you cool, but if zipped up after a capsize will at least slow the circulation of water next to your skin, which is the key to reducing heat loss.

Made-for-kayaking waterproof outerwear: an anorak with extra material in the shoulders for freedom of movement, an adjustable hood, double-protected zipper (with Velcro cover), big pockets, sealed wrist tabs, and adjustable waist; the pants offer articulated knees, roomy rear, and sealed ankles and waistband (both from Patagonia).

There are many excellent jackets and anoraks designed for sea kayaking. Most include elastic or hook-and-tape cuffs and neck openings, and good pocket space for safety items. I have a personal abhorrence of anoraks—I suffer claustrophobic heebie-jeebies getting the things over my head in a boat—but that's a personal lunacy. They work well for kayaking because the lower part of the torso has no entries for water slopping over the deck.

Over a base layer of Capilene or similar wicking underwear, synthetic fleece is the best material to increase insulation value. It absorbs little of its weight in water, and after a dunking needs only wringing out to regain reasonable effectiveness.

A fleece jacket or pullover is an essential clothing item for kayaking.

THERMAL STRETCH FABRIC

Here is a material that virtually eliminates your excuses for underdressing in marginal conditions. It used to be that you had to jump right from synthetic underwear and paddling jackets into wet suits once the water temperature dropped below 60°F (15°C) or so. If the water was cold but the air warm it felt like you were wearing Saran Wrap. Thermal stretch fabrics, such as Voyageur's Aquatech and Sport Suits of Australia's Thermalastic, bridge the gap comfortably.

Thermal stretch fabric comprises an outer layer of Teflon-impregnated Lycra for water repellency, backed by an elastic, waterproof/breathable membrane, with an inner layer of synthetic fleece. Garments made from the material are very stretchy and comfortable. When immersed, the material allows a layer of water to seep next to your skin; once your body heat warms that layer you stay comfortable. You can buy a farmer john and wear it alone, or put a full top over it. Sport Suits also offers a thinner material, without the fleece inner layer, for milder conditions. This material has a very versatile comfort range.

WET SUIT

When water temperature drops below 50°F (10°C) or so, the time you can spend in the water before losing coordination and presence of mind begins shrinking rapidly. If conditions are rough or currents are flowing the heat-robbing effects are magnified. It's time for serious protection, which a wet suit can provide. A wet suit functions by trapping a thin layer of water next to your skin, which quickly warms and stays warm due to the insulative properties of the neoprene.

Wet suits, made from neoprene and often backed with nylon, come in various thicknesses, from 1.5 millimeters (mm) up to 7 or more (most paddlers use 1.5mm to 3mm to ensure freedom of movement). They are also available in various configurations, from farmer johns to shorty suits to

Take into consideration what you know about your own physiology when you dress for kayaking. Everyone has different tolerances for cold, so don't feel foolish if you put on a dry suit when your companions are wearing wet-suit farmer johns.

full-body suits. The farmer john is a good basic wet-suit garment for kayakers, because it doesn't restrict upper-body movement but protects your core temperature. However, you should wear neoprene gloves to retain dexterity in your hands. You can also buy a fairly thick farmer john, and augment it with a thin top to increase protection but retain mobility.

Wet suit farmer john keeps your torso and legs warm while allowing freedom of movement in your arms.

A wet suit is very buoyant (that's why divers wear weight belts). It's an additional margin of safety for a kayaker, but don't think of it as a substitute for a PFD.

DRY SUIT

Because it completely isolates your torso and limbs from contact with the water, a dry suit is suitable for the coldest water—the Arctic Ocean, the Drake Passage, the Alaskan coast, the Faeroes. But winter conditions in more southern regions can be nearly as challenging.

A dry suit is made from waterproof fabric—either fully coated or utilizing a waterproof/breathable laminate such as Gore-Tex—with stretchy latex seals at ankles, wrists, and neck. You enter the suit through a waterproof zipper, which can run up the front or the back of the suit. Front zippers are infinitely preferable, not so much because they're easier to get into but because it's easier to work the zipper pull. The whole operation resembles some Houdini-esque escape act in reverse.

Dry suits *isolate* you from the water, but they do little to *insulate* you from it. You need an insulating layer underneath, usually some sort of wicking underlayer with a fleece midlayer. Often the biggest problem with dry suits is that they keep water *in* as well as out, meaning

A dry suit offers this kayaker the protection she needs in Arctic paddling conditions.

Look for neoprene kayaking gloves that have articulated (pre-bent) fingers and grippy patches on the palm.

Pogies—neoprene coverings that fit over the paddle shaft, and into which your hands slide—offer excellent additional protection in really cold water. But they should never be used alone, because in an emergency you will have to take your hands out of them to effect a rescue.

HEAD PROTECTION

One of the chief causes of the cold-shock syndrome I mentioned earlier in this chapter is icy water rushing into the victim's ear canals and hitting the sensitive tympanic membrane (eardrum). You could prevent this by never washing out your ears, so they filled up with wax and were rendered effectively waterproof, but your friends and family would become annoyed at having to shout to communicate with you. Much more convenient is a hat or a hood. Even a wool watch cap

perspiration has no place to dissipate. Gore-Tex suits alleviate this problem greatly, although they by no means eliminate it. Beware: The "ex" in Gore-Tex stands for *expensive*.

Since it traps air inside, a dry suit adds even more buoyancy than a wet suit. For years I've heard a horror story regarding dry suits, about someone who enters the water upside down and finds that the air trapped inside the suit has ballooned up his legs, so he is held head-down. I've never been able to find an actual documented case where this occurred, so the story might be apocryphal. It's a great one to tell other people wearing dry suits though—especially if you see someone in a nice Kokatat Gore-Tex model. Maybe they'll sell it to you cheap.

GLOVES

You could consider your hands to be your most basic rescue tool—without them you're helpless. Yet, when cold, the first thing your body does is shut down circulation to its extremities to protect the vital core area. So your hands need to be well protected to retain their dexterity. Neoprene gloves perform well in a variety of conditions, and are very comfortable. Buy ones with grippy material on the palm, and that are contoured to the shape of a grasping hand.

In cold weather and cold-water paddling, always wear gloves and a hat; you think with your head, which means a lot of blood circulates up there (and cools off fast) and you need your hands to work properly during a rescue.

pulled down over your ears will slow the rush of water. Fleece or pile caps and hoods, made to be worn under a jacket hood or waterproof hat if needed, are excellent, and a neoprene wet-suit hood offers nearly complete protection.

NOSE CLIPS

We're talking about *very* serious paddling here. Water up the nose is another factor in cold shock. Nose clips are the solution, but a damned uncomfortable one. Still, a set hung around your neck would be smart on a really exposed cold-water paddle; if conditions get nasty you can clip them on. "Heyb," you can then call to your companions, "I thig we od to lad sood."

FOOTWEAR

Neoprene booties offer good protection against cold, and are comfortable to paddle in. More versatile, though not as warm, are the new breed of so-called water shoes, which are built to walk and hike in, but can be immersed without harm to the shoe. In a situation in which you were cast on shore and had to walk out for help, several of the water shoes I've tested would serve nearly as well as good approach shoes.

If you like to keep your feet dry, nothing beats a genuine pair of British "Wellies." Be sure to wear an insulative layer underneath, however.

Footwear for cold-water paddling includes neoprene booties, like those scuba divers wear, and water shoes, like these kayaking shoes from Patagonia, which have neoprene collars, well-drained uppers, and grippy treads (see Appendix A for source information).

Hot-Weather Paddling

When air and water are both warm, your priorities change. Sun protection becomes the number-one goal.

A good, medium-brimmed hat is indispensable in the sun of tropical waters. I don't like hats with really wide brims, because they flop around in the wind and try to fly off. Two to 3 inches is about right—enough to shade your nose, ears, and neck. I've worn an Ulti-

Food and Water: Another Item of Clothing

Whether you're paddling in cold or hot weather, eating enough and drinking plenty of water are just as important as dressing properly. Your body functions best when its metabolism is properly fueled and hydrated.

It's easy to remember to drink when it's hot (although few of us actually do), but you can also dehydrate dangerously in cold weather without realizing it. Medical reports of hypothermia victims almost always list dehydration as a related condition. Keep a water bottle handy and remind yourself to sip often; likewise, a handy bag of snacks will keep your energy at peak levels.

Sunscreen

Don't neglect sunscreen: even body parts shaded by a hat can be burned by glare reflected off the water. You don't want to experience a burned septum (the divider between your nostrils). It's excruciating.

For hot-weather paddling, a medium-brimmed hat is essential (you don't want it so big and floppy it catches the wind), and a long-sleeved lightweight and well-ventilated shirt will be better than a t-shirt for sun protection.

Amphibious sandals are great kayaking footwear for hot-weather paddling. Buy an adjustable, open-toed model like this Teva so you can put on socks at night when the temperature drops.

mate Hat for several years, and it's held up well. The cinch strap keeps it on through the worst Baja *norte*.

It's tempting to wear short-sleeve shirts when it's hot, but holding your arms out the way you must while paddling is like putting them on a spit. I stick with lightweight long-sleeve cotton or nylon shirts in white. Brushed nylon shirts with mesh ventilation panels, such as those made by Tarponwear and ExOfficio, are excellent—you'd never know they weren't cotton.

Shorts are the order of the day for most people, but be careful if you paddle with your spray skirt loosened—your thighs will toast. Long pants made of similar material to your shirts are the best alternative. Patagonia makes nice, quick-drying shorts called Baggies, with a long-pants version as well. Tarponwear and ExOfficio also make good synthetic pants. If your paddling destination offers chilly nights and hot days, take along a pair of Lycra tights to wear under your shorts; you can shed them later when it gets hot.

Sunglasses

One last item to add—even for cold-weather paddling—is a pair of sunglasses to cut the glare and protect your eyes from damaging rays. Buy a truly dark pair, not those pastel-tinted fashion glasses. The double-gradient lenses from Ray-Ban are excellent.

PART

TWO

TECHNIQUES FOR TOURING

5

PADDLING TECHNIQUES FOR TOURING

Sea Kayaking with Sir Isaac Newton

A kayak with 150 pounds of gear inside is a different animal than the unburdened shell you learn to paddle in. Schools don't teach surf landings or rolling techniques in loaded kayaks, and many books show rescue procedures that would be at best useless, and at worst dangerous, with a loaded boat.

At the same time, a load actually enhances several of the kayak's natural handling characteristics. The theory behind this chapter, then, is to make the load work for you as much as possible.

The Physics of a Loaded Kayak

A loaded kayak floating on the ocean is, from a certain point of view, weightless—a 50-pound boat with 150 pounds of gear, plus a 150-pound paddler, say 350 pounds total, is supported on the water's surface effortlessly.

But that kayak still carries its full 350 pounds of *inertia*. Getting it moving from a standstill requires overcoming that inertia, and stopping or turning it in a hurry does too. If a wave picks it up and throws it at

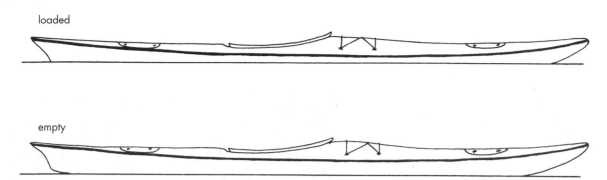

loaded

empty

A loaded kayak sits much lower in the water, reducing the effects of wind. Also, the waterline length increases, enhancing directional stability.

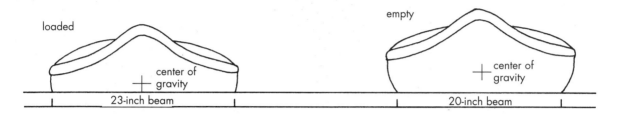

loaded

empty

center of gravity

center of gravity

23-inch beam

20-inch beam

The same kayak from the front, showing how the waterline beam also increases with a load. Note how much lower the center of gravity is.

the beach or a partially submerged boulder, you've got 350 pounds to control and aim.

Luckily, that inertia works for you at times. Once it's moving, a loaded kayak will tend to punch through small waves with little loss of momentum. Confused, choppy seas will knock it around less, and sudden gusts of wind will affect it less than they would an unloaded kayak.

A loaded kayak has other advantages. Provided it is properly distributed, weight greatly increases the stability of the boat (see Chapter 10, page 149, on loading). This results both from lowering the center of gravity, and from the fact that as the boat sinks in the water its waterline beam increases, enhancing initial stability. One advantage of practicing with an empty boat is knowing it will feel more stable when loaded.

The lower it sits in the water, the less of the boat there is for the wind to grab, in addition to the extra inertia gusts have to overcome to move it off course. This, combined with the longer waterline of a loaded kayak, means significantly enhanced tracking in a breeze. One of my wife's first sea kayaking experiences

was in an estuary sheltered from large waves, but raked by a 20- to 25-knot wind. She simply had no directional control over the (empty) plastic boat she was paddling, until we took it back to shore and loaded it with rocks. Problem solved.

Efficient Strokes

One of the most noticeable differences watching an expert kayaker paddling alongside a novice is the apparent lack of effort on the expert's part. This is no illusion, and it's not solely due to better conditioning—an experienced paddler simply uses less energy to move the kayak.

The secret—well, one of the secrets anyway—is smoothness. As your level of skill increases, your paddling style will shed itself of excess movement; your paddles will enter and leave the water with less splashing; your cadence will probably slow.

When I teach beginning kayakers, I concentrate less on forcing them into some standard style of paddling,

Good paddling form includes an upright posture, relaxed hand positions, and a slight twisting of the torso to maximize efficiency.

and instead work with them to refine whatever stroke comes naturally. This comes from my own early kayaking days, when I taught myself from books and thus had no personal analysis or input on my paddling technique. Years later I was paddling with an experienced instructor, who watched me for a while before commenting, "You have a very strange paddling style." He then paused for a moment, and said, "But it works."

One of the best ways to refine your stroke is to watch how much splashing your paddle blades create as they enter and leave the water. Every bit of water you splash is water you have shoved out of the way or even lifted into the air for no purpose whatsoever. Therefore, concentrate on getting your blade to knife smoothly into the water in front of you, and lift out cleanly behind you.

Don't worry if your paddle shaft whacks the side of the boat now and then, or if your stroke seems awfully splashy at first. Everything comes with time.

Most sea kayaking manuals advocate a low paddling stroke; that is, keeping the blade that is out of the water as low to the surface as possible. This both conserves energy and makes it easier to control the paddle in wind. However, there are times when a slightly more upright stroke is useful, with the blade planted in the water closer to the kayak. The reason for this is that the farther away from the boat the paddle blade is as it is pulled through the water, the more it tries to turn the boat instead of push it (imagine if you mounted the outboard engine to a powerboat on the end of a long bracket on the side of the boat—the boat would just spin in circles). The sweep stroke, a semicircular stroke accomplished with the paddle held as far out from the boat as possible, is designed to turn the boat quickly. It follows, then, that the closer to the boat the stroke, the more pure forward movement results. You can gauge

Whenever possible keep your paddle strokes low.

Forward strokes: 1. Plant the blade as close to the boat as possible without holding the paddle upright; note the relaxed hand positions (avoid a completely upright, energy-wasting whitewater-style stroke).

2. When drawing, avoid submerging the paddle more than a couple of inches beyond where the blades meet the shaft (pulling the shaft through the water creates turbulence but no propulsion).

3. Remove the blade from the water with as little splash as possible to reduce drag.

4. This paddler is moving too much water on the release.

Some Ocean Terminology

- Following sea: the wind and waves are coming from behind you.
- Soup: the relatively calm foamy water between breaking surf and the shore.
- Dumping surf: surf that breaks heavily right up against a steep beach; no soup, strong undertow.
- Spilling surf: surf that breaks more gradually farther offshore.
- Set: a number of large waves followed by several smaller waves; characteristic of most surf.
- Window: the period when the smallest waves of a set are breaking; the best time to launch or land.
- Broach: the stern of the kayak is snapped suddenly sideways by a wave, turning the boat broadside to the wave.
- Upwind: the direction from which the wind is coming.
- Downwind: the direction toward which the wind is blowing.
- Offshore breeze: a wind blowing from the land out to sea.
- Onshore breeze: a wind blowing from the sea to the land.

this effect by the amount of yaw in the kayak; that is, the amount the bow swings back and forth as you stroke on one side or the other.

When conditions are calm and the wind is low, I raise my paddle slightly to plant the blades closer to the boat, while avoiding a completely upright, energy-wasting whitewater-style stroke, and also avoiding submerging the paddle more than a couple of inches beyond where the blades meet the shaft (pulling the shaft through the water creates turbulence but no propulsion). As the wind rises, I lower my paddle, accepting the slight loss in efficiency for reduced wind resistance and a lower center of gravity.

Maneuvering

Many, many people never learn more than the simplest kayaking strokes. While they may still get where they want to go, they are missing out on about 80 percent of the capabilities of their boats, and thus, to be safe, must pass up 80 percent of the horizons open to them. In Chapter 1 I talked about the fusion between boat and paddler as the key to the kayak's capabilities. It's this *active* seaworthiness that makes the sea kayak such an awesome craft. It's the difference between hitting a tennis ball and being able to apply spin, between a

snowplow turn and a carved Telemark, between—dare I stretch it this far?—driving the minivan to the store and finessing a Porsche 917 around the Nurburgring.

USING RUDDERS AND SKEGS

As I mentioned in Chapter 1, I think the biggest disadvantage to foot-controlled rudders is the tendency to rely on them in place of basic boathandling skills. If your kayak has a rudder, by all means practice with it, so you can exploit its strengths to the fullest. But paddle without it too, in as many conditions as you can, so you'll know how your boat behaves should a cable or fitting snap.

Some kayaks—particularly those with long, straight keels—turn better with the help of the rudder, but don't need much tracking assistance from it. Other boats with more rocker (see Chapter 1, page 12 for an explanation of rocker) might actually turn faster with the rudder retracted, using simple paddle strokes, but need the rudder to hold a straight course. Experiment with the rudder up and then down to see which personality your boat displays. The revelation of just how horribly one of my kayaks handled crosswinds without its rudder led me to replace the cables and hardware with tackle stout enough to anchor a North Sea oil rig. The boat simply would not hold a course perpendicular to the breeze with the rudder retracted (or, by extrapolation, with it broken).

If you buy a kayak with a rudder, make sure you practice maneuvering in all conditions with the rudder up.

You'll find that, in any boat, a rudder can turn only so sharply before it stalls; that is, it assumes such an acute angle to the water that it acts as more of a brake than a rudder. You will be able to feel the transition as a decrease in speed, and hear it as well as the turbulence bubbles around the stern. At this point you need to back off on the pedals.

Be alert when using a rudder in rough seas. If the blade lifts out of the water as a wave passes under you, you will momentarily lose directional control, then regain it with a jerk as the blade submerges again.

Skeg-equipped kayaks require tuning to perform optimally. For example, in a crosswind most skeg boats will turn upwind *(weathercock)* with the skeg retracted,

Kayaks as Windvanes

A kayak left to itself will almost always turn broadside to the wind and waves. In any other position, the force of the weather will act more on one end than the other, so the boat swings until the forces are equalized.

However, if you start paddling that kayak broadside to the wind, without using the rudder or correcting strokes, it will usually try to turn *up*wind, until it is pointed about 30 to 50 degrees from a straight upwind course. The reason for this is that, as the kayak is pushed through the water, water pressure on the downwind side of the bow is greater that on the downwind side of the stern, so the wind pushes the stern farther downwind. This effect is called *weathercocking* or, in sailing terms, *weather helm* (as opposed to *lee helm,* meaning the bow wants to turn downwind). Virtually all kayaks weathercock to some degree.

Weathercocking can be controlled with a rudder, by simply turning in the opposite direction the bow is swinging. It can also be controlled with a skeg, which increases the lateral resistance at the stern. The skeg can be adjusted up or down to balance the handling of the boat on different points off the wind.

Load distribution in the boat affects weathercocking too. A sea kayak is usually loaded with about one-third of the load in the front compartment and two-thirds in the rear. Too much weight in the front will increase weathercocking. (See Chapter 10, page 150, for proper loading instructions.)

and turn downwind with it all the way deployed. So, to gain neutral handling, the paddler must adjust how much skeg is exposed. After a while you get used to the feel, and can adjust instinctively for any conditions. On long crossings in calm conditions, dropping the skeg will reduce yawing; skirting boulders along the coast you'll want it retracted for sharp handling.

TURNING

Minor course corrections and gentle turns are easy in any sea kayak. If you have a rudder, you just paddle normally while pushing with the foot that's on the side you want to turn to. Without a rudder, you simply stroke on the side opposite the desired change of direction.

Quite often, though, you need sharper response—skirting rocky coasts, handling currents and waves, or assisting another kayaker. A bit of sophisticated paddle technique and some body English will dramatically increase the responsiveness of your boat.

When you enter a turn on a bicycle or motorcycle, even when running, you lean into the turn. It's a natural reaction to keep your balance. So it is difficult to overcome the same instinct when turning a kayak. However, the underwater shape of most kayaks is such that they turn more quickly if leaned in the direction opposite the turn. Note that this does not mean that *you* lean. The idea is to keep your upper body vertical, and simply lean the boat with your knees and hips. You stay perfectly balanced throughout the turn. Combining such a lean with a *sweep stroke* will significantly decrease the turning radius of any kayak.

A proper sweep begins with the paddle planted in the water far forward and close to the bow. Sweep outward and back with the blade. This pushes the bow in the direction of the turn. As the stroke sweeps out and around, it acts as a normal turning stroke, but then you finish by pulling the blade all the way behind you and back toward the stern. The last movement actually pulls the stern around, furthering the new heading.

In rough seas you can increase the speed of the turn even more by turning when the boat is poised on the

A proper sweep stroke begins with the paddle planted in the water far forward and close to the bow. Sweep outward and back with the blade (shown in photo). This pushes the bow in the direction of the turn. As the stroke sweeps out and around it acts as a normal turning stroke, but then you finish by pulling the blade all the way behind you and back toward the stern.

crest of a wave, so its ends are out of the water. This move requires concentration, however, to make sure your paddle blade stays *in* the water.

Another way to turn with the paddle is to use it as a rudder when you have some momentum going, such as down the face of a wave, trailing the blade vertically in the water near the stern on the same side to which you wish to turn. (The original rudder was nothing more than an oar trailed similarly; on Viking longships it was mounted on a pivot on the right side of the sternpost. The term *starboard*—the right side of a boat—comes from *steer*board.) While a sweep stroke maintains the speed of the kayak, a *rudder stroke* slows it—in fact, a rudder stroke will work only if the kayak has sufficient speed to start with.

Using the paddle as a rudder to turn left.

To drastically slow and turn a kayak at the same time, employ a *reverse sweep,* which is exactly what its name implies—a sweep that starts at the stern, then arcs out and around to the bow. The bow turns toward the side on which you are sweeping.

Either a forward or reverse sweep can also be used to spin a stationary kayak nearly in place.

You can use a backstroke to stop, or to speed turning. Remain upright but twist your torso to the side on which you will perform the maneuver. Plant your paddle as far back as comfortably possible, and close to the hull; then, draw the blade back toward the front of the boat parallel to the hull or with a slight sweep.

DRAW STROKES

You've made a perfect approach to a low dock or rock, or a friend in another kayak holding out a Snicker's bar. You stopped directly opposite the goal—but you're still 10 feet away.

You can move a kayak sideways through the water in one of two easy ways. One is to reach out to the side with your paddle and plant the blade vertically in the water, with the face of the blade toward the boat. Pull the paddle toward you, and the boat will move toward the paddle. This is called a *draw stroke*. Repeat until you can reach the candy bar.

A more stylish technique is to place the paddle the same way, but instead of pulling move it back and forth in a figure eight, so that in each direction—back and forth—the blade planes through the water and pulls the kayak toward it. This is called a *sculling draw stroke*.

The only caution with both techniques is that you don't get too excited by the candy bar and capsize yourself.

To execute a sculling draw stroke, instead of pulling the face of the paddle straight back toward you, move it back and forth in the water in a figure eight, so that in each direction—back and forth—the blade planes through the water and pulls the kayak toward it.

Safety techniques, such as rolling, solo rescues, and assisted rescues, are covered in Chapter 6.

Bracing

Most people practice bracing less than any other kayaking maneuver except actual rolls and rescues. Too bad, because braces are easy to learn, quickly become instinctive, and will prevent the *necessity* of a roll or rescue about 99.9 percent of the time.

If you sit stationary in your kayak, place the blade of your paddle flat on the surface of the water, and push downward firmly, the boat will tip in the opposite direction. Similarly, you can lean the whole boat toward the paddle and push down, and right yourself instantly. This is the essence of a brace.

LOW BRACE

The low brace is the most useful, since it requires no change from a normal paddling stance except for a twist of the wrist to turn the paddle blade parallel to the water's surface. With the blade against the surface, a short, firm downward push will provide a surprising amount of support to right a tipping boat or lean into a wind gust. By planing the blade across the surface, the support from the brace can be extended for several seconds.

If you are paddling across the wind, always try to brace on the upwind side of the kayak. This helps you lean into the weather, and keeps the upwind paddle blade low. If you are caught off guard and must brace downwind, a quick, forceful "slap" brace will often suffice.

Low brace: With the blade against the surface, a short, firm downward push will provide a surprising amount of support to right a tipping boat or lean into a wind gust. By planing the blade across the surface, the support from the brace can be extended for several seconds.

Remember that virtually any standard paddling stroke can be turned into a partial low brace, by angling the paddle blade so it partially planes as you pull it through the stroke. In this way you gain both propulsion and bracing support at the same time.

HIGH BRACE

The high brace is rarely needed unless waves coming at you are head-high or larger, and very steep. It is thus useful when landing through surf (see section on surf landings later in this chapter). To perform a high brace you raise the paddle to the level of your shoulders, or even higher, and either plane the blade over the top of

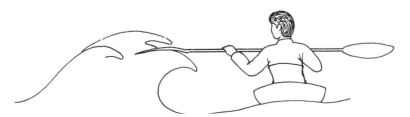

Using a high brace to steady the kayak against an oncoming wave.

the approaching wave, or actually stick it right into the face. The amount of downward force that can be applied in a curling wave is amazing.

SCULLING BRACE

The skulling brace is a very powerful brace that can safely support a kayak right at the edge of capsizing; it is very useful if a quick low brace doesn't do the trick and you need a few more seconds to get yourself righted.

The sculling brace uses the same principle as the sculling draw stroke—a back-and-forth figure-eight movement of the paddle—except in this case the paddle is held nearly flat against the water, so the planing back and forth results in support instead of propulsion.

You can use a normal grip on the paddle to perform a skulling brace. Extend the paddle out to the side of the boat, keeping the shaft as low as possible across your lap. Place the blade flat on the surface, then plane it back and forth. Lean toward the brace so a little of your weight is supported by the blade. Practice with the movement and the angle of the blade until you can commit more and more weight to the brace. With practice, you will be able to lean until your whole outboard arm is under water, and your head nearly so. A quick downward push will right the boat.

Launching and Landing

CALM WATER

Launching and landing in smooth sea conditions is mostly a matter of minimizing wear on the boat. If you're launching from the beach, load the boat right at the waterline to minimize dragging it over sand or rocks. I put my paddle across the deck on the *paddle park* (a pair of cleats immediately fore of the cockpit to which the paddle is temporarily secured by a loop of deck bungee), and use both hands to scoot the boat into the water, lifting it as much as possible with each shove. Even better is to enter the boat after you have it afloat in a few inches of water. The safest way to do this is to straddle the kayak at the cockpit and slowly lower your butt into the seat, then lift your legs in. If you have a very small cockpit opening you might have to sit on the rear deck and lift your legs in first. As long as you keep your weight centered you'll be okay. You can also use the paddle to steady the boat during a wet launch by bracing it against the bottom.

If the kayak is afloat in deep water next to low rocks (or a low dock), use your paddle to bridge the gap and

Preparing to launch: 1. The kayaker has donned and adjusted her spray skirt and steadies the boat before climbing in (the best way is by straddling it first, then sliding the rear, then one foot at a time). Next she will secure the spray skirt, beginning at the rear. 2. She launches in between wave sets using powerful strokes (rudder up, to avoid dragging).

steady the boat. Rest one end on the rock, and wedge the shaft against the rear cockpit coaming, gripping both shaft and coaming with one hand. Then you can step into the center of the cockpit and lower yourself in.

When landing, avoid the temptation to blast straight at the beach and slide half the boat out of the water; the gelcoat on the front edge of the bow will suffer. Instead, angle in and swing the stern around at the last second to put the boat parallel to shore. Or you can reverse the wet launch procedure, lifting your legs out in shallow water and straddling the boat, then standing up. Don't try to swing your legs out on one side, or you will capsize most ungracefully.

LAUNCHING AND LANDING THROUGH SURF

Dealing with surf is a little more complex, but not as difficult as you might think. Planning and commitment are the keys.

It's almost always easier to launch through surf than to land through it. That's a vital point to remember if you're debating whether to go out or not. If you feel the surf is on the edge of your ability to launch through, and you're not absolutely certain there is a more protected landing site at your destination, make another pot of coffee and get out a book.

Launching through small to moderate surf, on a gently sloping beach with plenty of "soup"—the foamy shallow water between the breaking waves and shore—is uncomplicated and usually uneventful, if frequently wet. First, look for an area along the beach where the break is gentlest, and launch there. Position yourself in the boat, spray skirt fastened, right at the edge of the water, so wash from the bigger waves almost lifts the boat. If there is enough soup for you to get afloat, do so—some gently sloping beaches have 50 yards or more of it. Watch the waves carefully until you determine the duration of the sets—a number of large waves followed by several smaller ones, characteristic of nearly all surf. The relatively calm period between large groups of waves is called the *window.* At the end of a big set, push off and paddle strongly straight out through the break. If a wave curls up at you, lean forward and punch right through it, avoiding the temptation to raise your arms over your head. Bring the paddle in under one arm to point it through the wave, so the wave doesn't smack it back into your chest, but be ready to stroke strongly once through the other side.

Be *very* cautious of dumping surf. Dumping surf is caused by a steeply sloping beach, causing the waves to tip and break right on the shore, often with heavy, shocklike sounds. There is no soup, and the undertow is often fierce. While it can become routine to launch through normal surf with waves 4 or 5 feet high or higher, a dumping surf with waves only 3 or 4 feet high can be extremely dangerous.

Landing in surf involves more variables than launching. First, it's harder to determine wave sets from the seaward side of the break. You must get as close to shore as possible, while staying behind the waves breaking farther out, and watch carefully, including back over your shoulder to gauge the incoming swells. Sometimes it's easier to *hear* waves sets than to see them. When you've determined that the last big wave of a set has passed, paddle hard toward shore on the back of the next wave, just behind the crest if you can, trying to keep the boat straight. If the wave gets ahead of you, continue to paddle strongly, but as the next wave overtakes, try to catch its back as well. The best way to hit the beach is on the gently collapsing back of one of these smaller waves.

Often, things won't go this way. Many times a wave coming up from behind will lift your boat and surf it toward shore at a furious pace. If you can keep control with rudder or a rudder paddle stroke, angle the boat slightly to one side or the other to plane down the face of the wave. Lean back to keep the bow from "pearling,"—burying its nose in the trough of the wave or even the sand underneath. If you angle to the right down the wave, you'll probably have to use some left rudder, or a stern paddle rudder on the left, to keep the boat from broaching parallel to the wave, but keep the boat itself leaned into the wave. Sometimes you can surf right up the beach. Other times, though, the kayak will broach no matter what you do, snapping quickly right or left on its own until it is broadside to the wave, bouncing along in crashing foam up to your nose. If the kayak broaches, immediately brace strongly into the face of the wave to keep the boat upright. Again, the wave might carry you all the way to shore; if instead it leaves you behind, turn straight toward shore again and resume paddling to catch the next wave.

The best rule for landing through dumping surf is, *don't.* If at all possible find a better spot. If you're forced to go through with it, time the wave sets carefully and paddle at top speed on the back of the smallest wave you can find. Forget taking it easy on the gelcoat; you want to get as far up the beach as possible. When the boat hits the beach, immediately leap out and get it out of the way or the next wave will suck it right back to sea.

If you are part of a group, the paddlers should launch and land one at a time, to avoid possible collisions. It's axiomatic that the most experienced paddler should always launch last and land first. This way he or she can help push off the less experienced paddlers at the right time, and can ease landings by timing wave sets from the beach and waving in succeeding boats, ready to grab the bow toggles and help them out of the water. Also, if the group sees the experienced paddler crash and burn on the way in, his kayak broken in two, barely dragging himself alive from the water, they know to go find another landing spot. The trouble with this situation is, it's difficult to get anyone to admit being the *next* most experienced paddler.

What if the surf is just too high to land through—and yet you have to anyway? This is when a sea anchor could be a lifesaver (see Chapter 3, page 39, for a description of the sea anchor).

Steph Dutton, who paddled the entire Pacific Coast of the United States, experimented successfully with deploying a sea anchor, and letting it slowly *back* him through very high breaking surf. He was able to control the boat as the surf came at him bow-on, the long line from the drogue flexing enough to keep the movements from being too abrupt. He was even able to back two kayaks at once through the surf on one drogue, by tying an additional line from the stern of his boat to the bow of another, so the kayaks went through the break line one at a time.

If you practice in surf, *wear a helmet.* If you're touring where surf landings might be frequent, *take* a helmet and have it accessible. If you capsize in surf you could hit your head on the bottom (see Chapter 7 for more on seamanship).

Paddling in Wind and Waves

I enjoy those occasional days when the ocean seems to sleep—when the largest waves in sight are the ripples from your bow, and you can hear the drips from your paddle blades as they splash back and shatter the mirror surface of the water.

But let's face it: if every day were like that, the challenge would vanish from sea kayaking, and with it the sense of accomplishment that comes from safely rounding a windswept point, crossing a turbulent channel, or negotiating a wave-battered, rocky coast. The days that test your limits provide the greatest reward. So you need to learn to deal with, to accept, even to welcome those days, and make sure your skills are up to them.

Wind and waves usually, though certainly not always, go together. If you can handle both at once, you can easily handle either one separately, so in this section we'll assume that you're faced with the combination.

HEADWINDS

Wind and waves coming straight at the bow are almost always the easiest—that is, safest—to deal with. Of course, if you're trying to *get* somewhere upwind, that's another problem. But right now we're just concerned with keeping your head above water.

Pointing into the wind takes advantage of the best profile of the kayak, it allows you to see what's coming, and you can lean strongly forward to lower your profile, while still paddling effectively. Your chief concern is to keep the bow on track. A drifting kayak will turn to lie broadside to wind and waves. The same kayak under power will usually assume a heading about 30 to 45 degrees off the wind, so if your bow veers right or left conditions will try to keep forcing it off course. The rudder can help, but only as long as you are able to maintain forward progress. If the boat stalls

Kayak tourers should be prepared to deal with all kinds of conditions. A morning of glass-smooth water can, by afternoon, become a wind-tossed frappé.

and begins to drift backward, the water will catch the rudder blade and force it over to one side, furthering the kayak's off-course momentum. If this happens and you can't force the rudder straight, you must lift it out of the water at once.

It's best to keep paddling when on an upwind course. Letting the boat drift for even a few minutes will erase significant portions of your forward progress. It's easy to be fooled; because with the wind and waves coming at you forward progress seems rapid, but a check of the shore will give you a real measure of your speed. Consider carrying a sea anchor, which reduces drifting to a minimum and allows stress-free breaks.

DOWNWIND PADDLING

Downwind paddling in mild conditions is easy and fast, although it doesn't *feel* fast unless there's a coast nearby for perspective. In low seas and breezes of 10 to 15 knots, you can cover an amazing amount of territory.

When wind and waves kick up, though, controlling the kayak becomes more challenging. As seas coming from behind get bigger and steeper, the effect is as though you were paddling toward shore in surf—except it goes on for miles. The trick, then, is to use surf techniques to keep the boat on course.

Steep waves coming from behind will try to broach the kayak just as surf waves will. Often the paddler will retain control until the crest of the wave lifts the boat's stern out of the water (along with most or all of the rudder), and it is blown suddenly sideways, sending the kayak skidding down the face of the wave until it trips and capsizes. A paddler in such conditions must have instantaneous, instinctive bracing skills. The first defense is to keep the boat headed straight downwind. Keeping up speed actually helps, because speed increases the responsiveness of the boat to rudder and paddle input. The resulting rides down the faces of big waves can be exhilarating or terrifying, depending on your state of mind, but if you stay pointed downwind you should be okay. If the stern starts to snap around to the left, apply left rudder (or a left paddle rudder) to

head downhill again. If the boat doesn't respond, and starts to slide sideways down the face, brace on the upwave side. This will keep you upright, but it also slows the boat so the wave passes under you. The instant the crest passes, stop bracing and get the kayak pointed downwind again before the next wave lifts it.

Sometimes it is not possible to stay with the waves passing you. In this case you can let the wind push you at a moderate pace while using most of your paddling effort to stay on course. The kayak will naturally yaw as the waves push it around; you'll need to use rudder and sweep strokes to maintain heading.

If you are caught out in really dangerous conditions, with the only safe landing downwind, and are having difficulty controlling the kayak, turn it around and keep it pointed into the seas. The wind will drift you backward toward your goal. It will be slower, but safer. When you are close to your goal and need to turn around, do so either in the trough or on the crest of the wave, not on the face. Turning in the trough offers you some protection from the wind, but turning on the crest lifts the ends of the boat out of the water and assists a quick sweep to spin the boat toward its new heading.

CROSSWINDS

Strong crosswinds are simply no fun to paddle through. They require constant attention to keep the kayak on course and upright, and the whole time waves are slapping you upside the head in a most rude manner.

Paddling in crosswinds and beam seas tests the seaworthiness of a kayak. The easier your boat is to rock side to side with body English, the easier it will be for you maintain an even keel as waves try to tip the boat first one way, then the other. The idea is to keep the kayak essentially level with the horizon at all times.

Your rudder pedals, if you have them, should be adjusted so you can work them with your knees braced firmly under the deck. Your knees are the key to the fusion between you and the boat. When a wave approaches, say from the left, the kayak will attempt to tilt to the right. As the boat begins to slide up the wave and tilt, press up with your right knee, at the same time rocking your hips left, to keep the boat level. As the crest passes, the boat will tilt the other way, and you reverse the procedure. (I made the mis-

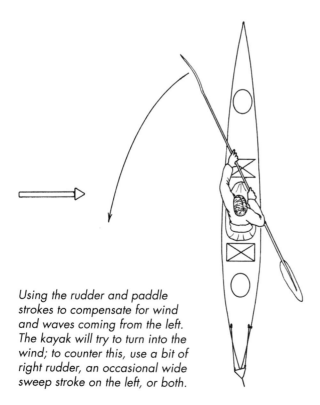

Using the rudder and paddle strokes to compensate for wind and waves coming from the left. The kayak will try to turn into the wind; to counter this, use a bit of right rudder, an occasional wide sweep stroke on the left, or both.

take of asking my wife for an analogy to this action. She thought a moment, then said, "Sure—it's like a dog lifting his leg to pee: up goes the knee; down goes the opposite hip." Thanks, honey.)

On paper, it sounds like a consciously orchestrated series of events, but it becomes absolutely automatic with time. I can sit beam-on in good-size waves while photographing or reading a chart—not because I have superior skills, but because these motions become ingrained in any experienced kayaker.

In most seas, leaning the boat will be enough to maintain control, and you can devote your paddling

The Windward Stagger Formation

This sounds like something three sailors leaving a seaport bar would do. It's actually a formation for a group of paddlers, which allows the leader to keep an eye on everyone, while a sweep paddler brings up the rear.

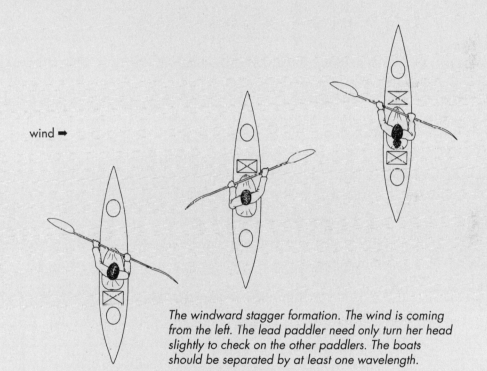

wind ➡

The windward stagger formation. The wind is coming from the left. The lead paddler need only turn her head slightly to check on the other paddlers. The boats should be separated by at least one wavelength.

As you can see from the illustration, this formation puts a strong paddler in front, while succeeding paddlers place themselves slightly behind and to windward of the leader, with a sweep paddler last. The leader has only to turn slightly to check on the group. If one of the paddlers capsizes, the leader can easily stop and place his or her kayak where the capsized boat will drift down on it for a rescue. It's easy for the rest of the group to assist or raft up.

Paddlers in a group should always stay within whistle range, but not bunch up too close, so waves don't cause collisions. Usually one to two wave lengths between paddlers is about right (except in the Pacific, where a whole party can often fit on the face of a single swell).

to forward movement. As the waves get larger and steeper, though, you might have to employ the occasional brace on the top or even into the face of the wave to help support the boat. You can turn the power stroke on the upwind side into a semibrace, by angling the blade so it partially planes as you pull.

It's vital to time your paddling cadence to coincide with the wave pattern. You don't want to be stroking on the downwind side of your boat as a wave lifts you; your paddle blade will likely meet thin air, or, worse, if it makes it into the water the wave might push the kayak right over it. Plant your stroke in the face of the wave as it lifts you, then stroke into the back of the wave as it passes. If the waves are farther apart, you can paddle in the troughs and brace/paddle over the crests.

Of course, while you are bracing and leaning and body Englishing over the waves, the wind is going to be trying to knock you over as well. Offer it as little surface area as possible, by crouching to keep your profile low, and your paddle as close to horizontal as you can. If, despite your grip, the wind snatches the paddle away from you, let go with the upwind hand and let the paddle flip up and over, spilling the force.

Perhaps the most difficult of all situations in which to paddle is a quartering wind, coming from about 45 degrees on either side of the stern. In this situation, waves will be constantly trying to broach the boat, and you have a hard time keeping watch on what's coming up behind you. Close concentration is needed, along with quick bracing skills.

Paddling in crosswinds requires some special navigational techniques to accurately reach your destination; for more on this, see Chapter 8, page 119.

DOWNDRAFTS

One other direction from which wind can arrive unexpectedly is straight overhead. If you are paddling close to cliffs, and a strong wind is blowing out to sea, very often downdrafts will punch the surface with astounding force, scattering in different directions and

One other direction from which wind can arrive unexpectedly is straight overhead. If you are paddling close to cliffs, downdrafts can punch the surface with astounding force, scattering in different directions and knocking you every which way. Paddling farther offshore is safer.

Kid Kayakers

Children love boats. They seem especially attracted to kayaks—perhaps because kayaks are small compared to a lot of other types of boats, and thus not so intimidating. Sea kayaking is a wonderful sport for children, but they should be self-sufficient in the water, with good swimming abilities, before coming along.

- Always outfit kids with proper life jackets and safe clothing appropriate to weather and water temperature.
- Outings with young children should be limited to very sheltered waters, close to shore.
- Several models of double kayaks with a center compartment can be used as triples, with the center hatch converted to take a seat. These are perfect for carrying children—but in the event of a capsize, the child must be capable of self-rescue. Don't count on your own ability to be able to help them; you'll be busy enough on your own, or could even be injured or otherwise hampered.
- Many people put young children in the seat with them in a single; this is an unsafe practice because you both could be trapped in the cockpit. Likewise, those who put a child in the rear compartment of a single have eliminated the flotation in the rear of the boat, also very unsafe. Even the triple kayak sacrifices flotation in the center compartment.
- This shouldn't scare anyone off from including their children in the sport. It's just common sense to be sure your child is as ready as you are for any situation that might arise.
- Older children can take advantage of kayaks made especially for them. This is when the real enjoyment starts, because no child loves anything better than a little bit of independence. The only problem arises when they start outpacing mom and dad!

knocking you every which way. Even though the sea might be a bit rougher farther out, you will probably be safer there, in the more predictable conditions.

Kayak Sailing

I might as well admit to a slight prejudice—I think sailing with a kayak retains just the faintest whiff of cheating. Once, on a long downwind Baja paddle, my companion brought out a small, triangular sail. He erected it on a collapsible aluminum mast that fit through a hole in the foredeck and into a fitting glassed into the floor of the cockpit. His speed immediately jumped about 2 knots, and he pulled away from me effortlessly. I remained behind, feeling quite superior that any mileage *I* covered that day would be honestly gained. This went on for about three rest stops—where

he would be relaxing as I pulled up exhausted. Finally I decided that, in the interests of possible magazine articles on the subject, I should get some photographs of his setup in action. So, with many sidelong smirks, my friend rigged a line from his stern to my bow, and away we went.

Well, it was all well and good to scoot along with no effort at all, but I remained steadfast in my determination to proceed on my own, and as soon as I had enough photographs I insisted on being cut loose. Of course, I'm not sure how long it's going to take me to sell seven 36-exposure rolls' worth of the back of my friend's kayak. . . .

Kayak sailing has evolved radically in the last 10 years. The early attempts to gain downwind speed consisted of flying a parafoil kite, which dragged the boat along at the edge of control in even a moderate breeze. Today, Easy Rider offers as an option for their

A sail on your kayak can increase your speed dramatically in a downwind situation.

double kayaks a system with twin outriggers and a batwing sail setup on *three* masts. This rig is fully capable of tacking upwind. The only thing missing is a carved mermaid on the bow.

The whole-hog Easy Rider setup, while amazing, certainly goes beyond my definition of sea kayaking. However, for touring use, it's possible to equip a kayak with a compact collapsible mast and sail that will significantly increase your speed downwind. For example, Primex of California makes a triangular sail that erects on a three-part fiberglass-wand mast, and stores on deck.

A sail on a kayak obviously plays havoc with stability. Here you are

Primex sail rig.
(Courtesy Primex of California)

in this craft that you've carefully loaded to keep weight as low as possible, and you're going to stick this big piece of cloth up in the air. It's like carrying a sheet of plywood in a breeze. Common sense as well as sea sense are called for.

Sailing directly downwind involves nothing more than letting the wind push you along. The more sail you have up, the closer your speed will approach that of the wind, until you near your theoretical hull speed (if you've forgotten this already, see Chapter 1, page 12). Stability isn't affected too much in reasonable conditions, but gusts and eddies in the wind can create sideways instability.

Once you try to move off the wind's course, the main force of the wind starts pushing the boat over sideways as well as forward. Unlike a sailboat, a kayak doesn't have a weighted keel, so there is little to resist this force (unless you've got Easy Rider–type outriggers, which give the effect of a trimaran). So a kayak with a downwind touring sail can effectively sail only very nearly straight downwind.

Sailing across the wind, and tacking upwind, involves entirely different science than going downwind. To move the boat at right angles, or closer, to the direction of the wind, the sail has to function as a wing, just like the wing on an aircraft. The slightly bellied shape of the sail, and its proper attitude just shy of parallel to the breeze, creates a low-pressure area on the back of the sail, which translates to forward motion on the boat. In a sailboat, the keel keeps the boat from sliding downwind; on a kayak, leeboards or outriggers serve the same purpose. Several manufacturers besides

Easy Rider are making sailing systems capable of reaching and tacking. Keep in mind, however, that most of these rigs aren't things you can put on and take off during the course of a trip. You have to pick whether you want a kayak or a sailboat before you launch.

While all this innovation among hard-shell kayaks has occurred, the folks at Klepper have just been chuckling. The Klepper Aerius folding kayaks have had optional full sail rigs for decades.

Skills such as dealing with currents and tides, reading the patterns of waves, the rules of shipping and rights of way, techniques for crossings, navigation, and other seamanship topics are covered in Chapters 7 and 8.

The Klepper, with its wide beam, can take advantage of a sophisticated sail rig. The system consists of a mast with both mainsail and jib, and leeboards on each side of the cockpit to resist downwind slipping when reaching. There is even a tiller available for the rudder, so the paddl . . . uh, sailor can perch up on the windward edge of the cockpit to ballast the boat, just like you see dinghy racers doing. Yet the Klepper rig can be disassembled at any time so you can resume paddling—when your conscience gets the better of you.

By the way, the new, open-cockpit double from Feathercraft will be available with a sail rig as well. At a trade show recently, the Feathercraft folks reacted with surprisingly good humor when I referred to the new design as the "Feathercraft Aerius."

6

RESCUES AND RECOVERIES

Simply put, a *rescue* in sea kayaking means that someone has capsized and exited the kayak (what we call a *wet exit*), and needs to right the boat and get back in. If the capsize occurs within the surf zone, the rescue usually involves getting paddler and boat safely back to shore. Some people classify Eskimo rolling as a rescue, but it's really more of a *recovery*, since the paddler never leaves the cockpit and can usually resume paddling immediately. We'll cover both rescues and recoveries in this chapter.

Many, many people explore thousands of miles of coastline in sea kayaks without ever capsizing. Some are skillful, some are lucky, and some just never put themselves in a position in which a capsize is likely. The stability intrinsic to most modern sea kayaks has kept many other paddlers out of trouble, even in situations that were beyond their abilities. But if you bought this book I'm assuming you are eyeing broader horizons with the desire to meet them fully prepared (I like to slip in these compliments now and then). Trust me on this: if you prepare yourself ahead of time with the knowledge and skills to handle emergencies, you will not only be better equipped for real adventuring in your kayak, but your confidence will also result in much greater enjoyment of those challenges.

Two Ways to Approach Kayak Touring

You can go to sea in your kayak with one of two attitudes. The first is the blissfully ignorant approach, practiced successfully by thousands of paddlers each year. You don't think about capsizing, because it's unlikely. You don't worry about safety equipment or protective clothing or rescue techniques because you'll probably never need them.

Statistically, very few people who take this approach get into trouble. When they do, however, it is usually *big* trouble.

The other way to kayak is to be aware of the possibility of trouble, prepare for it, and then relax and enjoy yourself. Very few people who take this approach get into trouble either—but when they do, they analyze the situation, handle it calmly and competently, and go back to having fun.

Take your pick.

What to Do After a Capsize

Capsizes come in two basic kinds. The first is the absentminded capsize, when you're simply not paying attention in moderate conditions and a wave catches you unaware. The second is the dire-straits capsize, when you're caught in truly bad weather and dumped despite your best efforts. The results are the same, although recovering is more difficult in the latter instance.

If you do capsize, there are several courses of action available to you. In decreasing order of preference (mine anyway), they are:

1. **Rolling back up.** This is by far the best option. It puts you back upright in a few seconds, minimizing exposure to the water; it results in little or no water in the cockpit, since the spray skirt remains attached; it requires no extra gear to be deployed; and it doesn't require assistance from companions who might be having difficulty themselves.

2. **Reentering and rolling.** Even if you have good rolling skills, you could be caught off-guard by the capsize, or otherwise unable to roll successfully the first try, and wind up in the water. Reentering the upside-down kayak and rolling back up is a useful strategy. It's quick, requires no help, and you can time the reentry to take advantage of a lull in waves, and to make sure you have a lungful of air. The disadvantage is greater exposure time, and significantly more water in the cockpit, which will need to be pumped out.

3. **Reentering and rolling with a paddle float.** If your roll is marginal, or conditions are fierce, inflating a paddle float on the end of the paddle and using it as an aid to roll back up (as in number two above) will greatly increase your chance of success.

4. **Reentering with a paddle-float outrigger.** Properly done, a paddle-float self-rescue can be accomplished in very rough conditions, especially if you also employ a drogue. Since the boat is righted first, this technique usually scoops less water into the cockpit than a reentry and roll. On the other hand, the outrigger system must be secure and reasonably rigid to ensure rapid success, and there is a certain amount of time, when the paddler is squirming across the deck into the cockpit, when the stability of the whole operation is marginal, even with the help of the float.

5. **Assisted reentry.** I listed this option last, but depending on conditions it could be number two. The first condition, of course, is that you have someone to assist you. Then, conditions must not be so bad that your companion or companions are fully involved in their own struggles to stay

upright, or would put themselves in danger trying to reach you. Otherwise, an assisted reentry can be fast and easy, resulting in very little more exposure time than a reentry and roll. An added advantage is that your companion can continue to stabilize your boat while you fasten the spray skirt and pump out the cockpit.

The most important thing to remember about this list of options is that at least one of them will work in virtually any situation, provided you have practiced it thoroughly and are wearing clothes that will keep you warm enough to continue functioning for the time you are in the water. (See Chapter 4, beginning on page 50, for tips on the right clothing for kayaking.)

Wet-Exit Etiquette

Before you can learn any recovery or rescue techniques, you have to learn how to fall out of your kayak gracefully. Yes, you should practice wet exits for a couple of reasons—first, to learn how to retain control of the boat and paddle; second, to get comfortable with the feeling of being upside down in the kayak. Once you try it, you'll lose your fear of it.

So. Get in your kayak without the spray skirt first, in calm water near shore, or in a pool. Wear your PFD, and a dive mask if you wish. Have someone nearby to assist you, and to take your paddle for the first few tries. Brace your knees under the deck to anchor yourself in the boat, take a breath, and lean over until you capsize. Now, hang there for a second or two and look around. Not so bad, is it? Now grasp the front of your cockpit coaming with both hands, and tuck-roll out of the cockpit to the surface. You will come up facing the rear of the kayak, still holding onto the coaming.

Next, try it with the spray skirt fastened. Make sure the release loop is out, and that the skirt is not too tight around the cockpit opening. Try yanking off the skirt a few times on land to make sure you can do it quickly. Now, capsize again, yank the release loop to free the skirt, then grab the cockpit coaming again and surface.

Once you've done this a few times, practice while holding a paddle, releasing the skirt and grabbing the boat with one hand while holding the paddle with the other. Then try it without a mask. Now you'll be able to relax when you practice further recovery and rescue techniques.

Practice falling out of your boat and reentering; you will feel much more confident, more relaxed, and have more fun when touring.

You can learn to roll on your own, but you'll learn much faster if you take a class from a qualified instructor. A day-long course will do it, after which you'll be sore as hell, but able to practice with a better grounding in technique.

The Bombproof Eskimo Roll

I'm going out on another limb here: I don't think any expedition kayaker needs to know more than two styles of Eskimo roll: the screw roll and the pivot roll. The myriad arcane techniques illustrated in books and articles are interesting, and occasionally historically pertinent, but they confuse a lot of people, and further the misconception that rolling requires some sort of black magic. I also think that, in most circumstances, if a screw or pivot roll doesn't work, it's very unlikely that switching to a King Island roll or a Steyr roll or a vertical storm roll will work either. I am not putting down those techniques, or even claiming they are less effective—they are just redundant. If you become expert at the screw and pivot rolls, and want to try different styles for fun, great. If you just want a reliable method of righting yourself and your kayak, keep it simple.

When you do practice, it's helpful at first to use a diving mask, to keep water out of your nose and provide a better view of the proceedings. But practice without the mask later, unless you plan to wear one every time you paddle. It's also very helpful to practice with a loaded boat once you've done so with an empty one.

One thing to remember when practicing rolling is that you don't have to succeed on the first try. In fact, you can use a sculling brace stroke (see Chapter 5, page 67) to bring your head to the surface to catch your breath and get oriented before beginning the actual roll.

THE SCREW ROLL

The screw roll is so called because if you try it once and miss, you're . . . no, just kidding. It's called that because you twist yourself to the surface and back upright, using leverage rather than brute force.

The advantages to the screw roll are several. First, you don't have to shift your grip on the paddle. Second, the sequence of moves is simple and instinctive. Finally, because it relies more on technique than strength, even people with marginal upper-body strength can accomplish it. In fact, I know an instructor who claims women on average learn the technique much quicker than men, because they concentrate on the moves rather than thinking they can just muscle their way up.

The screw roll is diagrammed in the accompanying illustration. In step 1, the kayaker positions the paddle as shown, with the forward blade nearly flat on the surface. In step 2, he begins to sweep the blade out and around. As it planes across the surface, he begins to rotate the boat to a partially upright position. The buoyancy of his PFD is assisting him too. By step 3, he can lift his face from the water to take a breath—but under no circumstances should he try to lift his entire head out of the water. Instead, in step 4 he uses his hips to "flick" the kayak upright. This is the crux move of any roll, and the hardest part to get straight, because your instincts are screaming at you to forget about the boat and get *yourself* out of the water. However, by step 5 the kayak has snapped to an upright position, and combined with the last sweep of the paddle (step 6) is helping to pull the paddler's torso out of the water.

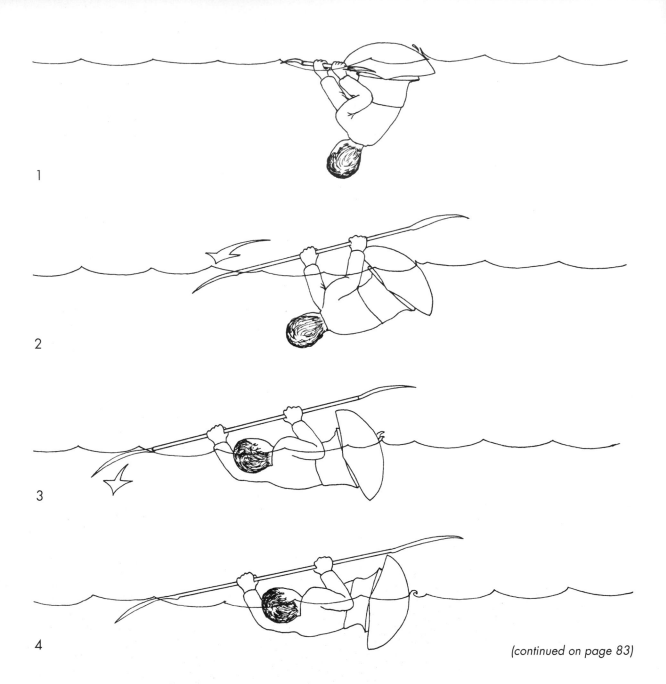

1

2

3

4

(continued on page 83)

Note that by this step the paddler is leaning well back, both to provide clearance for the sweep and to keep his center of gravity low.

The screw roll can be accomplished in less than 5 seconds, and is forgiving of imperfections in the path of the planing paddle blade—if it planes just under the surface, the roll will still work. If you attempt the screw roll in rough water and have the presence of mind to stay oriented, try to roll up on the upwind side. That way you'll emerge leaning into the wind, and if a wave hits as you roll, it will help you up instead of slapping you back down.

5

6

A screw roll (1–6). Note how the demonstration sequence was accomplished with such style that the model's hair remains perfect.

THE PIVOT ROLL

The pivot roll requires you to shift your grip on the paddle, but it gives you more leverage than the screw roll and requires less finesse in the placement of the outward blade. The pivot roll is also excellent when used with a paddle float. This roll has several permutations and names ("Headstand" is one), but I think "pivot roll" best describes the action.

Rather than the planing support provided by the paddle blade during the screw roll, the pivot roll relies on simple resistance of the blade to being forced straight down into the water, as when you perform a brace. To initiate the roll, as the illustration on page 85 shows, you move the paddle out until one hand is grasping the blade, and the other is gripping the shaft at about midpoint. Reaching up to the surface, extend

the outward blade as far as you can, and pull down firmly, using your near hand and the end of the paddle as a "pivot" for the lever, holding it tightly against your side. Done quickly, with a good hip snap, the outward blade will not sink far at all, but you still need to pull it out of the water by the shaft, rather than trying to force it straight back up. Otherwise you will pivot yourself right back over. You can set yourself up for the roll by first using a sculling brace to bring your head to the surface. A sculling brace utilizes the same grip on the paddle, so you don't have to shift your grip for the final push.

The pivot roll is often taught using part of the kayak deck to anchor the tip of the pivoting paddle blade. I prefer gripping the blade with my hand to minimize the chance of slipping; however, if you use an unfeathered paddle, the paddle park cleat just in front of the

Practicing with an Audience

I have a kayaking friend named John who is a physical therapist by trade. A couple of years ago he was working at a nursing home, a fulfilling position for him because his expertise had such an immediate effect on the comfort and health of the residents. He became fast friends with a group of very elderly ladies who were wheelchair-bound, and who delighted in both John's skill and his zany sense of humor.

At the time, John was just learning how to Eskimo roll, using an old whitewater kayak. He got permission from the manager of the nursing home to use their indoor pool, and a few evenings a week he practiced rolling. One night after he plonked the kayak in the pool and wiggled into the cockpit, a door opened, and John saw several orderlies wheeling his fan club of little old ladies out to the pool's edge to watch. A little self-conscious, he nevertheless paddled around a bit to get the feel of the boat, then took a breath and capsized.

John described his first efforts to roll with an audience as "flailing, thrashing, and cursing"—but he finally managed to struggle upright. Shaking his head, he looked over to see the effect of his performance on the ladies.

Each one of the old dears was holding up a large white card, on which was scrawled a number with a felt-tipped pen: 6.8, 7.0, 6.7. . . .

The capper came after their giggling fit subsided, when one of the ladies leaned to her neighbor and, in a whisper loud enough to register through a hearing aid—as well as carry across the pool—said, "If he tries that in a river, his ass is *drowned*."

cockpit on many American kayaks can provide a reasonably secure base.

You can also combine the screw and pivot rolls (uh-oh, this is starting to get complicated), by shifting your grip on the paddle to the pivot position, but then doing a sweep to roll back up. This results in tremendous power, but requires more strength as well.

Incidentally, I should offer a general apology for our use of the term "Eskimo" roll. As you might know, the word *Eskimo* was originally a derogatory term meaning "eater of raw meat." The preferred inclusive term for northern indigenous peoples in Alaska, Canada, and Greenland is Inuit—but there's little likelihood of getting everyone to say "Inuit roll." As a matter of fact, the native people of my own region, the Tohono O'Odham, were long called Papago, meaning "bean-eaters," another put-down at the time. Recall that these epicurean belittlements were adopted by a society whose own gourmands, to properly age a chicken carcass, hung it by the head until the body decomposed enough to fall off.

Self-Rescues

In many capsizes the victim is completely unaware of the impending event until he or she is upside down. There is no sense of "Uh-oh, I'm about to capsize," no time to take a deep breath or attempt to brace. This suddenness, combined as it often is with the shock of cold water, means that even experienced paddlers with good rolling skills sometimes find themselves treading water next to their upside-down boat.

Two things you must *never fail* to do during a wet exit: hang on to the paddle, and hang on to the boat. In rough conditions either one could be blown out of your reach quickly. Of course, if it's an absolute choice of one or the other, *stick with the boat, even if the paddle is floating just feet away.*

Traditional wisdom has always urged staying on the downwind side of the kayak, so it can't be blown away from you. This strategy has its own disadvantage, however. In high winds and waves, the boat will attempt to run you down with each passing sea. I've also found that the boat, with its higher windage, tries to pivot around the swimmer, who is acting as a drogue. If conditions are so bad that you are having trouble controlling the boat from the water, the solution is a real drogue (sea anchor), which will not only slow the boat's drift, but keep its nose into the wind. With the boat held into the wind, any rescue is much easier. (For more on using drogues, see Chapter 3, page 39.)

It's been suggested that a drogue exacerbates the dangers of getting separated from the kayak, because it essentially stops the boat's drift while you can still be blown downwind. This is a moot point, because without a drogue the boat can be blown downwind much faster than you can swim. Either way, you should never let go of the kayak. But never tether yourself to it, or even put your hand through the bow carrying loop. If the boat rolls over in the waves, your hand could become trapped or injured.

REENTRY AND ROLL

For paddlers with good rolling skills, this is the quickest way to recover from a wet exit. You can be back in the boat and rolled up within a minute.

The best way to perform a reentry and roll is to position yourself next to the cockpit, facing the rear of the boat (which is the way you come up after a wet exit). Watch the wave patterns for a window, then take a breath and tuck-roll up into the cockpit. Quickly

A pivot roll, using the right hand as the pivot. Pull the left hand straight down sharply while using a hip flick to right the boat.

lock your knees in under the deck, position the paddle, and roll back up, using either a screw or pivot roll. Then, depending on conditions and how much water has entered the cockpit, you can refasten the spray skirt and pump out while bracing, or deploy a sea anchor for a little more control. If you are paddling with someone, you can also raft up, positioning your boats side by side and having your companion hang on to your cockpit while you pump. The rafting technique provides solid stability in all but the biggest seas.

REENTRY AND ROLL WITH
A PADDLE FLOAT

With a little practice, this technique can get you back in your boat in really bad conditions. It takes more time to set up, but you are almost assured of a successful roll as a result, in addition to which the paddle, with float attached, can serve as an outrigger to steady the kayak while you pump out the boat.

This rescue is accomplished similarly to the previous one, except you first attach the paddle float. Make sure you know in advance the proper way to attach the float, because styles differ.

Once you have the float attached, tuck into the cockpit and roll back up, using a simple pivot roll (a screw roll will work as well, but the sweep is largely unnecessary). The float will provide tremendous leverage to right the kayak. Reattach the spray skirt, then brace the paddle across the cockpit rim in front of you, so the float forms an outrigger. You can do this reasonably well with just one hand by pressing down on the shaft at the side of the boat, freeing the other hand to pump.

PADDLE-FLOAT OUTRIGGER REENTRY

Ahh, the famous paddle-float rescue. It has been described as "an excellent way for a novice to reenter a kayak in calm water"—a backhanded compliment if I've ever heard one. On the other hand, I know of paddlers with absolutely no rolling or rescue skills who pop a paddle float under the deck bungees and head out on exposed crossings, assuming they'll figure out how to use it when the time comes. The biggest danger of the paddle float is the false sense of security it engenders among fools.

Properly used, a paddle float will get a kayaker back in the boat in very rough conditions. The correct procedure is vital, though, and at best the paddler is in the water for much longer than the rescues described above.

Sea conditions make a big difference in the effectiveness of, and the strategies best employed with, a paddle-float outrigger. In big ocean swells the procedure is actually more manageable than in fast, steep, wind-driven waves. In the latter situation a drogue could help considerably by keeping the bow nosed into oncoming waves, preventing them from broaching the boat down onto you as you attempt to climb in. A properly set-up drogue takes only seconds to release, after which you can begin setting up the float while the drogue line is still deploying. You must be

Realistic Practice Sessions

Start out practicing rescues and rolls in the calmest conditions, and with as few things to get in the way as possible. However, as you progress, try to make your dry runs as realistic as possible.

Experiment with your rescue equipment to find the best places to secure it for access. Try rescues in a windy, but enclosed, harbor or lake. And finally, try adding some weight in the kayak to get a feel for recovering a loaded boat.

To reenter a kayak with a paddle float used as an outrigger (front-of-paddle entry position): 1. After securing the float-equipped paddle in the deck webbing, the kayaker grasps the cockpit with the left hand and shaft with the right hand while pushing down on the paddle to heave the body up. 2. The kayaker will hook her right knee over the paddle shaft as she swings her left leg into the cockpit, then brings in the right leg, remaining lying face-down on the rear deck. 3. Keeping her center of gravity low, the kayaker slides her legs down into the cockpit and carefully twists around until she is facing forward, keeping her hand on the paddle and using the float to remain steady.

ready for the elastic jerk when the drogue bites the water, however.

It's sometimes possible to succeed in reentering the kayak by simply bracing the floated paddle across the back of the cockpit, gripping the shaft with your thumb, and hooking your fingers under the cockpit rim. But a harness system on the rear deck makes a much more stable platform. Many kayak manufacturers include a bungee arrangement to secure the paddle shaft, but I have found bungees practically worthless for adding any real rigidity to the system. Much better are nonelastic cords or nylon straps, which are becoming more common. If your kayak is equipped with bungees, I recommend rigging your own straps and testing them in the water. The only danger to a rigid outrigger setup is the extra stress on the paddle, which is why you bought a good paddle and have a spare secured to your deck.

One key to a successful paddle-float reentry is doing it quickly. The less time you spend sprawled across the deck of your kayak, the better. So set it up right the first time, watch for a window in the sea conditions, and then get in fast. Some procedures show the paddler entering from in front of the paddle shaft (as in the accompanying photos), others show entry from behind. The rear-entry position works better with a small cockpit.

To perform a paddle-float outrigger rescue, first right the kayak by heaving up on the edge of the cockpit. This will scoop some water into the boat, but don't worry about it yet. If you cannot right the kayak by lifting it away from you, scramble over the hull until you can grab the other side of the cockpit rim, and pull the boat over toward you. This is a surefire technique, but because your weight is added to the boat, it scoops more water in.

With your elbow hooked over the cockpit to control the boat, install the float on the end of your paddle. Rigid-foam floats are easy to secure using their attachment straps; inflatable floats are sometimes easier to put on if you put a couple of breaths in them first, to make them more rigid, then finish inflating once they're on.

Slide the other end of the paddle through the rigging on your rear deck. Tighten the straps if so equipped, to lock down the paddle. Let's assume you have installed the paddle extending out to the left side of the boat as you look forward. Position yourself behind the paddle, with your right hand over the deck and your left hand holding the cockpit rim. Kick upward and hook your left knee over the paddle shaft, and scoot your torso face down onto the rear deck. Move your right foot up to hook over the paddle shaft, while swinging your left leg over and into the cockpit. Swing your right leg in as well, so you are lying face down on the kayak with your legs in the cockpit. At the same time, move your right hand down to grasp the paddle shaft to lean on it and control it. Now scoot down into the cockpit, and twist around to face forward. You've done it.

If you enter from in front of the paddle shaft, you grasp the back of the cockpit with your left hand, and the paddle shaft with your right. You kick up and over the cockpit, hooking first your left and then right leg into the cockpit, then twisting around and forward.

Once you're back in, make sure the paddle is still well secured in the rigging, so you can continue to lean on it. Look for a lull in the waves to let go of the paddle and secure your spray skirt, then lean on the shaft again with your left hand, while pumping out the boat with your right. If conditions are really rough, consider deploying a drogue, or having a companion steady your boat or even give you a tow, to keep the bow into the waves while you pump.

Wet-Exit Mantra

Two things you must *never fail* to do during a wet exit: hang on to the paddle, and hang on to the boat. If, for some reason, you *have* to choose one or the other, stick with the boat.

Bow Toggles

The toggle at the bow of your kayak is not just a carrying handle; it is an important way to retain a hold on your boat in many rescue situations.

The toggle itself—usually a section of PVC pipe—should extend *beyond* the bow of the boat, so you can hold on to it even if the boat rolls over in surf or other rough conditions. But never put your hand through the loop; in fact, it's a good idea to wrap the loop with cord or a piece of tape to prevent your accidentally doing so.

Some kayaks have the bow loop positioned so far back on the deck that lengthening it is impractical. I would consider consulting the manufacturer, and then drilling crossways through the bow, through the solid "end pour" that most fiberglass boats have, to mount a separate rescue loop.

SEA WINGS AND OTHER FLOAT RESCUES

Float systems that strap to the kayak, adding buoyancy on one or both sides of the cockpit, take more time to set up than a paddle-float outrigger. Their advantage is in the semipermanency of the resulting structure—an injured or exhausted paddler could ride out nonbreaking seas with little or no effort by simply sliding down into the cockpit as low as possible. I think this type of device would be especially useful for groups, as a means to secure an injured member for towing.

Care must be exercised with such systems, however, as they effectively add up to a foot to the beam of the kayak, with a resulting loss of responsiveness in steep waves. If a float-equipped kayak did capsize, righting it would be troublesome.

See Chapter 3, page 36, for more on Sea Wings.

Surf-Zone Rescues

If you capsize while launching or landing through surf, rolling back up will be difficult in the tumultuous water. If you wet-exit, your strategy should be to get back to shore to regroup.

If you have managed to hang onto the kayak, get to the bow and hold on to the bow toggle. Do not, under any circumstances, put your hand through the loop. If the kayak is tumbled by a wave, your hand could be trapped and severely injured. Keep the boat between you and the shore, and, if possible, keep the kayak upside down, which prevents more water being dumped into the cockpit. The waves will push the boat ahead of you, and carry both you and the boat to the beach. If for some reason you lose control of the boat, swim away from it and continue to shore. It will probably be carried in and you can recover it then.

Assisted Rescues

A pair, or group, of paddlers well practiced in rescue techniques enjoys a considerable advantage, both real and psychological. The main benefit of an assisted rescue is that two or more kayaks rafted together are far more stable than a single boat in almost all conditions.

SIDE-BY-SIDE RESCUE

This rescue is quick, easy, and can be performed in almost any seas short of actually breaking. I have accomplished the technique on the first try with a complete novice paddler, in pretty bouncy conditions.

The rescue is set up in one of two ways:

1. The paddler in the water positions himself next to the cockpit of the upside-down boat, and flips it upright by heaving up on the cockpit rim, or by climbing over the hull and pulling the boat over toward him. The rescuer then pulls her boat

A side-by-side assisted rescue. The rescuer steadies the empty kayak while the person in the water climbs back in. Note the paddles are tucked under the front deck bungees of the rescuer's boat.

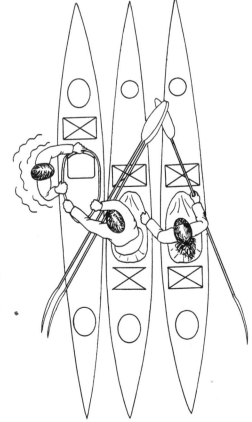

A third person can hold the middle boat, adding even more stability to the system.

alongside, facing the stern of the empty boat, to a point where she can grasp the front of the cockpit.

2. If, for some reason, the paddler in the water cannot right the kayak, the rescuer positions her boat where she can reach under to grab the cockpit rim. The rescuee, meanwhile, pulls himself around to the opposite side of the rescuer's cockpit. He can then provide stability while the rescuer pulls up on the cockpit of the capsized boat.

After the kayak is righted, the rescuer steadies it by holding on to the front of the cockpit rim while the swimmer enters from the other side, by grasping the cockpit rim and, with a powerful scissors kick, pulling himself up on to the rear deck, facing down and toward the stern, so he can slide his legs into the cockpit and twist around to drop into the seat.

The effect of the rescuer's hold on the rescuee's cockpit serves to steady both kayaks, and to enable the other paddler to reenter. It is the job of the rescuer, from her better vantage point, to watch for an opportune window in the conditions and to signal her companion to climb in. The rescuer continues to steady both boats while the other fastens the spray skirt and pumps out the cockpit.

The rescuee can slide his paddle under the deck bungees to keep it out of the way during the procedure; the rescuer can do the same, or position hers across both boats to further steady the system.

There are a couple of ways to accomplish the side-by-side rescue with three paddlers. I prefer to begin with the basic setup described above, and have the additional kayak next to the primary rescuer's boat, on the opposite side from the empty boat, to provide additional bracing. This gives the paddler in the water plenty of room to maneuver when climbing back in. The other method is to position the rescuing kayaks on either side of the victim's boat, and have him slide up onto the deck between the other kayaks by hooking one arm over his own deck and the other over one of the rescuer's decks. While this method might work better for a weak or injured paddler, more sliding and squirming are necessary.

ALL-IN RESCUES

British kayaking writer and pundit Derek Hutchinson used the delightful term "infectious" to describe capsizes. It's true—conditions leading to one capsize can very well lead to several, particularly immediately following the initial upset, when everyone stops to gawk or help and stops paying attention to their own situation.

Two paddlers in the water can still perform an assisted rescue for each other. Each paddler rights his or her own boat, then they swim and push them together bow to stern. One paddler gets between the cockpits, hanging on to each, while the other enters from the outside. The paddler in between the boats can provide sufficient downward force to counterbalance the entering companion. When one paddler has reentered, he or she can then assist the other with a standard side-by-side rescue.

DOUBLE-KAYAK RESCUES

Double kayaks are somewhat more resistant to capsizes than singles, but they are by no means immune. Fortunately anyone paddling a double has a built-in assist for a rescue.

Rescue of a double kayak is similar to the all-in situation, except both paddlers cooperate to recover one boat. The best way to proceed is to get the stern paddler back in first—the rear cockpit usually has the rudder controls, and the boat is normally wider near the stern, so stability is better there. The paddlers position themselves on either side of the rear cockpit, and one steadies the boat while the other climbs in. The stern paddler can then brace with a scull on one side of the boat while the bow paddler climbs in the opposite side.

Questionable Rescue Techniques for Touring

Many, many other rescue techniques have been described in books and articles, but I think the options we've covered so far are the most solid for

boats that are loaded with gear. Some of the others are useful in certain situations; on the other hand, some I've seen endorsed just look plain dangerous for loaded boats.

Several rescue strategies illustrate the capsized paddler remaining upside down in the cockpit, banging on the hull and waving his or her arms to signal a companion (it's always both arms; where the paddle has gone is a mystery). Let's assume several things for a moment. First, let's assume the capsized paddler has enough air and presence of mind to remain in the cockpit and signal calmly. Then, let's assume a nearby paddler sees the signal within the necessary 30 seconds or so, and can reach the capsized boat within another few seconds. Some books show the rescuer's kayak approaching at 90 degrees, bow pointed directly at the side of the rescuee's hull. The idea is that the capsized paddler can grab on to the approaching bow and right the kayak. But in any sort of surging wave conditions—the very ones most likely to result in a capsize—this approach is risky, to put it mildly. Remember our 350 pounds of inertia? What if the victim manages to dog-paddle to the surface to grab a breath at the instant the boats meet?

An approach parallel to the victim's boat makes much more sense, but is still difficult to perform quickly and accurately with a loaded kayak. British Canoe Union coach and writer Nigel Foster endorses what he calls a "rapid approach" rescue, paddling in quickly on a parallel course, and grabbing the upside-down hull to slow your boat and position your bow near the victim's hands. This makes good sense, but I still think of it as a rescue for highly experienced paddlers paddling lightly loaded boats.

Other techniques show various ways of sliding the capsized kayak out of the water onto the deck of the rescuer's boat, to empty the cockpit or even repair a leak. Again, I don't think these suggestions are intended for loaded boats. At least I know no one could lift *my* boat when it's packed for an average Baja trip—I can barely drag it up the beach.

Towing

If one of the members of a group becomes sick or is injured, or capsizes near a rocky lee shore and is in danger of being blown onto it, the other members should have the equipment and knowledge to rig a tow line.

The most efficient tow lines are ready-made systems (see Chapter 3, page 41), but any length of stout line will do in a pinch. To be safe and allow a bit of elasticity, the line should be at least 20 to 30 feet long. The line should be clipped or tied to the rescuee's bow toggle, and fastened to the towing kayak's deck near the cockpit. The paddle park cleats installed on many

American kayaks will serve, but the jam cleat that comes with a towing system is better. With a jam cleat, the line can be cast off instantly in an emergency, or if the person being towed isn't showing the proper gratitude. If the line must be tied to the towing kayak, a sharp knife should be nearby.

It is difficult for one kayak to tow another, but it is virtually impossible for one kayak to tow another kayak plus a person in the water who is hanging on to that kayak. So, first get the paddler back in the kayak if there has been a capsize. To subsequently increase the pulling power, you can add another kayak in front of the first with an additional tow line. This method is safer than putting the towing kayaks side by side, especially in rough seas.

Another element to consider in rescues and safety is seamanship: in order to most quickly and efficiently deal with capsizes and rescues, you should know the basics of tidal currents, wave patterns, and other hydrologic features. See Chapter 7, beginning on page 96, for details.

After the Rescue

Getting a capsized paddler back in the boat and away from a danger zone is only half of a complete rescue. The second half is to ensure the paddler is uninjured and not hypothermic. If the water is cold, the group should head to shore immediately if possible, to dry out, change clothes if necessary, and brew some tea or coffee.

If the rescue happens in the middle of a long crossing, check the victim thoroughly for signs of disorientation, severe shivering, or loss of coordination. A spare, dry fleece cap, and even a jacket, are good things to have available to warm the head and torso, and a thermos of something hot will help raise the core temperature. Rescues in rough conditions are frightening, and everyone (not just the victim) will be pumped full of adrenaline and potentially shocky, so keeping an ongoing assessment of the situation—if your group is still in danger—is crucial to remaining safe.

All kayak tourers should have basic first-aid training, although I strongly recommend wilderness first-aid training as well—most Red Cross first-aid courses simply teach you how to stabilize someone until the paramedics arrive in a few minutes. In the wilderness, help could be hours or even days away. And if you know how to deal correctly with things such as hypothermia, you might not need to call in for help. See Appendix A for listings of wilderness first-aid schools and books on first aid in the wilderness and for mariners.

Failed Rescues

If you have practiced recovery and rescue techniques, are dressed properly, and have the right equipment, it is *extremely* unlikely that you will be caught out of your boat and unable to reenter it. But the possibility, however remote, should be considered. It is in this situation that you will want to attract outside assistance.

How you go about alerting potential rescuers depends on your location. If you are near other boat or ship traffic, you should stay with the kayak if at all possible, because it is a much larger target than your head and shoulders sticking out of the water.

Try the VHF radio first, using the emergency channel. If you can raise another vessel, help is assured. If no one answers the radio call, leave it on so you can monitor voice traffic, and look for a boat or ship that is angling your way (so the pilot will be looking somewhat in your direction). Fire off a meteor flare, aiming in a high arc across the bow of the ship, then use your signal mirror, if it's sunny, to flash right at the bridge or helmsman. If it's dark, first switch on your personal strobe, then fire a flare. Don't waste all your flares at once—if no change of course is evident immediately, look for another boat, or wait a couple of minutes before firing another flare. If you are carrying a See/Rescue distress banner, deploy it so passing aircraft might spot you. Continue to try the radio at intervals, because boats might be moving in and out of range.

The only reason you should leave the kayak is if you are swept *very* near land, and are otherwise in danger of being carried out to the open sea by a strong tide. You will conserve energy and warmth by having the kayak to cling to.

The chances that you'll have to swim for land increase when you are alone in a remote area, away from possible outside assistance. If you do make the decision to abandon the boat, now is the time to clip a survival kit to your life jacket (see Chapter 10, page 155). The most energy-saving stroke is to lie on your back and frogkick, which both keeps your head out of the water and allows you to use just your feet to kick, while keeping your arms folded to conserve warmth. Alternatively, you can face forward while hugging a dry bag that might contain extra clothes or food and that will support your head farther out of the water.

STASH AN ITINERARY

A "just-in-case" idea that's really smart is to make sure your name, phone number, and address are attached somewhere permanently in your kayak. Then, each trip, store a copy of your itinerary in the boat as well. That way, if you ever become separated from the boat and it is found drifting, the authorities will know where to search along your course, to find you either swimming or, hopefully, warming your hands in front of a fire on some island.

7

S E A M A N S H I P

Mastering the Elements

Seamanship is a wonderfully evocative word (despite its faintly sexist suppositions—but *seapersonship* just wouldn't have the same ring). It implies a consummate skill, a broad-ranging knowledge and instinct for the sea and its moods, and for the ships that move upon it.

The basics of seamanship can be taught—the arithmetic for currents and tides, the patterns of waves and the types of clouds, the rules of shipping and rights of way—but the wisdom that gives the word its real meaning can be gained only through time and experience. If your passion for sea kayaking develops beyond the occasional weekend trip, you will find yourself developing a "feel" for the sea that goes beyond tide tables and barometric readings. Is it a mystical bond that is formed, or does our subconscious merely correlate and collate past experiences into an accurate synopsis? Who cares, as long as it works!

Judgment, Caution, and Common Sense

I was camped in a small, sheltered bay south of Bahía de los Angeles, in Baja, with a group of clients. Around the point, between us and our next landing, was about 5 miles of rocky lee shore, at the moment being pounded by a *norte*—a characteristic northerly wind that can blow for days in the Sea of Cortez. This one was fairly mild as they go, about 20 to 25 knots or so, but I still wasn't about to lead six inexperienced paddlers along that coast. Several of the group, noting that the conditions didn't seem worse than what we had already encountered, voiced a mild protest, but I remained firm.

About midafternoon another group of kayakers paddled past our cove, headed straight for the bad stretch. I recognized them as a group from a university outdoor program, the leader of which I had talked to earlier. These were also novice paddlers, and although they were all in double kayaks, I was shocked to see them go by—until I remembered the instructor's mentioning their schedule, which required them to be back in Bahía de los Angeles by the next day.

Noting several sidelong glances from my group ("If *they* can do it, why can't *we*?"), I climbed to the top of the bluff overlooking the rocky shore, and watched through my binoculars the progress of the six kayaks as they bounced and slammed across steep four-foot seas.

And what happened? Well, they made it just fine, which is how such situations usually turn out. Did I regret my decision? Heck no! It took but the mildest of luck to get that group through what were only marginally bad conditions—but luck it was. The leader had the boats ferrying properly to maintain a straight course—that is, they paddled slightly into the wind to cancel its push—but the course he picked was barely 200 yards off a jagged volcanic shore being pounded by surf. Had one of those boats gone over, I seriously doubt the group could have organized a rescue before it hit the rocks.

It has been said that airline schedules result in more kayaking accidents than any other cause. As our lives get more hectic, vacation time gets more precious, and the urge is overpowering to cram in as much recreation as possible. With no slack in the itinerary, no safety margin, when the last day before the return flight produces dicey weather, we think there's no choice but to go for it.

The solution isn't to miss the flight and pay a thousand bucks extra for a one-way ticket home; the solution is to plan for bad weather, so you've got leeway to catch your plane. When I guided clients with airline tickets, I made sure we were at least within hiking distance of the put-in two days before the flight. That way, if worse came to worst, I could take them back cross-country and collect the boats later.

Don't ever—*ever*—let anyone talk you into paddling in conditions in which you don't feel safe. The corollary is, don't ever even think about coercing someone else to paddle when he/she is uncomfortable. In his book *Commitments and Open Crossings,* about the first kayak circumnavigation of Great Britain and Ireland, author Bill Taylor mentioned the pact he and his two companions made: to abide by the decision of anyone in the group who didn't want to paddle—for whatever reason. Despite a few tense moments, they stuck by that pact, and it helped keep the group together for the entire expedition.

Every time you paddle you make a conscious decision that it is safe to do so. This decision results from a score of inputs—the look of the water and sky, your knowledge of the coast ahead, weather reports from the radio, and so on. If you are part of a group, make sure the whole group agrees with the decision. If you are alone, make sure your whole brain agrees with it.

Tides

Most people know that tides are caused by the gravitational pull of the moon and, to a lesser degree, the sun. Beyond that, things get hazy. But tides, which cause tidal *currents*, are important to people in self-propelled boats. So let's cover a few basics. "Oh no! SCIENCE!" you groan. Not to worry. The next measly 400 words will make you an expert on tides, able to bore friends and acquaintances with fireside lectures and improvised flip charts.

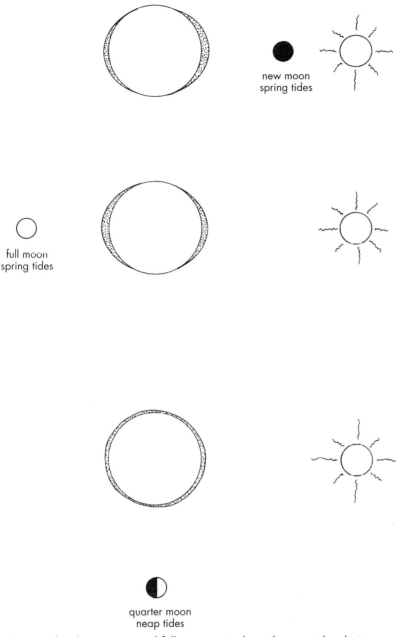

new moon
spring tides

full moon
spring tides

quarter moon
neap tides

Spring tides during new- and full-moon periods, with neap tides during quarter-moon phases.

A *tide* is simply a bulge of water pulled out from the earth by the moon (the sun pulls its own, smaller bulge). The bulge always follows the moon; the earth, as it were, rotates under the bulge. It's easy to see that when the moon and sun are on the same side of the

earth *(new moon),* their gravitational effects are combined, producing a higher high tide and a lower low tide. This is called a *spring tide*—no matter what season it is. When the moon is on the opposite side of the earth from the sun *(full moon),* the two are pulling in opposition, and we also get a spring tide.

It follows that, when the moon is at right angles to the sun (which we perversely call *first-* or *last-quarter moons,* even though you see *half* the full face of the moon), the pull is somewhat nullified, producing moderate tides, which are called *neap tides.* Since it takes about 14 days for the moon to go through a cycle from new to full, spring tides occur every two weeks, alternating with neap tides.

So far so good. Now, many people know that there are two high tides and two low tides every day. Their actual duration is about 24 hours and 50 minutes, corresponding to the time it takes the moon to appear in the same place in the sky each day (if you watch the moon rise on successive nights, you'll find that it rises about 50 minutes later each night). So a low tide is followed by a high tide in a bit over six hours, followed by another low tide in another six hours, and so on.

Now, the big question: Why are there two whole up-and-down tide cycles in a day, when the moon is "going around" only once? Ah, because of the sun, you say. Good answer, but remember, when the moon and sun are on the same side of the earth, there are *still* two tides. There is another tidal bulge on the opposite side of the earth from both the moon and the sun.

To understand the reason, you need to dispense with the notion that the moon orbits "around" the earth. By astronomical standards our moon is more like a second planet than a mere moon—its diameter is one-quarter that of earth's. So, as the moon orbits the earth, the earth *wobbles,* like a top about to fall over. What is actually happening is that both the moon and the earth are orbiting around a common point about 1,000 miles beneath the earth's surface. As the moon pulls up a tidal bulge, it is also pulling the earth itself, which leaves another bulge of water sticking out on the opposite side. That's all there is to it. Well, not *all,* but that's the basics.

Tidal heights vary dramatically around the globe. In parts of the Arctic the total variation is only a few inches. In the Bay of Fundy, off Nova Scotia, on the other hand, if you stand at the water's edge at low tide under a full moon and wait six hours, you'll be under 40 feet of ocean. Tidal variation at the north end of the Sea of Cortez in Mexico commonly exceeds 20 feet. What these two areas have in common is that they are both dead ends—as the front of the tidal bulge hits the landlocked end of a long bay or a big estuary, the water has nowhere to go, and the rest of the bulge builds up behind it, sometimes to tremendous heights. On some very flat beaches in Mexico, if you land at high tide and try to launch at low tide, you'll have a portage a half-mile long. And the Wadden Sea in Germany has tidal flats that stretch for miles.

Because of landmasses, bottom variations, and about 17,000 other factors, tides occur at slightly different times

Tidal variation at the north end of the Sea of Cortez in Mexico commonly exceeds 20 feet, which meant a quarter-mile slog with loaded boats across a mud flat for this group.

even within a hundred-mile stretch of coast. Tide charts, where they are available, are indispensable. They will tell you both the time and height for tides in your area (although even these can vary slightly), and will help you predict such things as tidal currents.

TIDAL CURRENTS

There are several types of currents in the ocean, but tidal currents are the ones that most affect kayakers.

In the open ocean, tides cause negligible current. But near landmasses, especially where the tide is forced through straits, tidal currents are a significant factor in marine navigation—even for large ships. And in some places the effects can be apocalyptic. In the Gulf of Corryvreckan, off the west coast of Scotland, the tidal current exceeds 8 knots (nearly 10 miles per hour), and a rough, shallow bottom causes standing waves, overfalls, and a huge whirlpool known as the Hag. Even Corryvreckan pales in comparison with the Saltstraumen Maelstrom in Norway. Here almost 500 hundred million cubic yards of seawater is forced through a strait that at one point is only about fifty feet wide. A World War II German warship that blundered into the Maelstrom while chasing resistance fighters *broke in two.*

For kayakers, most tidal currents cause considerably less trouble. On coastal journeys where currents are gentle, you can even time your paddling to take advantage of the flow. If the tide is coming in, it is *flooding;* if it is going out it is *ebbing.* Between the two, at both high and low tide, is a relatively calm period called *slack water,* which can last anywhere from a few minutes to an hour or so. By juggling your route and

Near land masses, especially where the tide is forced through straits, tidal currents are a significant factor in marine navigation. This shows Canal del Infiernillo ("little hell") in the Sea of Cortez; when the tide is at full race, the tidal current here is over 5 knots and the waves can be short, very steep, and coming from all directions. Note also the submerged sand bars (shoals); current forced over a shallow bottom will be faster, and if the bottom drops suddenly there may be overfalls—standing waves where the level of the sea actually drops as if spilling over a ledge.
(Courtesy Brian Hagerty)

The Rule of Twelfths

Tidal currents don't always flow at the same speed. To gauge how fast the tide rises—and thus how fast any tidal currents are flowing—use the rule of twelfths:

- In the first hour after low tide, the tide will rise $\frac{1}{12}$ of its total height
- In the second hour, it will rise $\frac{2}{12}$ths of the total
- In the third hour, $\frac{3}{12}$ths
- In the fourth hour, $\frac{3}{12}$ths
- In the fifth hour, $\frac{2}{12}$ths
- And in the last hour before high tide, $\frac{1}{12}$th
- The tide falls at this same rate

From this you can see that any tidal current will be flowing fastest in the couple of hours midway between high and low tide, and that the best times to paddle to miss tidal currents are as close as possible to high or low tide—slack water.

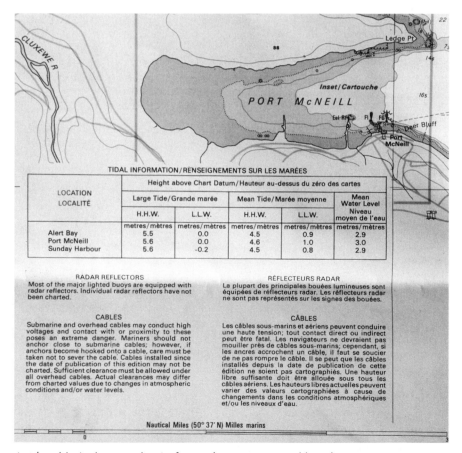

A tide table (in box on chart) of your destination is vital kayaking equipment.

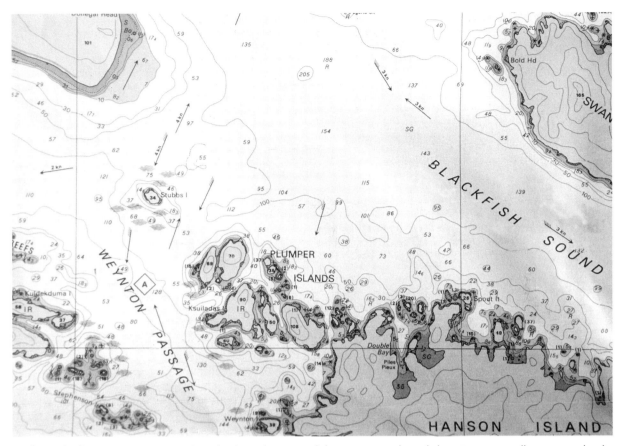

A chart of Johnstone Strait in British Columbia, showing tidal current speeds and directions, as well as water depth.

timing, you can make the tide work for you, or at least prevent it from working against you. Tide tables for the area you are paddling are vital equipment

If you have to paddle against the tide, keep in mind that eddy currents near the shore sometimes circulate in the opposite direction of the main flow, actually helping you along. Be cautious, however, because the interface between the opposing currents is often very rough. A kayaker surprised by the confused and choppy conditions could easily capsize.

The Vocabulary of Seamanship

- Spring tide: the period of great tidal fluctuation near each full and new moon.
- Neap tide: the period of low tidal fluctuation near each first- and second-quarter moon.
- Flood tide: tide is coming in.
- Ebb tide: tide is going out.
- Slack water: period of negligible tidal current near high and low tide.
- Fetch: the distance over which waves can travel and build in size.

Charts usually indicate significant or dangerous tidal currents. Areas to be especially cautious of include narrow straits between islands or between an island and the mainland, and points or peninsulas that jut into the current. These are best negotiated at or near slack water. See Chapter 8 for more on navigation and charting courses.

The sea bottom can affect conditions as well. Current forced over a shallow bottom will be faster, and if the bottom drops suddenly there may be *overfalls*—standing waves where the level of the sea actually drops as if spilling over a ledge.

If a tidal current is flowing one way and the wind is blowing in the opposite direction, dangerous seas can be generated quickly—short, but very steep and confused waves. You should avoid such situations at all costs.

For information about navigating across tidal currents, see Chapter 8, page 119.

Waves

Virtually all waves are generated by wind (exceptions include boat wakes and tsunamis). On a flat sea, a rising wind produces ripples, and the ripples, with greater surface area for the wind to push against, build higher and higher. Once created, a large wave can travel for hundreds of miles in windless conditions. Unless it is breaking, a wave actually moves very little water except for minor surface currents—a cork bobbing on big swells essentially goes up and down in an ellipse.

Wave terminology is pretty simple. The *crest* of a wave is its highest point; the *trough* is the depression between waves. Wave *height* is the difference in height between the crest and trough. The *length* is the distance between crests. *Fetch* indicates the total distance over which the waves can build; the longer the fetch, the higher the waves can get.

Related terms: a *lee shore* is a shore onto

which the wind, and thus waves, are blowing. It is usually more dangerous than a *weather,* or *windward, shore,* one from which the wind is coming, and thus where wave action is small. An *offshore wind* blows from land to sea; an *onshore wind* blows from sea to land.

Waves can be deceptive in the challenges they pose to sea kayakers. For example, the huge swells of the Pacific Ocean are terrifying to a novice, but as long as the crests are not breaking and you have access to sheltered launching and landing points, they are usually easy to handle, furnishing an exhilarating but safe roller-coaster ride. On the other hand, short but steep and fast-moving waves blown up in a narrow and shallow channel can present a serious danger of capsize to a paddler. Generally, any conditions that produce breaking waves of any size should be treated with extreme caution.

Waves—whether they be water, sound, or electromagnetic—share certain characteristics. They can reflect, refract, and bend. In the illustration, for example, waves hitting a cliff or seawall reflect, bouncing back into oncoming waves and creating chaotic patterns. When a big wave crest reflects into an incoming large crest, the violent collision can shoot skyward for tens of feet. These waves are called *clapotis.* A paddler traversing such an area must move farther out to sea to avoid these dangerous conditions.

In the second illustration, waves approaching a small island refract around it. The area in the lee of the island, where you might think it would be calm, is actually very confused, as waves from either side meet, creating conditions similar to those in the first illustration. Only very close inshore will the sea flatten.

Waves reflecting off a cliff or sea wall can create confusing, unpredictable conditions when the crests collide. Paddlers should stay well offshore.

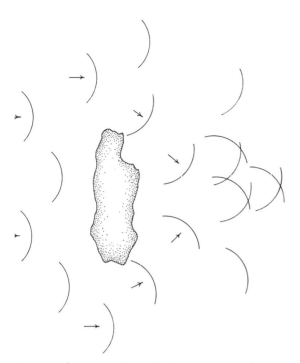

Waves refract around an island, creating rough water in the lee of the island where you might expect calm conditions. Only seas very close inshore will flatten.

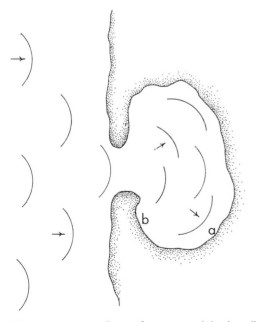

Waves entering a bay refract around the headlands, creating surf even out of the direct line of the mouth of the bay. The landing at "a" might still be rough. Better to land at "b."

In the third illustration, waves entering a bay refract around the headland, causing surf even out of the direct line of the incoming seas. The waves also bend, so that they curl and break from one side to another rather than in a straight line. Landing might still be rough even at *a*. The best landing will be at *b*.

The best way to handle waves in any situation is to pay attention. Waves are rarely completely uniform in size, and most people who get into trouble have let themselves get distracted for a moment; they let an out-of-the-ordinary wave take them by surprise (see Chapter 5, page 69, for launching and landing through surf).

Shipping Hazards

One thing you'd better get used to: in a sea kayak, you are at the bottom of the watercraft pecking order—a mosquito crossing the interstate highway of the offshore world. Sailboats and sportfishing boats will have a hard time seeing you. To most commercial and military craft, you're just not there at all. So forget about rights of way, and make sure you stay *out* of the way.

That doesn't mean you shouldn't do everything possible to make yourself visible—bright colors, lights, and so on—it just means you should never count on the other boat's seeing you and altering course to miss you.

BIG SHIPS

Remember our example of inertia in a loaded sea kayak—all 350 pounds of it? Consider the physics involved in maneuvering a medium-size 550-foot-long cargo ship, with a displacement of about 12,500 tons. Cruising speed with a full load is 18 knots—about 20 miles per hour. From that speed, a full-on emergency stop will take around 1,100 yards. That is well over a half-mile. Even at half-speed the ship would cover nearly one-quarter mile before stopping. An emergency 90-degree turn would describe a radius of hundreds of yards. And that is just a medium-size ship. Some supertankers take several miles to screech to a halt.

Now, consider that, from the bridge, the bow blocks the skipper's view of anything within about 1,000 feet of the front of the ship. Beyond that distance, in mildly choppy conditions, a sea kayak is invisible anyway. You get the picture.

The easiest way to avoid big ships is to avoid big shipping channels. In a kayak you can skirt the shallow edges of buoyed commercial channels, where the deep-draft vessels can't go.

If you have to cross such a channel, scout it carefully. Use your chart to estimate how long it will take you to cross the traffic lane, then time the passage of a ship from first sighting to past your route. This will give you an idea as to how much of a window you have. Don't be fooled by how slowly a big ship appears to move while it is far away—the size makes the speed deceptive.

SMALL POWERBOATS AND SAILBOATS

A kayak can navigate water too shallow for even small recreational craft, but you can't spend your whole time skirting the shoreline to stay in a foot of water. So you'll have to use an active defense against poorly piloted weekenders.

First of all, *never* assume the other boat has seen you. I was nearly run down in a river channel because I could look the pilot of the oncoming boat in the eye and would not believe he hadn't seen me. I assumed he was just being obnoxious—until he was 50 feet away and still coming straight on. I frantically waved my paddle, and it was apparent from the horrified look on his face as he swerved that he had no idea I was there. He passed within 5 feet of my port side.

Your ability to get out of the way of powerboats and sailboats is limited, because they are both faster than

Can you spot the kayaking hazard in this photo?

Books About Small Boats

These books aren't for further instruction; in fact, they aren't even about kayaks. They're for pure enjoyment and inspiration.

Swallows and Amazons, by Arthur Ransome. This book, the first in a series, was first published in England in 1930. It follows the adventures of four children with a small sailboat, the *Amazon.* Enchanting reading for adults or children.

Ice, by Tristan Jones. The astonishing account of a Welsh sailor who refitted an ex-Royal National lifeboat and attempted to singlehandedly beat Fridtjoff Nansen's farthest north mark by sailboat, off the east coast of Greenland. A rousing, terrifying, and wickedly humorous yarn. Jones went on to write *The Incredible Voyage* and many other books.

Shackleton's Boat Journey, by F.A. Worsley. Several books have been written about the desperate open boat voyage undertaken by Sir Ernest Henry Shackleton and his men across the Antarctic ocean, after their ship *Endurance* was crushed by ice. But the understated account of Worsley, the captain of the *Endurance,* is perhaps the best. This tale needs no superlatives.

you and very maneuverable too. If you see one headed toward you and it's too late to get out of the way, wave your paddle blade in an arc over your head while twisting the blade back and forth. This makes a very effective semaphore. Turn broadside if possible, to enlarge your profile.

When I paddle in a bay or other place with a lot of recreational-boat traffic, I keep one of my small meteor flares tucked under a deck bungee. If I ever feel really threatened, I'll fire it off as a last resort, right over the bow of the approaching boat.

Be especially watchful and considerate of small working boats—inshore trawlers, lobsterboats, and the like. Remember they are out there trying to make a living, and will be paying much more attention to their nets and pots than to a bunch of people on vacation. Working boats rarely travel on predictable straight courses, so you must watch for their overall pattern.

Weather

As we all know, even the most sophisticated weather reports are hopeful at best. And anyone who would

commit to a long crossing because Biff on Channel 9 said Mr. Sun would be smiling all day today, well. . . .

Your weather strategy as a sea kayaker should coalesce from a comprehensive, logical sequence of research, beginning with overall patterns for the region you're visiting and gradually focusing tighter and tighter in both space and time.

Start by learning seasonal norms for the coast, state, or even country of your destination. This information can be obtained from many sources: coastal piloting books, cruising guides for sailors, or magazine articles. You can also contact local paddling or sailing clubs. Such information will provide you with an overall history of climatic conditions by season—mean wind direction and speed, mean high and low temperatures, sea temperature, percentage of cloud cover, precipitation, and so forth. See Appendix A for sources.

This knowledge will help you plan a rough strategy for your trip, such as, obviously, what time of year to go, plus a general route to anticipate expected winds and tides, and finally what clothing and additional equipment might be needed.

When you reach the area, concentrate on learning recent weather patterns by asking at local shops or marine stores where you might be picking up tide

Using Barometers

Mechanical barometers are reliable, and a delight to anyone who appreciates fine craftsmanship. But electronic barometers are reasonably priced, and can include extra features. One I tried recently, from Oregon Scientific, has a digital bar graph that displays a 24-hour history of atmospheric pressure.

In general, rising pressure indicates improving weather; decreasing pressure indicates worsening conditions. A rapidly falling barometer might forecast a fast-moving storm. The bar graph of the Oregon Scientific barometer shows at a glance the trend for the previous 24 hours, plus a little changing icon of a sun or clouds, making it easy to do your own forecasting. In addition the instrument displays current temperature and relative humidity.

Oregon Scientific says that the barometric method of predicting weather patterns is up to 75 percent accurate—which is certainly a leg up on not knowing anything at all (or having to depend on Biff). Remember, however, that other 25 percent, and keep in mind Ambrose Bierce's definition of a barometer: "An ingenious device which tells us what the weather is like outside."

Oregon Scientific imports an electronic mini-weather station that is useful for kayakers; it reads temperature, gives barametric pressure in a constantly updated bargraph so you can track rising or falling pressure, and it even predicts the weather (it's pretty accurate). Consider carrying a mechanical backup barometer if you are relying on readings for your route planning.

tables, and listen for long-term forecasts on your VHF radio.

Once you have launched, you will be relying largely on VHF weather channels plus your own observations. Each day begins with a synopsis of the forecast, your analysis of sea and sky conditions, and possibly additional input from your barometer.

Watch for breaks in seasonal patterns to warn of impending weather changes. For example, in the Sea of Cortez in winter the normal pattern is calm early mornings, with a rising northerly breeze in late morning, subsiding again around dusk. If I wake up at dawn to a smart southerly wind, I know something weird is up. I can bet before I look that my barometer will show a drop in atmospheric pressure.

Knowing a few local tricks can sometimes help. If I can pick up a Southern California weather report from the beach in Mexico and hear a forecast for Santa Ana winds, I can be pretty sure a *norte* is on the way, meaning anywhere from hours to several unbroken days of fierce northerly winds.

Clouds can give you an idea of impending weather as well. I found a laminated card at a marine supply store that shows different types of clouds, and includes tips on forecasting using cloud patterns.

If you become fascinated enough with weather to go beyond basics, I recommend William Crawford's *Mariner's Weather* from Norton Nautical Books. It is an excellent and very in-depth look at weather from the boaters' point of view.

For a listing of more books, including a few about sea kayaking travels and travails, see Appendix A, beginning on page 208.

8

NAVIGATION AND PILOTING

It's Easier on the Coast

Route-finding for coastal kayak trips has one huge advantage over both open-water navigation and cross-country orienteering: no matter how lost you might be, at least you know *you're on the coast!*

That might sound flippant, but it's true. Your scope of error is reduced to a one-dimensional line, however squiggly it might be, that represents the interface between water and land. Your only problem can be whether you are farther *up* or farther *down* that line than you thought.

That realization took a lot of the tension out of kayak navigation for me. If you've never done any navigation yourself, coastal route-finding is an ideal introduction.

Lines of Position

To understand how the science of navigation works, you should first have an idea of the big picture—how cartographers (map and chart makers) organize the world so that with just two numbers you can find any spot on earth—and how that information is translated onto a map or chart.

What's a Knot?

A minute of latitude is equal to 1 nautical mile, about 1.15 land (statute) miles. A "knot" is 1 nautical mile per hour—or 1.15 land miles per hour.

Cartographers have overlaid the earth with an imaginary grid of lines—longitude and latitude—that form an immense pattern like avenues and cross streets, with each intersection precisely defining a location.

Lines of latitude encircle the earth horizontally; the equator is the central reference point at 0° latitude. Lines of latitude, which lie parallel to each other and are thus often referred to as "parallels," are measured either north or south of the equator. The North Pole and South Pole are at 90° north and south, respectively; Everett, Washington, lies at about 48° north.

Lines of longitude run vertically, north and south, but are not parallel. Lines of longitude, or "meridians," are spread out at the equator and converge at the poles. Because there is no natural reference point for longi-

tude, an arbitrary line through the Greenwich Observatory, in England, was chosen as the 0° mark in the seventeenth century. All meridians count east or west from Greenwich up to 180°, which is the international date line on the other side of the earth. Everett is about 122° west.

To provide more accuracy, each degree (°) of latitude and longitude is divided into 60 minutes ('), which is further divided into 60 seconds ("). When describing a position, latitude is always stated first, indicating north or south, followed by longitude, indicating east or west. So a precise location in downtown Everett is 47°59'07"N, 122°11'10"W. A location such as this, listed down to the seconds of a degree, is accurate to within 100 feet. When you look at a chart or map, you

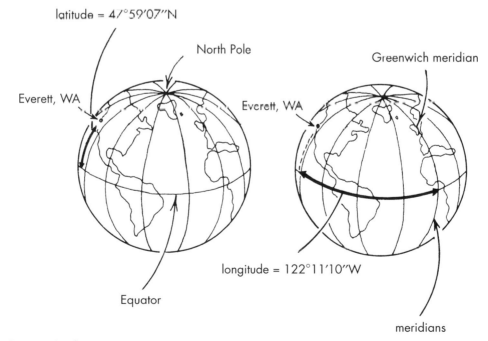

latitude = 47°59'07"N

North Pole

Greenwich meridian

Everett, WA

Everett, WA

Equator

longitude = 122°11'10"W

meridians

Locating Everett, Washington.
Courtesy Christine Erikson

will see lines of latitude and longitude inscribed over the image, with the numbers indicated in the margins.

How Compasses Work

The arrow that points north on a map indicates the geographic North Pole, "true north," the top of the axis around which the earth revolves. Roads that aim north, lines of longitude—all are oriented to true north. For precise route-finding, map and chart directions are described in degrees from true north. North is 0°, east is 90°, south is 180°, and west is 270° (this also puts north at 360° if you complete the circle). When you take a reading with a compass, you give the bearing in degrees; for example, if an island you want to describe is northeast of you, you would say the bearing is 45°.

North is 0°, east is 90°, south is 180°, and west is 270°. When you take a reading with a compass, you give the bearing in degrees; for example, if an island you want to describe is northeast of you, you would say the bearing is 45°.

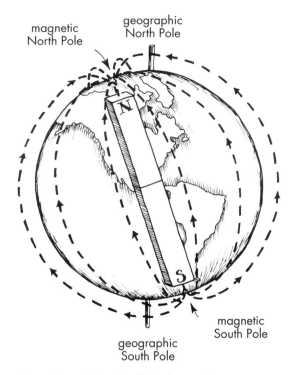

Magnetic variation is relatively easy to compensate for. (Courtesy Christin Erikson)

Unfortunately, the needle on a compass that points north points to a different North Pole, the magnetic North Pole, which at present is several hundred miles northwest of Baffin Island (it drifts very slowly over the years). The difference between true north and where the compass points is called *variation* on nautical charts and *declination* on land maps (the answer to your question is, I haven't the slightest idea). It is measured in degrees either east or west, and every chart will list variation for the area. In some places on earth where the magnetic pole is directly between you and the geo-
(continued on page 113)

Two Compasses

In addition to the compass on your kayak, you should carry a separate orienteering-style compass. It doesn't have to be fancy; it needs only a clear base plate and an adjustable arrow on the dial for variation. Use the orienteering compass for chartwork, and your boat compass for on-the-water navigation. That way you always have a backup as well, although if your orienteering compass bites the dust and your boat compass is built in, it's dang awkward to lay the whole kayak over the chart as a pointer.

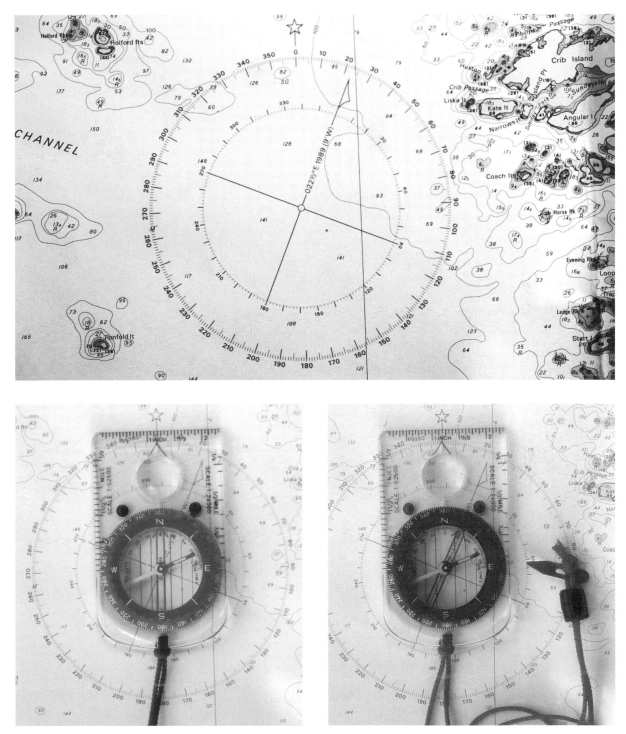

To figure in magnetic variation: 1. Refer to the compass rose on your chart which indicates local compass variation. This chart shows a variation of 22½° east. 2. Lay the compass over the rose so that the baseplate is aligned with true north (the star on the top). The needle will point at the 22° east line on its dial, and your 0° mark will be pointing true north. 3. If your compass has an adjustable variation arrow under the needle, move it so it points 22° east.

Taking a Bearing

Taking a bearing with your boat compass is straightforward. You just point the bow at the target and look at the degree reading on the *lubber line* (the line right in front of you that overlays the face of the compass). That is your magnetic bearing.

Taking a true bearing with a handheld compass requires a bit more juggling. Once you have set the variation arrow to your local variation, hold the compass in front of you, so the 0° mark is oriented to true north. To take a bearing, look over the face at your target. Then rotate the compass dial with your thumb until the needle is aligned over the variation arrow, which aligns the degree dial correctly with your horizon. Look down at the degree dial and see which number matches the direction you are looking. This is your true bearing. Better orienteering compasses have a sighting notch and a mirror that allow you to hold the compass at eye level and take very precise bearings.

To take a simple chart bearing, you can use a pencil to draw a straight line from your position to your target. Place the compass so the side of the base plate lies along your course. Turn the dial of the compass until the series of north/south lines inscribed on the face align with the north/south lines on the chart. The direction-of-travel line on the baseplate of the compass will align with a degree mark on the compass dial— this is your true bearing. See more about chart navigation below.

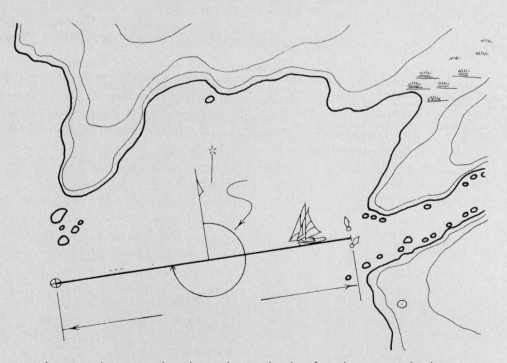

To go from one place to another, draw a line on the chart from the origin to the destination. The arc shows the magnetic bearing, and the length of the line gives the distance.
(Courtesy Rob Groves)

Compass Error

Don't confuse your deck compass by packing under the compass anything in your deck bag or in the kayak that is made of ferrous metal, which will throw off your compass needle.

graphic North Pole, variation is zero. In other places variation can be considerable. If you were kayaking the coast of Ellesmere Island in the Canadian Arctic, variation would be around 90° west—the magnetic pole is due west of you. Most places are somewhere in between—in San Diego Bay the variation is about 14° east; that is, a compass needle will point about 14° east of true north.

Variation is not only easy to compensate for, but at times you needn't worry about it at all.

If you are navigating by compass, without using a chart, you can use what are called "magnetic bearings." For example, if you decide to do a night crossing to an island, you use your compass to take a bearing on the island before dark (see sidebar for instructions on taking bearings). If the compass says 270°, you just paddle on a bearing of 270° and you'll get there (assuming there aren't any currents). Variation is irrelevant. If you leave a note for companions who are following you later, telling them to paddle to the island at 270° magnetic, they'll find you.

But if you need to translate what your compass tells you to a chart that is oriented to true north, you have to figure in the variation. If the chart says variation is 22° east, rotate the compass so the needle is pointing at the 22° line on its dial, and your 0° mark will be pointing to true north. If your compass has an adjustable variation arrow under the needle, move it so it points 22° east. When you move the compass so the needle aligns with the arrow, the compass will be oriented true north. You can then move it anywhere on the chart, or pick it up to take a bearing.

If the variation is 22° west, you have to subtract from 360 to set the variation—338°.

Because most kayak compasses have no provision for variation, if you want to translate a chart bearing to the boat, you have to convert back to a magnetic bearing. If, for instance, we wanted to head for that harbor shown on the chart at 45° true, and we know the variation is 22° east, we know the boat compass will be pointing us 22° too far east. So we subtract 22 from 45 and head 23° on the boat compass—our magnetic heading. As long as the variation is east, you *subtract* variation from the true heading to get the magnetic heading. If variation is west, you *add* the variation. To convert a magnetic bearing to a true bearing you do just the opposite.

GPS Units

I have a 1990 equipment catalog that lists a Magellan GPS unit—price $2,995. I also have a recent equipment catalog that lists a current Magellan GPS model—price $147.99. Not since the early days of VCRs have prices dropped so precipitously on an electronic device. And VCRs just play movies—a GPS unit reads the signals from orbiting satellites to determine your position anywhere on the earth to within a few yards.

When civilian GPS units first appeared, the accuracy with which they could pinpoint a location was astounding—often to within 5 feet. Our military, as you might imagine, positively *freaked* at the thought that any enemy agent with a Visa card could now target our missile silos to within an arm's length. So the signals were scrambled randomly, meaning that now your GPS can be accurate to within 50 feet or as much as 300 feet, depending on the degree of scrambling at the moment it gets a fix. This built-in inaccuracy is called *selective availability*. However, even 300 feet is plenty close for most navigation work.

GPS units have become nearly standard equipment for large sailboats, powerboats, and working vessels. For sea kayaking the applications are somewhat more limited. Most GPS units have several functions in addition to the simple fix, for example speed, estimated time of arrival, and graphic course representation. The problem is that, at the speed a kayak travels—combined with the random scrambling error—this information might not be accurate over a short course. Most units use a fairly short averaging period to compute speed and course; during that time a kayak might not have even moved out of the circle of error. Other units allow the user to modify the sample time, which would help.

If you're really into GPS navigation, many models can be equipped with an accessory known as a *differential beacon receiver,* which decodes low-frequency signals sent from Coast Guard transmitters and bumps the accuracy of the unit back into the 15- to 30-foot range. This also significantly enhances the accuracy of ETA, speed, and course functions. The differential beacon receivers, however, cost more than many GPS units, and work only when you are within range of the beacons. There are rumors that selective-availability scrambling might be coming to an end soon, but as I write this no one knows.

I view GPS units as interesting and somewhat useful accessories for sea kayakers, but certainly not substitutes for compass and chart navigation. If you do decide to buy one, check closely into claims of waterproofness (easily done—just look at the warranty). If it's not covered for water damage, buy one of the clear waterproof bags designed for VHF radios to keep it in. The unit will operate right through the bag.

Charts

A chart is simply a map of the ocean, as detailed in its own way and for its own needs as any topographical map of a state or county. Instead of contours of mountains and hills, charts list the depth of the water, speed and direction of currents, locations of navigation buoys and lighthouses, and so forth. This information is extremely detailed because it represents knowledge that could literally mean life or death for a mariner.

However, because charts are strictly concerned with navigation on the water, the only land features shown are those that would be useful to a mariner. If you want to do serious hiking inland, you'll need topographic maps in addition to your charts.

The legend on the chart tells you in which system the various measurements are shown. Older charts showed depths in feet or fathoms (1 fathom equals 6 feet), but most foreign charts and many newer U.S. sheets show depths in meters (1 meter equals 3.28 feet).

Nearly everything on a chart has a purpose. For instance, the style of lettering changes from land to sea. Land features are labeled in block letters; things in the water are shown with slanted letters.

Much of the information on a chart might appear to be overkill for a sea kayaker. Depths, for example, hardly seem important when you can tell if there's enough water under your keel by reaching over and feeling for the bottom. But water depth can significantly affect conditions on the surface. For instance, if a tidal current runs through a strait that is 100 meters deep at one end and only 15 meters deep at the other, the water is going to have to move much faster at the shallow end. The same effect occurs if the depth is constant but the strait is wider at one end than at the other. A chart plus a tide table will show bays that might be dry at low tide. These are things you need to know *before* heading out to cross a strait or explore

Large Scale, Large Features; Small Scale, Small Features

You'll hear charts referred to as "small-scale" or "large-scale." The difference is confusing. Just remember that on a small-scale chart, say 1:250,000 (where 1 unit of measurement on the chart equals 250,000 units of that measurement on land), the features the chart shows are smaller; on a large scale chart, such as 1:20,000, the features are larger. The number of the scale refers to the ratio of what is shown on the chart to real life. On the 1:20,000 chart, 1 inch on the chart equals 20,000 inches, or about $^3/_{10}$ths of a mile, on land or sea.

CONTENTS

Sample chart symbols.

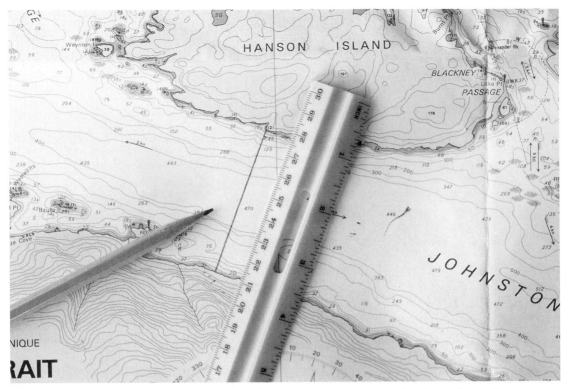

To plot a course from one point to another on your chart, 1. use your straight edge (ruler) to draw in a course line—say, from your camp in a cove to an island.

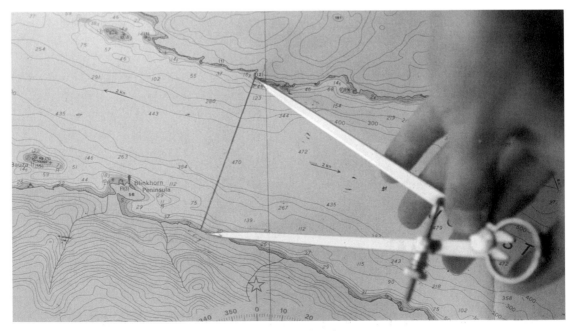

2. Spread the dividers until the points meet your start and end points

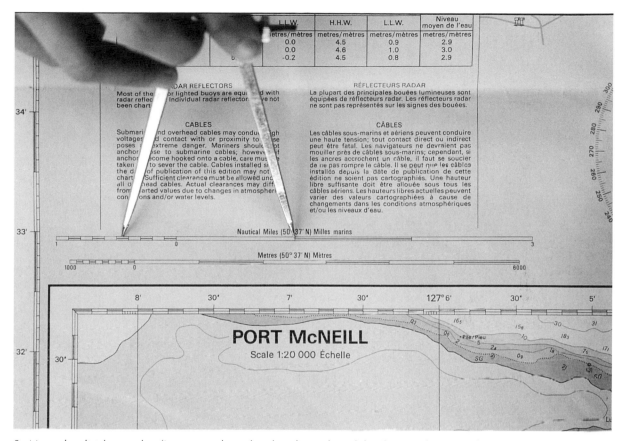

	L.L.W. metres/mètres	H.H.W. metres/mètres	L.L.W. metres/mètres	Niveau moyen de l'eau metres/mètres
	0.0	4.5	0.9	2.9
	0.0	4.6	1.0	3.0
b.	-0.2	4.5	0.8	2.9

RADAR REFLECTORS

Most of the ... or lighted buoys are equi...d with radar reflec... Individual radar reflector...ve not been chart...

CABLES

Submari...nd overhead cables may condu... igh voltages...d contact with or proximity to ...se poses ... extreme danger. Mariners should ...pt anchor...se to submarine cables; however ...f anchor...come hooked onto a cable, care mus... taken ... to sever the cable. Cables installed s... the d... of publication of this edition may not chart... Sufficient clearance must be allowed und... all o... head cables. Actual clearances may diff... from...arted values due to changes in atmospher... con...ons and/or water levels.

RÉFLECTEURS RADAR

La plupart des principales bouées lumineuses sont équipées de réflecteurs radar. Les réflecteurs radar ne sont pas représentés sur les signes des bouées.

CÂBLES

Les câbles sous-marins et aériens peuvent conduire une haute tension; tout contact direct ou indirect peut être fatal. Les navigateurs ne devraient pas mouiller près de câbles sous-marins; cependant, si les ancres accrochent un câble, il faut se soucier de ne pas rompre le câble. Il se peut que les câbles installés depuis la date de publication de cette édition ne soient pas cartographiés. Une hauteur libre suffisante doit être allouée sous tous les câbles aériens. Les hauteurs libres actuelles peuvent varier des valeurs cartographiées à cause de changements dans les conditions atmosphériques et/ou les niveaux d'eau.

Nautical Miles (50°37' N) Milles marins

Metres (50°37' N) Mètres

PORT McNEILL
Scale 1:20 000 Échelle

.3 Move the dividers to the distance scale in the chart legend, and the distance between the points will be translated into mileage. This shows 1.5 nautical miles (1.15 nautical miles = 1 land mile).

a rocky coast, so you can plan accordingly (here is also where you apply your seamanship skills, learned in Chapter 7, to choose the safest course and time your crossing to avoid hazards).

The shipping aids shown by charts—buoys, channel markers, lighthouses, and so forth—are useful route-finding markers for kayakers. Many symbols start with a generic shape—for example, a small triangle connected to an open circle for a buoy—but then have dozens of permutations to indicate specific shapes, sizes, colors, and lights. A nautical-chart symbol index, available for about three bucks from a marine-supply store, will explain all the different symbols used. (See the illustration on page 115 for examples.)

Basic course plotting on a chart is simple to do, because you're usually figuring straight lines instead of having to deal with big things such as mountains and ravines blocking your way. A 6-inch length of ruler or other straightedge, and a small pair of dividers, are handy for plotting courses. You use the straightedge to draw in a course line—say, from your camp in a cove to an island. Then you spread the dividers until the points meet your start and end points. Move the dividers to the distance scale in the chart legend, and you can directly translate the distance on the chart into mileage. If the course is longer than the dividers can reach, adjust the dividers first to a unit of measure on the chart scale—say, 1 mile—then "walk" the dividers along the course line, measuring off 1 mile at a time.

Another way to calculate mileage is with a *map measurer,* a tool with a tiny wheel you simply roll along your intended course. Some have simple dials with

Chart Protection

Protect your charts with a good waterproof case, such as those by Ortlieb (see Appendix A for source information) or others, available at boating and outdoor shops. These strap under the foredeck bungees to allow you a clear view of your chart while paddling. To safely store several charts in the boat, use 1½-inch PVC pipe cut to the length of your charts, then fitted on one end with a glued-on cap and on the other end with a rubber-fitted pull-off cap. Cost of materials—less than $5 from any hardware store.

Waterproof map case.

various scales marked on them; others are digital with a choice of scale. A measurer is handy because it can easily measure sinuous courses as well as straight ones, making it easy to follow coastal routes. Sometimes, however, none of the scales on the tool will match the chart scale and you have to perform a bit of arithmetic to figure the mileage.

If you're plotting a course to a destination you can't see—say, a hidden cove or a little island in a visually confusing group of islands—you can take a true bearing off your chart course and convert it to a magnetic bearing for your boat compass (see sidebar on taking a bearing). But read the section on crossings, below.

With these tools it's easy to plot a preliminary route for your trip before you leave home, giving you an idea of the mileage you'll need to cover each day, and the locations of potential camps. Of course, preliminary routes don't always bear much resemblance to the final one, but it's still a good planning tool. You can easily replot your courses en route.

Crossings and Ferry Angles

For the sea kayaker, crossings of major channels represent the culmination of applied seamanship. The skills you have learned in boat handling, weather evaluation, shipping hazards, chart reading, and compass use all come together when you commit to an open stretch of ocean that might take one hour, or five or six, to cross. And the feeling of accomplishment when your kayak scrapes the sand of the far side is immense.

Channels often have tidal currents running through them. If a current is running when you launch to paddle to a spot directly across the channel, you will be swept past your goal, and face a difficult upcurrent slog near the opposite shore. You must use your chart, tide tables, and timing to calculate an efficient crossing, combined with a technique known as ferrying, which we'll talk about in a minute.

The ideal way to deal with crossing a tidal current is to avoid the current altogether. If the crossing is not far, you can time your paddle to coincide with slack water (explained in Chapter 7, page 100). If the crossing is several miles, and will take longer than the slack-water period, you can cancel the tidal effects by launching near the end of one tidal current, paddling through slack water, and then letting the opposite current move you back.

Often, however, you can't avoid the current. Then it's time to ferry. No, I don't mean *taking* the ferry, although that's not a bad idea.

Ferrying means you paddle at an angle into the tidal current (or a crosswind) to cancel, or at least minimize, its push. You can ferry just by "feel," but a more precise approach is to perform a simple calculation before you launch.

You can calculate a ferry angle by drawing a diagram on the back of your chart with your 6-inch ruler. First, draw a straight line that represents your desired course (this line represents your direction, not any distance, so just make it as long as your ruler—long enough to work with). Then draw another line joining

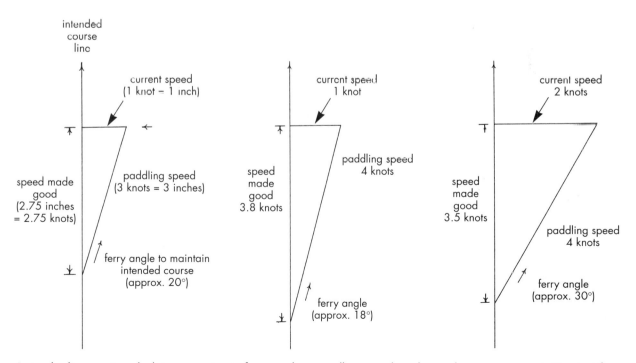

A simple diagram to calculate approximate ferry angles as well as speed made good across a current. (See text for an explanation.)

If you have trouble remembering your courses and bearings and angles for ferrying, there is a useful product for kayakers called the Nav-Board, an erasable waterproof plotting board for dead reckoning—tuck it beside your seat or in your deck bag for easy reference. (See Appendix A for source information.)

the right end of the current line, extending back down to your course line, thus completing a triangle.

The angle that your final line forms with your course line is the angle at which you need to paddle across the channel to maintain your desired course (see below for how to measure angles). The length in inches from where your final line meets the course line to where the current line meets the course line is the speed at which you will actually be moving, in the above case about 2.75 knots.

You can see how altering the parameters will result in different angles and measurements. For example, if you know you can paddle at 4 knots instead of 3, make the third line 4 inches long. You'll see that it meets the desired course line at a shallower angle, meaning you don't have to adjust your course angle as much to maintain your intended line across the current; also your actual speed goes up to about 3.8 knots (3.8 inches on the figure). On the other hand, if the current is running at 2 knots instead of 1, the current line extends farther out from the course line, and the third line forms a broader angle—you need to aim farther right to maintain your desired course.

You can lay your chart compass over the figure to get the exact angle to use for your heading.

Use your boat compass to determine the magnetic bearing straight to your desired destination, then lay in a course 20° right of your goal (if the current were coming from the left, you'd compensate to the left). You can pick a reference point on the opposite shore to aim at, but in order for you to maintain a consistent angle, the aiming point would have to constantly change as you crossed the channel, so it's better to use your compass course for paddling, and confirm your heading by using . . .

the first one near the end (see illustration), to represent the direction and speed of the current: for example, if the current is running at right angles to your course, draw the line perpendicular to the course line. Use inches to represent the speed of the current: if the current is running at 1 knot from the right, draw the line to the right 1 inch long.

Average paddling speed for touring is about 3 knots. To represent this, draw a 3-inch-long line starting at

Leading Marks

The use of leading marks is an essential, and easy, technique for making sure you stay on course during any sort of crossing.

Leading marks can be anything—lighthouses, anchored boats, hills, buoys. The idea is to keep two lined up to verify that you are maintaining a straight line. As an example, let's use a short crossing of a mile or so, where you can make out details of the harbor for which you are aiming.

Pick out something in the foreground, let's say a harbor buoy, and something directly behind and slightly above it, for example a flagpole at the harbormaster's. As you paddle, make sure you keep the two lined up. If the flagpole starts to move left of the buoy, it means you are drifting left and need to alter course to the right. If the flagstaff moves right, paddle left.

One of the hardest things about ferrying is maintaining the correct angle to your goal, because your brain is constantly telling you *you're going the wrong way, stupid!* If you use leading marks, you can continually verify that your ferry angle is correct and you are moving toward your goal—*even if your bow is pointed a different way.*

For ferrying over longer distances, you need to pick larger marks, such as bluffs, peaks, or small islands.

Despite all the fancy angles, ferrying is an inexact science. Currents vary in speed across a channel (they are faster in the middle than near the sides), as do wind speeds and even paddling speeds. But ferrying will get you much closer to your goal than any other technique, and after using the calculations a few times, you'll begin to get pretty good at guessing the proper angle.

Incidentally, you can read an excellent discussion of leading marks in Chapter 11 of *Swallows and Amazons* (see sidebar, page 105). And if you want to learn much more about kayak navigation, pick up a copy of David Burch's book, *Fundamentals of Kayak Navigation* (Pacific Search Press).

Other Navigation and Piloting Situations

NIGHT PADDLING

I'm supposed to tell you that paddling at night is dangerous. Indeed, it involves certain extra risks not associated with daytime paddling—but nothing can approach the sight of a sky full of stars from a kayak floating on a silent sea. So be careful, and be prepared, but try it.

For your first few night excursions, stick with a calm bay or coastal paddle with which you are already familiar, and go with a group. Make sure everyone has flares and a strobe, and at least two flashlights. Cyalume sticks bungeed to everyone's rear deck will not affect night vision too badly, but will keep the group cohesive. If the night is dark you can tape off most of the

Sailing Pilots and Other Guides

A very good source of detailed information about different paddling areas is a sailing or pilot guide, published in book form. These guides provide in-depth analysis of weather patterns, tides and currents, safe harbors, and even local maritime history.

Because they are intended for larger craft, not all the information translates perfectly, but it's easy to extrapolate what you need as a kayaker.

Look for them at sailing supply stores, called *chandleries,* near your destination, or through mail-order sailing catalogs (see Appendix A for contact information), for more far-flung destinations.

stick and still be able to see it from another boat (lighted compasses are okay for this too, but they're usually hooded and thus visible only from behind). Another Cyalume stick or lantern at your launch site will prevent embarrassing confusion about where you came from. Keep the group in frequent voice contact. If you want to sit quietly for a long time, have everyone raft up and then shut up, so there's no chance of a drifter turning up missing.

At night, especially when there's no moon, your ears are your best piloting device. Listen for the sound of water on rocks, or the hiss of approaching waves larger than the norm, or for the sound of boat motors.

Night crossings of channels are another universe. I would never cross a channel used for shipping at night unless I absolutely had to. A wilderness channel is better, but I'd still use extreme caution regarding waves and currents.

If you *have* to cross a shipping channel at night, learn how ships are lighted to help you determine their direction of travel:

- All vessels are required to show a red light on the port (left) side;
- green on the starboard (right) side, which must be visible from ahead and to the side of the ship; and
- white on the masthead, high and centered, and visible from in front and abeam (two masthead lights, one forward and one aft, are required on vessels exceeding 165 feet in length).

Night Crossing

Early in my sea kayaking career, my friend Michael and I took a trip to Tiburón Island in the Sea of Cortez. After several days exploring the virgin desert in the interior, we decided to make a night crossing back to the mainland.

We launched after dark, the correct heading memorized and the right star located to steer by, and headed east across the 2-mile-wide channel. It was a moonless night, utterly black; a blackness that precluded us seeing each other from even a few feet away. The water of the sometimes boisterous channel was calm, and only the sound of our paddles broke the peace. The stars swept overhead in an unbroken dome.

It was a night of spectacular bioluminescence. Each dip of a paddle blade left a vortex of green ghost-light swirling in our wake. A slap on the surface created an explosion like a supernova in deep space. A fainter comet trail led aft from each stern.

Soon our light began to attract attention. We began to notice other streaks of light shooting under the boats, as mullet looked for a possibly edible source of the luminescence. One hit the side of my boat with a *bang* that nearly stopped my heart. I looked over the side and saw another, more ponderous, trail of luminescence headed toward my kayak. As I watched, it passed slowly and silently underneath, until I could see the front end off one side while the back end was still visible over the other. Eight feet? Ten? It wasn't until later I learned that fish can leave luminescent trails much longer than their bodies.

A sudden thump, followed by a flapping sound and a shriek from Michael, indicated that one of the mullet had leaped clear of the surface and landed on his spray skirt. I dissolved in slightly hysterical laughter while the sounds of blind scrabbling ended in a splash. Had the mullet evicted my friend and taken his place? No, Michael's voice came, cursing me for my amusement at his discomfiture.

At last a quiet burbling pinpointed the water rippling at the mainland shore. We turned south, and paddled on. Our plan had been to camp and return to Bahía Kino the next morning, but the spell of the bioluminescence had us hooked. We felt our way down the coast in the dark for 15 miles, reaching the truck shortly after dawn.

So if you see a green light to the *left* of a red light, with a white light in between, that means a ship is headed directly toward you. To remember the light sequence, as well as the port/starboard confusion, just use another one of my confidence-inspiring acronyms:

SGR PRL—Starboard Green Right, Port Red Left. Or, (ready?) Ships Greatly Reduce Paddlers' Regular Life Spans.

Be cautious. Lights at night are misleading. Often one that looks far away turns out to be close, and vice versa. Don't count on being able to see all the running lights a vessel is showing. If you have a VHF radio, monitoring the local shipping channel can help you keep track of nearby traffic. If you live in a place where you will be paddling in traffic often—day or night—I urge you to buy a real piloting book, such as the classic *Chapman Piloting, Seamanship & Small Boat Handling*, and thoroughly familiarize yourself with maritime regulations.

FOG

I'm supposed to tell you that paddling in fog is dangerous. Happy to oblige. Paddling in fog is dangerous.

As with night paddling, the risk in fog goes up logarithmically with the presence of other boating traffic. And fog in shipping channels is really scary. At least on a clear night you can see navigation lights. Although ships are required to sound a foghorn at intervals of not more than two minutes, the direction of origin is often impossible to determine—and many small craft ignore the rules. If you choose to paddle during fog, stick as close to shore as possible, out of the reach of larger boats. Carry your own foghorn to use if you hear a boat approaching closely.

Some writers have urged the use of radar reflectors to make your kayak visible to ship radar. I've not yet read of any documented reports of the effectiveness of these reflectors on kayaks (although they have been proved useful on larger boats). The problem is they need to be as high above the waterline as possible to be effective, and so should really be mounted on some sort of mast on a kayak. In any event, I simply would not trust any such device to alert larger craft to my presence. The only exception I can think of is the Pains-Wessex Ocean Sentry Radar Target Enhancer,

which detects an incoming radar pulse and broadcasts a supercharged return pulse, approximating a target about 80 meters square. Now *that* would make 'em sit up and take notice. The target enhancer is a cylinder only 2 inches in diameter and 20 inches tall, and is available from Pains-Wessex or marine-supply stores. Oh, yeah—list price is around $1,500.

Applied Piloting and Seamanship

When you've learned how to handle your kayak in different conditions, have practiced rescues, are familiar with the basic theories of tides, currents, and waves, and have become comfortable with chart and compass, it's time to head out beyond sheltered routes and begin exploring more exposed stretches of coast, and open crossings. At last the drudgery of the early part of this book comes together in a shining climax, culminating in a competent, smoothly functioning system: you and your kayak.

A COASTAL JOURNEY

It is just after dawn on a fine, crisp morning. You stand at the water's edge with a cup of coffee, discussing the day's route with your three companions. The barometer is rising and the VHF had only good news, so you're looking at a promising cove indicated on the chart about 16 miles up the coast. A spring tide will be flowing your way for most of the morning, so you'll push the pace somewhat to start, paddle through slack water, then look for eddies to cheat the ebb current.

After launching, your group paddles out of the bay and meets a swell coming in from the Pacific. It's just big enough to add some fun to the paddling, but you watch for a line of cliffs that block any landings for about 3 miles. There they are, black in the shade of the morning sun. You paddle underneath, staying far enough out to avoid unexpected downdrafts and the waves rebounding off the rocks at the base. Gulls line ledges in the cliff, and a group of sea lions waits for the sun on their perches just above the booming surf. The tide helps you past the cliffs in less than an hour, and wooded slopes with sandy beaches stretch in front of you.

For tech-weenies, there's the Datascope, an electronic compass that includes a chronometer and rangefinder in a waterproof unit.

About nine o'clock you detour offshore a bit to look at a rocky islet. Waves refracting around the bit of land create a bouncy ride, and you all pay attention in the confused chop. Then you're beyond it, and entering a strait that is shielded from the ocean swell. The tide is really moving now through the constricted passage; moderate paddling makes the shore seem to zoom past.

Someone shouts "Whale!" and you turn to see the remnants of a spout hanging in the air a quarter-mile off to the left. Too far to tell—but then you forget the distant whale as several blows in rapid succession snap your attention forward. Orcas! A small pod of females, their short, curved dorsal fins identifying them. They cruise past within 50 yards of your group as you sit quietly and watch.

By lunchtime you have covered more than 12 miles, even with sight-seeing. A narrow beach serves as a stop, and you bring out the thermos of tea, and cheese, crackers, and summer sausage to slice up on the big plastic cutting board.

Afternoon brings a change. The tide has turned and is running south, while a southerly wind blows against it, creating a steep chop out in the channel. Your group hugs the shore, still catching sloppy waves over the deck now and then. But everyone is dressed warmly, so the splash is no more than invigorating. A gathering of bald eagles stares down at you from perches high in the pines above the water's edge.

As the sun begins to slant down in the west, you take a rest stop. More tea, a candy bar, a community huddle to examine some black bear and raccoon tracks near a stream. Just one more candy bar. Then back out.

Surprise! The wind was short-lived and the sea has calmed, although the current is still running against you. But an eddy underneath a long, low bluff runs your way, and in the windless conditions you can paddle within arm's length of the rock, which plunges straight down through the black water.

Suddenly, an opening reveals itself, a passage through the bluff to a perfectly protected cove. You're there. But it's even better than it looked on the chart. A semicircular beach of fine white sand slopes gently into the barely rippling water. Behind the beach the forest beckons, cool and mysterious. A jumble of logs promises benches and kitchen counters.

Your group of four paddlers executes a perfect simultaneous landing, bows scraping gently up the sand. You hop out and pull your kayak above the high-tide line, among the ferns. No scouting needed here; this is the most idyllic spot you've seen this trip. A 16-mile day, and it's only three o'clock—plenty of time for a hike and a protracted cocktail and hors d'oeuvres hour after you pitch camp.

But as you look around, you realize your companions are milling about in confusion instead of unpacking and setting up their tents. You ask why.

"Because," they reply in unison, "we haven't yet come to the camping section in *Complete Sea Kayak Touring*!"

THREE

CAMPING EQUIPMENT AND TECHNIQUES

9

CAMPING GEAR

A Home in Your Kayak

One of the most rewarding attributes of sea kayaking is being able to efficiently cover 10 or 15 or even 20 or 25 miles of coastline in a day, and at the end unpack a comfortable camp in which to relax and recount the day's adventures.

If you've done any backpacking, you probably have everything necessary to camp with your sea kayak. If, on the other hand, your idea of camping is slotting the Winnebago into space #34 between the Airstream and the pop-up tent trailer, you might need a few things.

Any sea kayak suitable for touring can carry at least 100 pounds of gear, and some will carry more than 200. Compare that to an average backpacking load of 45 pounds or so, and it's obvious you can travel in style compared with those poor folks who file down their toothbrush handles to save weight, and wear the same pair of underwear for a week. *Eeyuck.*

Seriously—any gear designed for backpacking will work well for sea kayaking too. But for short-range trips—say less than two weeks or so—the vast capacity of a sea kayak allows significant upgrades on the comfort quotient: a bigger tent, a shade awning, a full-length mattress pad, or more books.

Alternatively, that same tremendous capacity facilitates extended self-contained expeditions. With careful packing, it's possible to carry two months' worth of food and gear in many kayaks, allowing explorations along some of the most remote coastlines on earth. Imagine undertaking a 500-mile traverse of the Arctic coast of Canada, or a month-long expedition through the fjords of Chile, with no need for outside support.

I make no excuses for being as comfortable as possible while touring. The more secure and comfortable my camp, the more restful it is, and the better I perform on the ocean. When I plan for a trip, I first allow for the volume of food and water I'll need, then figure in the basics for shelter, cooking, clothing and personal hygiene, and first aid. Add cameras, tripod, and other equipment for photography; after that, whatever room remains can accommodate the luxuries. For me such options include a compact propane or gas lantern for really bright working light; an Outback Oven for baking brownies, cakes, and pizzas; a miniature synthetic-fill pillow for sleeping comfort; and extra reading material.

A group of kayakers willing to share a communal kitchen can get really deluxe on cooking arrangements. On my commercial tours each participant carried part of the communal gear in addition to his or her personal equipment. My fleet consisted of my own single, two other singles, and two doubles, one of which had a large center cargo hold. The kitchen outfit I developed eventually included a standard-height roll-up table, a two-burner propane stove with stand, a full-size lantern with stand, and two soft ice chests, in addition to full-size pots and pans, a griddle, a large cutting board, and an insulated coffee server. A Moss Parawing shaded the whole setup. This outfit dispersed easily

among the boats, and with it I could provide fresh meals for the group with comfort and efficiency. Of course, these trips were mostly of a week's duration or less, which allowed greater leeway, but it shows what is possible for a group to put together for short trips. Just remember—get the basics in first, then the extras.

Planning and provisioning for your sea kayak tour, as well as how to pack a boat efficiently and safely, are covered in Chapter 10, beginning on page 147. Sea kayak camping techniques and tips are covered in Chapter 11, beginning on page 160.

Shelter

TENTS

When I was leading kayak tours, my most anxious moments didn't involve taking novices out to sea for the first time. No, the real tension occurred later, when they unpacked their tents.

Wind is a near-constant companion on beaches. Be prepared for strong winds by choosing a good tent; a number of the tents in this photo collapsed after 12 hours of abuse by a Sea of Cortez Norte wind.

The tent on the right is a classic geodesic dome (a North Face VE25, a descendant of one of the first domes), equipped with a useful vestibule on the rainfly. The two tents on the left are hoop-style tents, and are single-walled, made from waterproof/breathable fabric (these are Marmot Takus).

I've never been able to figure out why so many people think a tent shouldn't cost more than lunch, but an inordinate number of them wound up on trips with me. The scene became all too familiar a breezy afternoon on the Sea of Cortez, a pristine sandy beach, and a half-dozen $39.95 dome tents collapsed like beached jellyfish, while their owners flailed around inside trying to prop them up. Ripped canopies and broken poles were common results. In self-defense I accumulated a tent repair kit of heroic proportions: duct tape, safety pins, pole repair sleeves, epoxy, you name it. I seriously considered discounting my tour prices for clients with good tents.

Buy a good tent. Yeah, I know, that's about the tenth time I've said "Buy a good. . . ." But few things are more annoying than having to mess with what is supposed to be your secure shelter from the elements, your home away from home—especially if it's three o'clock in the morning when you discover that the term "waterproof" has no legal definition, or that those fiberglass poles have the tensile strength of day-old pasta.

You don't have to spend a fortune on a tent. It will cost more than $39.95, though, and you won't find it in the sporting goods section behind frozen foods. Go to a specialty shop and look at name brands.

There are two predominant styles of tent in today's market: the dome, with crisscrossing poles that form a more or less symmetrical structure, and the tunnel, which is usually low at the foot and higher near the head, and has poles arranged in hoop fashion. There are also hybrid designs that combine elements of both. Each style has its merits. Domes offer tremendous interior room and are usually freestanding; that is, they don't need to be staked out to stand up. Tunnels use space more efficiently and are thus lighter and more compact when stored. Take into account your intended use when deciding on the general type. If you kayak where inclement weather might keep you in the tent for long stretches, a dome will minimize claustrophobia, especially if you share your tent with someone. If you have a low-volume kayak, or are planning long-range expeditions where space will be critical—or if your tent will do double duty for backpacking—you might prefer a lightweight tunnel. Either type can be made strong enough to stand up to just about anything you'll encounter. Domes, though, are essentially just as strong, no matter from which direction the wind is coming; tunnels usually perform better if pitched with the low end into the prevailing breeze. Whichever style you choose, make sure it is equipped with Easton aluminum poles.

Fiberglass poles are a near-sure giveaway of a low-budget tent.

Ignore the manufacturer's designations of one-person, two-person, and so on. Look instead at the square footage of the tent. For two people you'll want at least 30 square feet, and 35 or 40 is better. A single person should feel comfortable with 25 to 30. If you have kids, I recommend two tents rather than one big one. Kids love to have their own place, and smaller tents are generally stronger than larger ones.

A *vestibule*—a floorless area outside the door that is protected by the rain fly—is a valuable extra on any tent. Vestibules are great for storing shoes, clothes bags, and anything else you want accessible but not inside the tent with you. They come in handy at other times as well. On one Arctic trip, we were besieged by proverbial hordes of mosquitoes at a couple of camps. We were using a North Face VE25, which has an entrance with a large vestibule on one side and an additional entrance on the other side. We used the vestibule as a nearly mosquito-free space in which to cook (a procedure, by the way, strongly and rightfully discouraged by all tent makers because tents are flammable and stoves use up oxygen in enclosed spaces).

Most tents are built with a separate rain fly. The main body of the tent is breathable fabric, to allow condensation from breath and body warmth to disperse through to the outside; the waterproof fly fits over the top and provides protection from rain and snow. A tent made from just a single layer of coated fabric would condense moisture like a glass of cold lemonade on a hot day, soaking you as thoroughly as the rain. Some tents, though, are made from a single layer of waterproof, but breathable, fabric that keeps out precipitation but allows condensation to escape. Single-layer tents are generally much more

A great camp-enhancer is a caternary-cut tarp, such as this Parawing by Moss—a small, efficient, unflappable shelter for cooking, lounging, or sleeping.

expensive than traditional fly-equipped models, and designed more for high-elevation mountaineering than general use. However, I've used an old Gore-Tex Marmot Taku as a solo kayaking shelter for years (see photo, above). It's compact, roomy, and utterly bombproof—50-mph Baja *elefante* winds just roll right off it. It's back in production after an absence of 10 years. Marmot makes another nice single-wall design, the Asylum, and several high-quality fly-equipped models. I also like Mountain Hardwear's tents. For a good-quality tent at a lower price, take a look at Sierra Designs' extensive line.

When you shop for a tent, have the salesperson help you set it up, and sit and lie inside to judge the roominess. Some compact tents can be a little short on lying-down room for tall people. Lean on it a little to assess the structural integrity. Above all, look for nice taut fabric—a tight tent is usually a strong tent, and one that won't keep you awake by flapping on a windy night. Tent makers use the terms "three-season" and "four-season" to differentiate between designs intended for all-around use and those built to withstand really bad weather. A well-built three-season tent is usually adequate for sea kayaking; then again, its hard to imagine a tent being *too* strong. The only downside to four-season tents, besides price, is that they sometimes lack adequate ventilation for summer use.

The first thing to do with a new tent—before you even leave the store—is to throw away the worthless little peg stakes that come with even the best models. Buy a set of Black Diamond T-stakes, the large size, and your tent will stay put through anything.

Speaking of stakes, don't put too much value in the idea of a "freestanding" tent. Freestanding tents are easier to set up and to move around camp, and you can pick them up to shake sand out the door, but *any* tent needs to be staked down at all other times. Weighing it down with two sleeping bags and a daypack won't do it—I witnessed a tent thusly ballasted clear the top of a saguaro cactus by a good 15 feet after a gust launched it off the beach.

A ground cloth is a good idea to keep the floor of your tent in good shape. Many manufacturers sell ground cloths exactly sized to fit their tent models; these are well worth the investment. You can substitute a tarp, but if it extends beyond the tent floor it will collect and funnel rain water under the tent.

AWNINGS

If you've got room in the boat, a nice complement to the tent is a tarp to rig a front porch or cooking area sheltered from rain or sun. I carry a small Moss Parawing, which is sewn with a catenary cut to spill wind effectively. It pitches tightly, and can be tilted to block wind or late afternoon sun. In its stuff sack it takes up about as much space as a rolled-up shirt.

A regular nylon tarp works well too, although it will need more guylines to stay taut. A flat tarp can double as a work surface, for example to assemble a folding kayak on a sandy beach.

If you're not certain to have plenty of trees from which to tie your awning, carry a collapsible or sectional aluminum pole or two. And use T-stakes to secure it—awnings are more susceptible to wind than are tents.

Sleeping Comfort

SLEEPING BAGS

Even the generous gear space of most sea kayaks can be overtaxed. I once had a client family show up at the launch site with a pile of those gigantic Coleman sleeping bags with deer running across the flannel lining, despite having received my suggested gear list, which expressly prohibited sleeping bags with running deer and flannel linings. By the time we got all the deer stuffed in the boats there was little room for anything else.

One of the benefits of exploring a maritime environment is the maritime climate, which normally attenuates the large temperature swings common in the interior of continents. Thus, unless you're paddling in far northern regions, really cold temperatures on coastlines are fairly rare during the spring-summer-fall months. This means you can sleep comfortably in a lightweight synthetic or down three-season bag.

I am an unswerving fan of goose-down sleeping bags. A good down bag (uh oh, there's that word *good* again), with a rating of 20°F (−6°C) or so, can compress to the size of a 2-pound coffee can and will last at least 10 years with care, far longer than any synthetic-fill bag. On the other hand, if that down gets soaked it will retain the insulation value of sheet metal until it dries three months later or you find a commercial laundromat along your route. For that reason, synthetic-fill sleeping bags are an understandably popular choice for sea kayaking. And as the science of synthetic insulation advances, the warmth and compressibility of such bags continues to narrow (though not, as yet, close) the gap on down. Synthetic fill still has a limited life span, depending on how often it gets washed (less is better) and how long it remains compressed in a stuff sack (less is better), and thus is not the bargain compared to down it seems to be, but if it gets wet during a trip you can wring it out and regain a decent percentage of its efficiency.

For an excellent, thorough discussion of current synthetic fill types (and other outdoor equipment applicable to sea kayaking, often discussed by brand name), see Chris Townsend's The Backpacker's Handbook, *Second Edition (Camden, ME: Ragged Mountain Press, 1997 revised).*

Of course, you should avoid getting any sleeping bag wet—even a synthetic bag can take 24 hours or more to dry thoroughly. I put mine into its own coated nylon stuff sack, then put that inside a plastic kitchen garbage bag, and then put *that* into a heavy-duty dry bag. I've never had a leak, and so continue to use my fluffy goose-down bag.

If you do decide on a down bag, consider one with a shell of waterproof/breathable fabric, which not only gives a slight extra protection against water incursion, but also protects against sea fog and general dampness.

A valuable accessory for any sleeping bag is a machine-washable cotton or poly-cotton liner. These take up very little room, but are much more comfortable against your skin than nylon. Additionally, they help keep the bag clean, which reduces the frequency with which you'll have to wash it, which extends its life. On long trips you can hand wash the liner to keep it fresh.

SLEEPING PADS

What did we do before the Therm-a-Rest? Self-inflating foam mattress pads have nearly cornered the market on lightweight sleeping pads, and with good reason. They are comfortable and insulative, yet roll up into a small package. You can choose from the minimalist backpacker's model, three-quarter length and

A mummy bag is very efficient at keeping you warm (less dead air space), but some people find the cut too confining; a solution is this flex-kneed sleeping bag by Mountain Hardwear.

The Thermalounger is a slipcover for a Thermarest self-inflating mattress; it converts your sleeping pad into an extremely comfortable camp chair for cooking or relaxing, as this sea kayaker is demonstrating.

three-quarters of an inch thick, or luxuriate on a full-length, inch-thick pad. There are several brands on the market now, but Cascade Designs's Therm-a-Rest is the original and, I think, still the best, so I use their name to refer to the genre.

As with any inflatable device, the Therm-a-Rest's bête noir is pointy things. Keeping a Therm-a-Rest intact for the duration of a trip through Baja, the Land of Thorns, is a challenge. Fortunately repairs are straightforward with a factory kit, and even deflated the foam inside the mattress offers a bit of support.

The alternative to an inflatable mattress is a simple open-cell foam pad, puncture-proof but bulky. A series of nylon straps with friction buckles will help compress the rolled pad further. Thin, closed-cell foam pads take up less space than open-cell foam, but are correspondingly less comfortable.

My Therm-a-Rest goes in the boat naked, because it is coated nylon anyway. If you use an open-cell foam pad, it needs to be protected or it will take on water like a sponge.

An accessory that I think is a "Dahling, you simply *must* have one" necessity for the Therm-a-Rest is the Thermalounger (made by a different company, Crazy Creek). It is a heavy duty cover for the mattress, with straps that convert it into an almost unbelievably comfortable beach chair. I bought one of the first ones available, and could have sold them at three times retail if I'd brought extras on kayaking trips. People who tried mine simply refused to move, even when threatened with violence. The bonus to the Thermalounger is that it helps prevent punctures. Incidentally, Cascade Designs makes their own version, but I like the Crazy Creek product better.

Kitchen Equipment

STOVES

My old solid brass SVEA 123 backpacking stove didn't quite survive into my sea kayaking years—by then I had graduated to a more efficient, if less romantic, MSR (Mountain Safety Research) Whisperlite. It would have been interesting to see what salt air would have done to that well-polished finish.

Modern backpacking stoves are perfect for sea kayaking; they are light, compact, and burn with a hotter flame than a household range. You can choose from two basic types—those that burn liquid white gas, and those that use canisters containing isobutane, butane/propane, or a proprietary mix such as Coleman's Max Performance.

White gas is the most thermally efficient, and thus cheapest, fuel for compact stoves. In addition, many stoves that burn white gas can also operate on automotive gasoline, kerosene, even diesel fuel, making them ideal for travel in parts of the world that lack REI stores.

On the down side, white gas is messy (and even it's benign compared to diesel oil), often must be decanted into the fuel tank of the stove, inviting spills, and can leak from its container. Most white-gas stoves require priming, a process involving lighting a small quantity of raw gas in a priming cup on the stove, which can result in flare-ups. White-gas stoves are notoriously poor at simmering (a commercially available heat diffuser helps). And the burner orifice needs frequent cleaning to prevent clogging.

Canister stoves are neat and quick—you screw on a fuel canister, light a match (or press a button if it has

Modern backpacking stoves are perfect for sea kayaking—they are lightweight, very efficient, and simple to use.

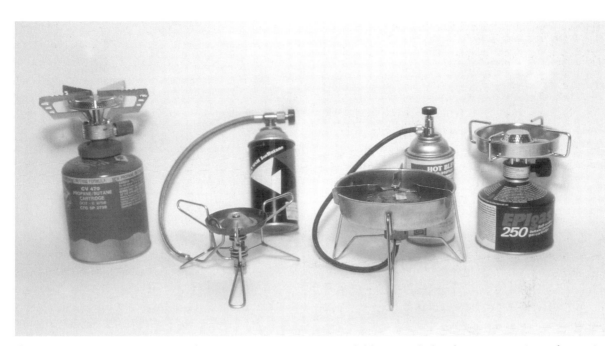

Canister stoves are convenient and some canisters are now recyclable—a real plus if you camp a lot. Left to right: Camping Gaz/Bluet, MSR Firefly, Scorpion II, and EpiGas. One of the most economical, efficient, and reliable stoves is the MSR Whisperlite, which burns white gas (or the International version will burn a variety of fuels). For longer trips, the Whisperlite is a real workhorse, and can be easily field-serviced.

an igniter) and turn a knob, and away it goes. No smell, no spills, and you can lower the flame to a bare flicker that won't harm the most delicate white sauce.

You pay for that convenience in fuel costs—three to five times that of white gas, depending on whom you believe. Few canister stoves burn as hot as white-gas models when all you want to do is boil water, and when you've emptied the canister, it's trash, destined to take up landfill space (although that's changing; see below). Also, it's difficult to guess the amount of gas remaining in a canister, so you're usually forced to take an extra for even a weekend trip.

Early canister stoves burned pure butane, which loses efficiency at below-freezing temperatures. Later mixes such as isobutane and propane/butane helped a lot. Pure propane is also a very efficient fuel, but must be stored at higher pressures, so the cartridges are heavier.

Coleman has attacked both major disadvantages of canister stoves. Its Max Performance cartridges are made of aluminum, and can be punctured and crushed

when empty, and recycled right in with your Coke cans. And the stoves that use the Max fuel employ a new vaporization system that significantly improves burning.

POTS, PANS, AND ACCESSORIES

You can use pot sets designed for backpacking on your kayaking trips, but they are usually made from very thin material to save weight, and thus are prone to scorching. I like to use thicker aluminum or stainless steel pots with a nonstick coating, which greatly reduces cleanup effort. There's rarely any need to have more than two pots along, or one pot and a frying pan—although if you're cooking for several people a large griddle can come in handy. Several retailers sell nesting pot kits that include a $1\frac{1}{2}$-liter and a 2-liter nonstick pot and lid; these are just right for one or two people.

One of the most useful accessories for a kayaking kitchen is a big plastic cutting board, or even two. I bought one huge one and cut it up into two pieces that would fit neatly in the rear compartment of my boat. They take up minimal space, but provide vital work surfaces for a beach camp, and can double as serving trays or small tables.

Plastic (Lexan) plates, bowls, and silverware are serviceable and easy to clean. A spatula and a large spoon should be all the specialized cooking utensils you'll need; however, I do like to have a real chef's knife along if I'm carrying fresh foods that need slicing and dicing, or if there's a chance of catching fresh fish that need filleting; make sure it has a slipcover.

Outdoor Research makes an excellent zip-up nylon kitchen pouch, with bottles for spices and cooking oil, and a mesh pocket equipped with eating utensils and cooking implements, including a spatula and serving spoon, measuring spoons, and a little whisk.

Speaking of fresh foods—for short trips, or longer ones during which you might replenish your food supply at local markets, a collapsible ice chest is a treat, good for bringing vegetables, fruit, heck, even a frozen steak or two. Depending on the level of chilling you need, you can use freeze-packs or dry ice wrapped in newspaper and sealed in bags to maintain perishable items for quite a while (*never* let unwrapped dry ice contact your boat or cooler—it can cause a lot of damage to plastic, fiberglass, and nylon). During winter paddles in Mexico, with daytime highs in the seventies, I found I could keep even butter and cream edible for up to a week.

One luxury I've become attached to is an insulated stainless steel coffee mug, which keeps the Colombian Supremo hot for an amazingly long time. For brewing the coffee, I bought a plastic filter holder that takes a number-two paper filter, and can be placed over a pot or a single cup. For cold-weather paddling, I carry a very slender, all stainless steel thermos that holds about a pint. A hot coffee break on the water at 10 A.M. or so is invigorating.

Other useful kitchen items: a cellulose camp towel, available at any outdoor store by the brand PakTowl, is good for spills, drying dishes, and picking up hot pots. A collapsible vinyl bucket is handy if you have to fetch water from a stream, and a collapsible wash basin is nice for doing the dishes.

Finally, if you can possibly squeeze it in, bring an Outback Oven, now manufactured by Cascade Designs. This cunning contraption packs in the same space as a frying pan, but functions just like a real oven. The Outback Oven can turn out cakes, brownies, and pizza from mixes made especially for it, or you can use grocery-store mixes nearly as effectively (see Chapter 11, beginning page 166, for more on cooking tips). From personal experience I can assure you that if you produce a hot pizza and brownies on the 10th night out, thereafter you will be worshipped as a god or goddess. (Another outdoor oven is the BakePacker, available from Adventure Foods; see Appendix A for more information.)

The Outback Oven is a portable, soft-sided baking oven that will convert your wilderness kitchen into a gourmet center: chocolate cakes, cinnamon buns, yeast breads, pizza, casseroles—your imagination is your limit. This setup shows the benefits of carrying two small canister stoves: one simmers the main course while the other bakes chocolate cake for dessert.

For a listing of camping equipment and accessories manufacturers and suppliers, see Appendix A, page 205.

Camp Lighting

My wife calls me Flashlight Man. I used to bristle at this nickname, until an inventory at her suggestion turned up 13 in my immediate possession, plus a couple I *knew* were around somewhere. So I conceded.

I always take two flashlights kayaking, plus spare batteries and bulbs. Sometimes three. Only *once* that I remember did I have four along—and guess who's only light burned out that trip, forcing her to beg one of mine. *Hah*.

Compact, waterproof, plastic-bodied flashlights designed for divers work great for sea kayaking. Models that take AA batteries do fine, though I like C-cell versions for their greater power and longer burn time. The Pelican Super PeliLite (also sold by Browning) is an excellent choice; with two of these along, plus a spare bulb unit and spare batteries, I feel very secure. Princeton Tec's AA models are really nice too, incredibly bright though hard on batteries. I like twist switches for their resistance to accidental turn-on; otherwise, I rubber band or tape down toggle switches to prevent dead-battery surprises.

Headlamps are a great choice for many uses. Their hands-free operation allows you to work with both hands while directing the light right where you need it. A couple of models are now waterproof. Some of the best and smallest are made by Petzl.

Flashlights, great for route-finding and pinpointing objects, are okay as a light for cooking or working, but lanterns throw a broader pattern. Compact fluorescent lanterns powered by AA cells function nicely. If I have room, though, I like to carry a real lantern,

Camp lighting options include (1) candle lanterns and white gas lanterns; (2) small flashlights (waterproof are best); and (3) headlamps.

either a Coleman Peak 1 white-gas type, or a canister model from Camping Gaz/Bleuet or Primus. These make easy work of late camp-pitching, and are bright enough for two or three people to read by. Kayaking is hard on the fragile wicks used by these lanterns, though; I carry at least a half-dozen spares. The lantern goes in its own dry bag, rolled in a piece of open-cell foam.

Candle lanterns are an option for those who prefer the simplicity and warm light of a flame. I like candle lanterns inside a tent, but find them too dim for general outdoor use. Also, I've never been able to get the little spring mechanism to work for the entire life of the candle; it burns only about halfway before clogging up with wax. Out comes the Swiss Army knife, and I get little wax turds all over the tent.

Water Carriers

For all your extended sea kayak cruising you will need to budget at least a gallon of water per person per day, to cover drinking, cooking, and cleaning. If you can't replenish your water reliably en route, you will need to carry it all with you—especially trips in arid lands such as Baja or the Arctic (where much of the fresh water is locked up in permafrost).

Unfortunately, choices for efficiently carrying water in a sea kayak are limited. Large hard-sided plastic containers don't pack well, and too many small containers can be a hassle to keep track of.

I usually use a combination of Nalgene or Olicamp 1- and 2-liter bottles and several 2½-gallon collapsible plastic water containers. If treated delicately, the collapsible containers hold up surprisingly well, but on one trip to Baja we did manage to put holes in two containers, lost about 5 gallons, and had to cut our trip short by a day. Someday I plan to make Cordura covers/carrying bags for these containers, which should greatly increase their life spans and my peace of mind.

If you have the money, MSR's Dromedary waterbags are stout and easy to pack, and the company's Waterworks water filter attaches directly to the filler opening.

Water Filters

Sadly, the days are gone when we could visit the wilderness and dip water out of any stream we crossed. A recent study suggests that, at certain times of the year, almost 90 percent of the surface water in the United States harbors intestinal pathogens of some sort. Even a pristine brook tumbling to a remote beach is suspect. Most disorders resulting from bad water involve nothing more than a few days of misery, but complications can include severe dehydration from diarrhea and vomiting. Such a condition could well prove life-threatening far from help.

Intestinal pathogens in surface water come in several flavors, as it were. Protozoans such as *Giardia lamblia* are well-known villains, common in many backcountry areas. Other protozoans include amoebas such as *Enta-moeba histolytica*, the perpetrator of amoebic dysentery, and cryptosporidium.

Bacteria, single-celled organisms like protozoans but of a more primitive form, include *Escherichia coli*, of Montezuma's Revenge fame. Although everyone carries *E. coli* in their intestines, the species has several thousand strains. It's when we ingest these unfamiliar variations that trouble occurs. Bacteria also include nastier beasts that cause typhoid, cholera, and salmonella.

An entirely different sort of nasty are the viruses, vanishingly small little packets of destructive DNA or RNA, that include the agents of HIV, polio, and hepatitis. Fortunately, few viruses can be transmitted through water.

Boiling water is a straightforward and effective way to kill unwanted hitchhikers. Contrary to some belief, the water doesn't have to be boiled for a certain amount of time; simply bringing it to a full boil will do the trick.

A water filter is an important tool, since nearly all surface water in North America harbors some microorganisms that could make you ill and ruin your trip. Left to right, choices include pocket filters from Sweetwater and PÜR.

But boiling is time-consuming, and inconvenient in the middle of the day. So increasing numbers of people are carrying water filters to do the job.

Water filters work by passing the water through a very fine-pored material, such as a block of ceramic or a microporous membrane, which simply blocks the passage of protozoans and bacteria. For most parts of the first and second worlds, the protection offered by simple filters is sufficient.

Viruses, up to 1,000 times smaller than the already microscopic protozoans, are another matter. They swim happily through any filter made (although First Need has recently introduced a model they claim will filter viruses). Most filters that claim effectiveness against viruses use an iodine matrix positioned after the filter element to kill, rather than block, any viruses present. But iodine should be avoided by pregnant women and anyone with thyroid trouble. Since viral contamination of surface water is extremely unlikely outside undeveloped countries, most kayakers will be served well by a plain old filter.

I have two favorites from several tests I've performed. One, the Katadyn Pocket Filter, has been around for decades. It's expensive, and takes some muscle to use, but will probably outlast its owner—the filter element is good for up to 13,000 gallons of water. My other choice, the First Need Guardian, is much less expensive as well as easier to work, although it uses an element that must be replaced every 200 gallons or so. The Sweetwater can be equipped with an optional iodine cartridge if you're headed to Burundi.

The most important thing to remember when using a water filter is to avoid contaminating the filtered water. Keep your container as far from the source as possible, and when you're through filtering, don't wrap wet intake and output hoses together.

10

PLANNING, PROVISIONING, AND PACKING

When the Horizon Beckons

It starts with a dream. A dream planted, perhaps, by a photograph, or an article, or a passage in a book. The dream could be of a forbidding, yet stunning, Arctic coastline, or a warm desert sea bordered by sand beaches, or a cool forested island chain where orcas roll from the water just yards offshore.

The dream is nurtured by further research—more magazines, perhaps a chart or two ordered from a marine-supply store, and a long, hard look at the savings-account balance. Then come telephone calls, housesitters, last-minute equipment needs and lusts.

The planning stage of a trip is one of the most exciting parts. It is also a vital key to ensuring a successful journey. No one can predict events once you launch, but the more thorough your preparation up to that point, the better equipped you will be to handle the unforseen.

Some of the special bonuses of adventurous travel to remote places include meeting wonderful people and learning about their cultures. These three Seri Indian children—whose ancestors plied the Sea of Cortez in reed boats with paddles—loved the author's boat. Roseann Hanson, the author's wife, samples muktuk, or whale blubber, in Tuktuyoktuk on the Canadian Arctic coast.

Keeping One Foot on the Ground

It's easy to be swept away by the romance of a history-making expedition. Easy, when you're sipping coffee on the sofa, reading about a solo circumnavigation of Australia or a rounding of Cape Horn.

You probably think I'm about to discourage you from such dreams, that I'm going to tell you about the superhuman qualities needed for such feats. Hah! You're wrong. The whole essence of sea kayaking lies in the almost unlimited possibilities open to an experienced paddler.

The operative word is *experienced*. You need to remember that the people who have accomplished outstanding feats in sea kayaks didn't do so after reading an inspiring article while sitting on the sofa, then jumping up, selling the house, and heading for Tasmania. They built their skills over years of shorter journeys, gradually honing both the techniques and the mind-set needed for epic exploration.

So don't be afraid to dream, but start slowly. Try weekend trips first, then week-long journeys to more remote areas. You will pass a critical threshold somewhere around the two- to three-week mark. If you're comfortable being out for that period of time, it's unlikely that adding significantly to the duration of a voyage will change your attitude. Then it's time to start planning for that epic journey.

Planning

It's likely your first few paddling trips will be in the company of a more experienced paddler who is familiar with your route. Eventually, however, you will start planning your own trips, and sooner or later you'll want to go places you haven't seen before. This is when advance planning and research become an art—the idea is that when you arrive at your launch spot, it will seem as though you've already been there.

If you're visiting a part of the world new to you, you'll be relying on the accounts of other people for advance information. Remember to rely on your sources in order of relevance. For example, an article in *Sea Kayaker* by someone who paddled the route you plan to take would obviously be ideal; a piece in *Travel and Leisure* by a passenger on a cruise ship that covered the same stretch will likely not be so germane. (By the way, did you know that some of those ships that ply the inside passage to Alaska have closed-circuit TV cameras mounted on deck to capture the view, which is then piped to monitors in the suites so the passengers don't have to get cold going out on deck to watch? Makes my skin crawl.)

Don't limit yourself to current or recent travel pieces. Look up historical accounts as well. It's good education, and the accounts of weather, sea conditions, and geography will be just as useful as more up-to-date sources.

An excellent source for paddling resources is The Whole Paddler's Catalog: Views, Reviews, and Resources, *edited by Zip Kellogg (Camden, ME: Ragged Mountain Press, 1997). It's chock-full of bibliographic information, phone numbers, addresses, and more tips than you'll know what to do with.*

Finally, if you're going to be visiting a new country, learn as much as you can of the customs, including manners and clothing. Nothing is uglier than the ugly American who expects other cultures to defer to American culture. If a different language is spoken, learn, and use frequently, four words: *hello, good-bye, please*, and *thank you*. You'll be astonished at the response.

Provisioning

I once had a deep distrust of books that include specific lists of food, calculated from mean caloric requirements of a representative human engaged in a typical exercise. I figured if you've grown up enough to drive your own car and have your own apartment, you know how much food you need to accomplish certain activities. But I've since learned that most people usually seriously underestimate the amount of food they will consume while journeying in the wilderness. Sea kayaking will definitely push the limits of your appetite, but once you've done a few overnight jaunts you'll have a good idea of your own mean caloric requirements. To

Kayaking the World Wide Web

If you have access to the Internet, you will be amazed at the wealth of sources for local contacts in many parts of the world. A recent browse by means of a search I titled "sea kayaking, Great Britain," turned up nearly two dozen shops, clubs, and symposiums—including the Outer Hebrides Sea Kayak Symposium. Local clubs are especially valuable, since they are by nature filled with people interested in sharing information. The best way to introduce yourself is to send an E-mail message to the club's address, explaining what you want to do and what sort of advice you'd like, and offering a return favor if anyone in the club might be interested in visiting your area.

Packing and Repackaging Food

It's easy to just dump all your food into dry bags and forget about it—until you get to the first night's camp and you can't find the basil, half the lunch items are in with breakfast, and one of the sharp corners of the chocolate-chip cookie box has ripped a hole in a dry bag.

Following are some tips for organizing and packing your kayaking provisions:

1. To minimize volume and maximize ease of preparation, look for packaged foods at your grocery store first, then your outdoor specialty shop. Canned meats such as chicken breast, tuna, and salmon are very versatile; refried beans are tasty and easy to whip up into burritos for lunch; and dried noodle, rice, and bean dishes are surprisingly abundant, cheap, and delicious.

2. Dried milk and buttermilk are excellent travelers. Take a little extra time before you leave home to prepare recipes for such things as buttermilk pancakes and biscuits so all you have to do at camp is add water; write the directions on a separate sheet of paper and slip inside the double zip-top bags.

3. Remove all packaged food from sharp-cornered fiberboard and cardboard containers, and repack them in zip-top bags.

4. A spice kit is an essential kitchen item. Some good staples include dried onion and vegetable flakes, garlic powder, chile powder, basil, oregano, cumin, salt, pepper, cinnamon, and nutmeg. Pack your spices in a zip-top bag for easy ID. (Note: it's not advisable to pack spices in used film containers, because of chemical residues.)

give you an idea of the quantities and kinds of food you'll need, refer to the tables in Chapter 12 of the *Ragged Mountain Press Guide to Outdoor Sports* (see Appendix A for bibliographic details). The tables list caloric requirements for various activities, and suggest packable and nonperishable foods that fill the bill with the least weight-for-calorie ratio.

With that said, following are more guidelines that will help you stay healthy and happy on the water.

- Familiar is best. The more drastic changes your diet suffers on an expedition, the more likely you are to suffer digestive complications. Eat as nearly as possible the same foods you enjoy at home.
- Fresh is best. The more fresh foods you can include in your trip diet, the better. Vegetables that travel well include potatoes, green beans, green and red bell peppers, carrots, and squash. Roma tomatoes survive well if you can protect them from being

Maxim's of Baja

Some people subsist happily on granola and Ramen while kayaking. On the other extreme is my friend Kenneth. A few years ago, he became infatuated with an English major from a prestigious eastern women's college, an alabaster-skinned waif who had never even been camping. He talked her into accompanying him on a kayaking trip to the Sea of Cortez, seeking to woo her with a taste of adventure under the velvet and diamond skies of Mexico.

Concerned, however, with what he assumed would be her upscale tastes, he hesitated at providing cold cereal and noodles for sustenance. So he enlisted my help to convert the entire forward cargo compartment of his kayak into a superinsulated freezer chest. We spot-glued sheets and wedges of thick closed-cell foam inside the hull and under the deck, not forgetting the hatch itself, until the whole space was utterly isolated from the savage February desert climate. The day before Kenneth's friend was to arrive for their trip, he spent the entire day shopping, and that evening I watched in awe as he packed the compartment with alternating layers of dry ice, Cornish game hens, dry ice, smoked duck, dry ice, salmon fillets, more dry ice, and the pièce de résistance, two pints of Häagen Das ice cream. In the bow, at what Kenneth had calculated was the thermally perfect distance from the ice, he stuffed an enormous bottle of Veuve Clicquot, probably worth more than the boat. In front of the rudder pedals went fresh vegetables and several flats of repulsive-looking fungi with italicized names.

When the couple returned five days later, the English major bubbled enthusiastically about the trip, and radiated an affectionate glow toward Ken—who, in contrast, seemed strangely subdued. Not until her plane left could I get the rest of the story. Yes, the trip had gone well—the skies were clear, the food had survived in fine style, and Kenneth had spent the major portion of each day creating fantastic meals, which disappeared with an alacrity that belied the slender figure of the diner.

There was just one problem. Having no frame of reference, the object of Kenneth's desires naturally assumed that this epicurean extravaganza was *perfectly normal* for a sea kayaking trip. When, under a romantic moon, aperitif in hand, she began brightly discussing possible menus for their next kayaking adventure, he started to doubt the wisdom of his plan. When she mentioned that she had always wanted to try *backpacking,* he knew he had made a horrible mistake. Visions of himself staggering up the Appalachian Trail under a hundred pounds of champagne and shitake mushrooms deflated his ardor with the effect of a slammed door on a soufflé.

Poor Kenneth spent the next two months dodging phone calls, until a mutual acquaintance informed him that the woman, impatient and hungry, had started dating a *sous*-chef from Club 21.

smashed. Cabbage makes good a salad base. Fruits such as apples and citrus are great. Cantaloupe for breakfast is wonderful. The trick is to look for tough travelers.

- Carbohydrates are good. You will burn a lot of calories while paddling. The best fuel to replenish your energy is a carbohydrate-rich diet. In cold climates you can consume more fat than you're used to, because fat provides more calories (energy) per gram than any other food.
- Stick with one-pot meals. Casseroles, stews, and other recipes that combine all the ingredients in one pot make for easier cooking and much easier cleanup. Choose foods that don't require cooking—carrot sticks, crackers, and cheese—for side dishes.
- Shop your grocery store first for packaged meals, then the specialized outdoor stores. You'll be surprised at how many easily prepared dishes are available at a regular supermarket, for much less money than typical freeze-dried or dehydrated backpacking food. These include tuna helpers, pasta dishes such as fettuccine Alfredo, rice and bean dishes, pizza mixes, simmer sauces for canned meat (although look into the excellent dehydrated meats and entrees from Adventure Foods, if weight and space is at a premium).
- Include fruit-drink mixes or fruit-juice-in-a-box. In any climate it's vital to drink lots of fluids. If you get bored quickly with water, the fruit drinks add welcome variation. Sorry—coffee and tea, and especially alcoholic beverages, don't count. They are all diuretics and can actually increase dehydration.
- Pick out lots of snack foods, then buy extra. Small, frequent quantities of food are excellent for maintaining energy levels throughout the day, and you'll consume far more than you think. Energy bars are good, but don't depend on them—some of them include high fructose corn syrup and a lot of fiber (one brand recommends drinking 16 ounces of water with *each* bar). Instead, buy nuts and dried fruit, crackers, pretzels, and durable cookies such as oatmeal raisin, ginger snaps, and the like. We once returned to our trucks a day early because we had run out of cookies. . . .

Many books are available that offer delicious, healthy, and economical recipes suitable for kayaking. Among them are *Trail Food*, by Alan Kesselheim; and *Good Food for Camp and Trail: All-Natural Recipes for Delicious Meals Outdoors,* by Dorcas Miller. For a more extensive treatment of cooking and provisioning tips for wilderness camping, refer to the *Ragged Mountain Press Guide to Outdoor Sports.* See the Appendix A for further reading suggestions and bibliographic details.

Gear and Food Lists

I make enough copies of lists every time I go paddling to qualify as a government agency. If I don't have a list, I won't just forget my toothbrush and comb—I'm likely to wind up at the water's edge looking forlornly at the roof of my truck and thinking "Wait; I *know* I put the kayak up there, didn't I?"

I am what defense strategists would call a worst-case scenario, but even a mainframe computer like that which resides in my wife's tiny skull can forget things in the press of expedition preparation.

The nearly foolproof solution is a three-stage list, a packing aid that covers all the spots in the sequence of trip preparation when you're most likely to overlook something.

It begins with a master list—a permanent document that can be stored in the hard drive of your computer, or on a hand-written sheet of legal paper—it doesn't matter. What does matter is that this list include *everything* you take on a kayaking trip. Right down to Chapstick, bandannas, and oregano. It helps to divide it into major areas—clothing, sleeping, cooking, and so forth.

I keep a separate inventory list for my first-aid kit and my tool/spare-parts box. Since my list is on my computer, I also keep several "addendum" files for specialized gear to take for differing environments. For example, my Arctic list includes cold-water paddling clothes and bear spray; my desert list includes a Sawyer Extractor (see Appendix B) for stings and bites, and a solar still for making emergency water. I can import the specialized list into the main list before I print it.

As you pack your vehicle for the trip, refer to your lists and use a transparent highlighter marker to draw a line over each item after you put it in the vehicle or duffel bag. The bright color makes it easy to see which items haven't been loaded.

When you're ready to leave for a trip, print out a copy of the master list with the relevant addenda. The procedure then goes like this:

- Use the list to organize all the gear in one spot. As each piece is added to the pile, put a check mark next to the item on the paper.
- When you're ready to load your vehicle, or your luggage if you're traveling by airplane, use a transparent highlighter marker to draw a line over each item *after* you put it in the vehicle or duffel bag. The bright color makes it easy to see which items haven't been loaded.
- Take the list to your launch site, and as each item goes in the boat, scribble a line through the item to obscure it.

Don't take anything for granted. My master list begins with big block letters that say:

1. KAYAK

2. PADDLES

3. PFD

4. SPRAY SKIRT

Make a separate list for your perishables, including food and staples such as cooking oil, spices, and stove fuel. Check this list off in the same fashion as the master list.

You can shorten the procedure if you pack some dry bags at home, so your master list is reduced from "underwear, 4 pair; socks, 4 pair; Capilene shirts, 2" etc., to "clothes bag, blue." Same with food and the first-aid kit. If you do this, add a tally of the total number of dry bags you've packed.

See Appendix B, beginning on page 211, for sample lists.

Rules of Expedition Planning

- Be honest with yourself—push your limits, but don't exceed them.
- Research thoroughly—magazines, books, Internet, paddling clubs, and shops near your destination. Buy charts, coastal pilots, tide tables. Check plane fares and cost of shipping/renting kayaks, if applicable.
- Modify basic equipment list for local conditions. Immerse yourself mentally in the climate and topography of your destination.
- Check and tune or repair equipment. Check spares and tools.
- Prepare master list of everything you'll take.
- As you pack (vehicle or luggage for plane), check off each item as it goes in—not before. Check list again as you load kayak.

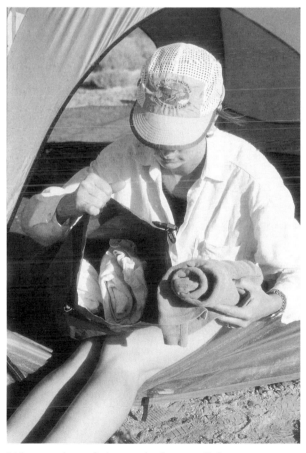

When packing clothes in dry bags, roll them up into tubes about 8″ long and slide them in like pencils in a case—it's easier to rummage for shorts or tops or outerwear, and they also get less crumpled.

Pack your boat carefully so it is balanced side-to-side, and most of the heavy items are near the bottom and toward the cockpit. Make a diagram of the final packing configuration, to refer to throughout your trip.

Packing the Kayak

HOW NOT TO PACK

My worst packing experience occurred on the second trip of my kayak guiding career. I met a group of six in Bahía Kino, Mexico, and we caravanned to the launch point at Punta Chueca, a Seri Indian village. We were a bit late and the temperature was rising, and I had some business I needed to do with the Seris, so I made the decision to let the group—self-proclaimed experienced kayakers—pack the two singles and two doubles I had brought for them, after they assured me they were "almost" within my guidelines of three dry bags per person for personal gear.

When I returned they were finished. But virtually all the "community gear"—food, stove, water, etc.—was stacked by my boat. With no time to argue I stuffed and strapped and piled on deck until my poor 17-foot single resembled a Haitian refugee craft. When we launched, my view over the bow looked like one of those films taken from a submarine's conning tower, shortly after the "dive" Klaxon has sounded. It appeared I had slightly exceeded the design displacement of my craft, and the effect was alarming—but we made it to our destination on Tiburón Island and set up camp.

The group had actually done a really good job of packing their gear. A colorful beach umbrella was well wedged into a front compartment, along with two folding chairs and a multisport whiffle-ball set in a string bag. The rear of a double held the other four chairs, several sleeping bags that looked to be good to at least −40°F (−40°C), and an enormous dome tent. Another single held the volleyball net and poles. I suppose they could have saved some space if they'd deflated the volleyball itself, since they had prudently brought along a sturdy metal pump anyway. Two roll-up tables and an equal number of soft coolers filled with unmentionably cheap beer completed the kit. As the three couples frolicked in the sand, it became obvious where they had scrimped in order to bring so much recreational gear: clothing. Throughout our stay Seri fishermen frequently cruised by offshore to admire the scene, which I privately christened Venice Beach II.

FIRST THINGS FIRST: SAFETY

The most important parameter to keep in mind when packing a sea kayak is safety. There are several aspects to this, including weight distribution, load control, windage, flotation, and access. Everyone will pack a boat a little differently, but certain rules should be inviolable.

The heaviest items in your boat—water containers, canned food, and the like—should be kept *low* and *centered*. This more than anything else will determine how the boat handles on the water. Placing heavy objects low helps the stability of the craft immensely; in fact, a kayak so loaded will be considerably more stable than an empty one. Keeping weight away from the ends of the boat does a couple of things: it helps the bow and stern climb waves rather than punch through them, and it makes turning easier (this is why the best sports cars are midengine; in engineering terms the desired effect is called a *low polar moment of inertia*). Weight should be centered from side to side as well—an easy detail to overlook, but paddling a boat canted to one side is no fun, as it will want to turn endlessly in circles.

Once the weight is in its proper place, make sure it doesn't go elsewhere. The cargo in your front and rear compartments should be immovable. Usually this is not a problem on long trips, because the boat will be packed full. If there is loose space, it can be filled with a spare dry bag, rolled to capture air—which serves the double purpose of providing extra flotation. As your gear volume decreases throughout the trip, more air can be added to the bags to keep things tight.

Many people assume that their "watertight" compartments will keep the contents dry and provide flotation in the event of a capsize. But much can happen to destroy the integrity of those spaces—hatches can come off, bulkheads come loose, or the hull can be punctured. And almost all compartments will leak a little over the course of a bouncy paddle. So it pays to keep *all* your gear in dry bags, thus providing both protection and flotation. It's surprising how little trapped air it takes to turn a dead weight into a flotation device. A rolled tent, for example, which many people stuff in the bow without a dry bag, will sink if dropped in the water, but even in a tightly compacted dry bag it will float nicely.

MINIMIZING DECK CLUTTER

When the boat starts filling up, it's tempting to strap gear on the deck. But not only does this decrease stability, it also creates windage that can prove hazardous in a blow. If you're knocked over because of your high

Packing Diagram

Tip: Keep a pad of paper handy in your personal gear, and after you've loaded your boat (and it's well-balanced), sketch a rough diagram of where everything went—refer to it throughout your trip, and repacking each morning will be a breeze.

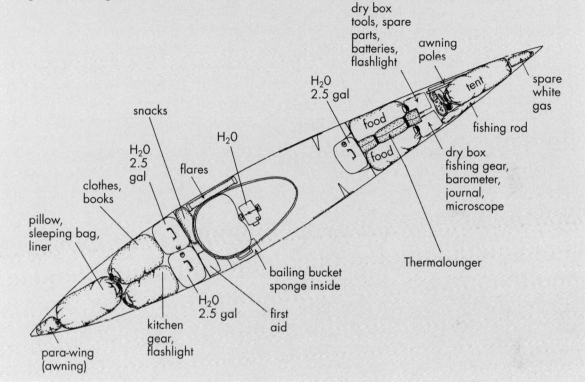

profile, and the deck gear comes loose, you've got real trouble. Try to limit the deck load to a single deck bag in front of you, for cameras, snacks, a water bottle, and your VHF radio (see the information on a deck-mounted survival kit, page 155, for an exception). And while we're on the subject, don't, as so many people do, just slide your spare paddle under the deck bungees. Wrap the elastic around the end of the shaft to secure it, making sure you can reach and free it while sitting in the cockpit. Position the spare paddle so it will not have to be moved to rig a paddle-float rescue. I prefer mine on the rear deck, where it throws less spray, but your deck configuration will determine whether or not that's possible.

ORGANIZING

Remember all those colorful dry bags you bought (discussed in Chapter 2)? Now you can use them to organize your gear by type—blue for clothes, red for food, and so on. Laminated tags are helpful to specify contents; for example, if all the food bags are one color, tags can denote breakfasts, lunches, and dinners.

It would be extremely helpful to practice loading your boat at home before each trip, but I don't know *anyone* anal retentive enough to actually do such a thing (of course, for a serious long-distance expedition the rules change, and trial packing at home becomes a necessity). The best alternative is to plan plenty of time at your launch point to go slowly and pay attention to the inviolable rules listed in the safety section.

Pack with the boat as close to the water as possible, to avoid long drags. A corollary of this: beware when loading hard or sharp-edged objects. Keep them away from direct contact with the hull, as they can create a wear point or even a puncture.

Keep in mind your itinerary. First things in will be last out. Camping will be the last thing you do each day, so the tent, which is usually a good bow-filler and fairly light, can go in first, followed by sleeping bags and clothes. Keep snacks and/or lunch items easily accessible. And do *not* pack away any safety devices such as first-aid or survival kits, radios, or flares. These should have well-secured spots in the cockpit, on deck, or on your person.

One of the most helpful things I do each trip is to make a diagram of my load arrangement right at the water's edge (see sidebar, page 151). This allows me to replicate the loading sequence painlessly each morning, and also to know where any particular bag is in the boat, in case I need something odd (such as the whiffle-ball set). It doesn't have to be a work of art; just a rough sketch will do.

PACKING FOLDING KAYAKS

Folding kayaks have no bulkheads or watertight compartments. Most of your reserve flotation, then, comprises the air trapped in your dry bags (some flotation is provided by the inflatable sponsons found on most folders). Keeping those dry bags in place is mandatory. The gear in the rear compartment is usually held in securely by the seat assembly; not so the front. Fortunately, with the exposed ribs of the frame for attachment points it's simple to rig security straps from ¾-inch flat nylon webbing, fastened with Fastex

When loading your boat at a busy seaport or marina, make sure you stay clear of loading ramps meant for bigger boats. This launch site in popular Vancouver Island's Telegraph Cove was reportedly closed to sea kayakers for a while because a few unthinking paddlers clogged the boat ramp used by paying customers of the marina (the cove now charges sea kayakers for any launching/landings).

buckles, which crisscross in front of the rudder pedals to secure the bags in the bow.

Packing folding kayaks can be a bit of a pain. No, I take that back—it's a *real* pain. The access hatches of the Feathercraft help immensely, but getting gear into a Klepper equipped with an expedition spray skirt (which is semipermanently attached to the cockpit rim, leaving only a small opening) is frustrating. On any folder, the ribs add to the difficulty of sliding in gear.

The secret tool here is half a paddle, which can be used the way a baker uses a long wood spatula to load bread in an oven. With care you can slide a dry bag

Deck Bags

A deck bag allows you to keep things like water bottles, snacks, and charts handy without creating a hazardous mess on deck, or having to peel off your spray skirt each time you want something.

You can stuff things such as water bottles and VHF radios under your front deck bungees, but if a good wave comes along it could slap everything off instantly. Tethering the expensive items helps, but increases clutter.

A better solution is a deck bag, available from many different companies (see Appendix A, page 209). Most are not designed to be waterproof, but merely organize and protect your gear. A couple, such as the top-quality Voyageur deck bag, use a dry-suit zipper and coated fabric to ensure a truly watertight seal. I've used a Voyageur bag to carry otherwise naked, and extremely moisture-sensitive, electronic cameras and lenses with complete confidence.

(continued on page 154)

A deck bag allows you to keep several things handy without creating a hazardous mess on deck. Even a small model will hold a water bottle and snacks, plus a VHF radio, a paddle float, and a waterproof camera or binoculars.

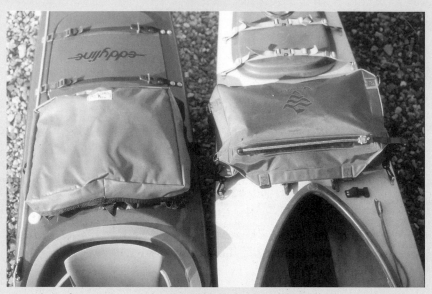

A number of companies make them; shown here are the Voyageur (right) front deck bag, and the Long Haul Products rear deck bag, which is made for Kleppers but can be retrofitted to other boats.

partway into the end of the boat, then use the blade of the paddle to scoop it the rest of the way in, with a final push to seat it.

An immense help is to tie to the deepest bags a retrieval line with which you can pull them out; in fact, this helps with longer hard-shell boats as well.

Just as I was finishing this section, I received a new catalog from Mark Eckhart of Long Haul Products. Mark makes exquisite accessories for Kleppers and other folding kayaks, and has just introduced a modification for the Klepper Aerius, consisting of modified front and rear decks that *unzip* to allow not just good access, but better access than any hard-shell boat, to the bow and stern areas. I guarantee this feature will increase the utility of a Klepper by 100 percent, and probably add significantly to the usable cargo space, because you can pack from the top and reach every

corner. It is, however, a truly custom modification and is thus expensive. Long Haul Products also sells a nice rear deck bag for folding kayaks that augments the interior storage (for lightweight items only), cockpit bags that take advantage of a folder's wide beam to secure small things near the paddler, and many other accessories. Quite a few would be equally useful in a hard-shell kayak.

USING WASTED SPACE

I began noticing years ago how much space is wasted in the cockpit. Most of us stuff what we can behind the seat, but that leaves a lot left over in various nooks and crannies. There is often empty space in front of your feet, under your thighs in front of the seat, between your hips and the side of the boat, and under the cockpit coaming.

In order to exploit this space you must find ways to secure the items to be placed there. Nothing can be allowed to come loose, even during the most violent roll or self-rescue. Usually this involves gluing or fiberglassing tie-down loops in various spots, although stainless bolts can be used through fiberglass bulkheads, and rivets through the deck. Just make sure no sharp bolts or eyes are in a position to cause injury during bracing with your legs.

Under the deck in front of the cockpit is a good place to mount a tube for charts. You can glass-in a piece of plastic pipe, or mounts to hook it on with bungees can be glassed-in, or riveted through the deck. Even better is an underdeck bag such as those by Mark Pack Works, which attach to a track under the deck so you can pull them out to access the contents.

On boats with hanging seats it is a simple matter to attach hardware or use bungee loops to secure items between the side of the seat and the hull. I mounted a waterproof tube on one side that holds a parachute flare; on the other is my bailing bucket with a large sponge stuffed inside.

On many boats there is a lot of room in front of your feet, behind the front bulkhead. I find this a good spot for backup water because it helps centralize the weight—but it takes very strong mounts to safely secure such a load, and access is awkward. If you have fiberglass bulkheads, stainless marine eye straps bolted through the bulkhead with large backing washers do the job; if you have foam bulkheads, you'll have to glass or glue loops to the hull and deck just behind it, a dif

ficult task. You could use this space for anything you don't expect to need frequently but that would take up space elsewhere. Make darn sure whatever it is doesn't interfere with the rudder pedals.

Under my thighs I glued in four small loops to secure a 2-liter Nalgene bottle with bungies. This serves as my daily water, and adds significantly to my overall capacity. This would also be a good place for a survival or rescue kit in a mini Pelican case. Dagger sells stainless rings with vinyl bases that can be securely epoxied to plastic or fiberglass.

Even the stuff behind the seat should be secured. On my boats with hard bulkheads I used stainless eye straps to which I can hook bungees. Something I've thought of, but not yet implemented, on a boat with a hinged seat back would be to attach stainless spring clips to the back and secure waterproof flares there, easily accessible if needed.

A DECK-MOUNTED SURVIVAL KIT

This is something I've put together over the course of several expeditions. Everything fits in a small dry bag. Usually it rides inside the kayak, but if I'm paddling solo, and facing a long crossing or a traverse of a rough coast with no landing sites, I secure it under the bungees just behind the cockpit. A short line with a stainless spring clip is wrapped around it. My theory is, if I ever capsize and for some reason have to abandon the boat, I can clip the bag to my PFD and swim for shore. Assuming I can make it to land, I'll have the basics for survival until rescued.

Rules for Packing

- Keep weight low and centered.
- Keep cargo secured against shifting.
- Keep the deck as clear as possible.
- Keep hard-edged objects away from the hull.
- Keep everything in dry bags.
- Keep safety gear accessible but secured.
- Keep a diagram of your packing arrangement.

The contents of the kit vary by trip, depending on where I am. For a desert trip, the most pressing need would be water, so I include not only a 2-liter water bottle but the materials I need to make several solar stills (see sidebar, below). If I'm in bear country it would include a can of capsicum spray; in rattlesnake country an Extractor. If I were on a really remote journey, the EPIRB would be inside.

Other items include:

• A tube of fire-starting paste and a waterproof container of matches

Emergency Solar Stills

A solar still uses a "greenhouse effect" to evaporate brackish or salt water and condense fresh water. A single still can produce up to a quart of water a day; you would need several stills to subsist for any length of time.

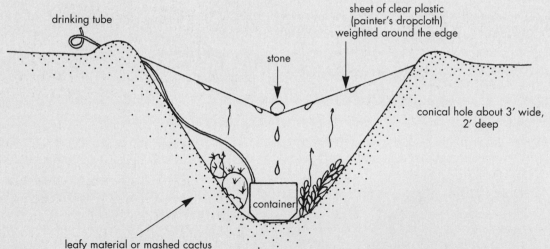

A single solar still can augment your water supply in an emergency. Two or three stills can supply enough water for one person to survive on. Solar radiation evaporates the water in the soil or plant material, which then condenses on the plastic sheet and drips into the container. Clear plastic works better than black. A drinking tube obviates the need to remove the plastic to retrieve the water.

- Fishing kit with line, hooks, and jig lures
- Space blanket (silver on one side, red on the other)
- Swiss Army knife (or, lately, a Gerber Multi-plier) and a small sharpening stone
- 50 feet of 4mm nylon line
- A coil of wire for snares
- Basic first-aid kit

See Appendix B for a list of essential first-aid items.

I eschew such survivalist nonsense as condoms for water containers. There are people who can live for weeks off a hip pocket full of trinkets, and I have great respect for their knowledge, but it's of little relevance to the rest of us. Then again, guys, it would make a great excuse if you were caught in a compromising situation: "Uh, I was just, uh, I was—RESTOCKING MY SURVIVAL KIT!"

Extended Expeditions

Just what constitutes an "extended" expedition is somewhat ambiguous. For example, I would consider a two-week trek along the coast of Antarctica, with no availability of rescue assistance, to be extended. But a journey of the same length through the lochs of Scotland, with semihourly pub stops, would be a lark. So various parameters such as length, remoteness, climate, and number in the party figure into the definition. Often I don't know if a journey on which I've embarked is "extended" until I'm launching, and a little voice asks, "Uh, are you *really* sure you want to do this?"

The commitment required to undertake a long voyage by sea kayak is matched only by the reward of successfully completing such a journey. It is likely the closest we can come in our time to duplicating the exploits of the great Canadian voyageurs, who challenged the unknown wilderness of America in open canoes, cut off for months at a time from their known world.

Much of the preparation for an extended kayak trip involves simply expanding the parameters of shorter trips. But several elements differ in significant ways, and require close attention.

COMPANIONS

If you launch on a three-day kayak trip with someone you don't know very well, and things don't work out, it's no big deal. But what if you discover, two hours into an eight-week trek along a wilderness coast, that your recent friend is one of those infuriating tuneless whistlers? Best to quickly arrange a tragic accident, then finish the trip yourself in tribute to the courageous memory of your lost companion.

Obviously, I'm going to tell you to choose your companions carefully for a long trip. But I'm going beyond that—you need to be *brutal* in choosing companions for a long trip. If you have a buddy who's been with you on several three- and four-day trips, who has a few habits that are annoying but which you were able to grit your teeth and bear for a half a week, think very carefully before committing to a month-long relationship. If you decide to go ahead with it, make sure neither of you carries any sharp implements.

You want to look for complete compatibility in your companions. That doesn't mean you can never argue, or even fight. You don't have to both keep your tent the same way or even like the same foods. It does mean you have to have similar outlooks on life in general, and kayaking life in particular. My best kayaking friend, Michael, has many different habits and opinions than I, but when we paddle we mesh perfectly—neither of us has any goal-oriented obsessions, we both enjoy paddling challenging conditions but know when to quit, and we're both happy to blow off a day of paddling and take a hike inland. He can paddle faster than I, but I can paddle farther, so if either of us tries any showmanship, the other has an ace to play.

I have a theory about the most propitious number of companions for extended expeditions, which has in no way been proved but which seems to have a resonance of truth in it, judging from both my own and others' experiences. Since all great psychological theories have names, we'll call this one The Hanson Principle: *The ideal number of companions for an extended journey is either none, one, or five or more.* Below are my postulations.

- If you have the right temperament and skills, traveling solo is an inspiring and satisfying experience. There are no conflicts to worry about, because you always agree with everything everyone present has to say.

- Two compatible people can usually travel well. Every conflict is one-on-one, and as long as both participants are reasonable, a fair resolution is possible. If personalities clash on any one day, it's easy for two to be agreeably separate.
- A critical threshold seems to appear at the three- to five-companion level. A group totaling four to six seems to be more prone to temporary cliquishness or us-against-them resentment by one pair. If a third of your group is mad at the other two-thirds, it's difficult to ignore.

Once group size exceeds a half-dozen or so, the weight of group opinion—peer pressure—begins to outweigh the unreasonableness of a small minority. If one person or two finds their attitude entrenched against five or six, they are more likely to do a little self-analysis. It's unusual for a big group to split right down the middle on any touchy issue. There may still be resentments, but they will be more diluted, and it's easier for one person to avoid another if worst comes to worst and there is a rift.

Obviously, this doesn't mean you should refuse to kayak with your spouse and four friends. It just means you should be aware of group dynamics.

Group leadership is a touchy subject. Believe it or not, in many ways a benevolent dictatorship is best. If one of the group is more experienced than the rest, it can prevent much confusion if everyone can look to a single person for leadership. This is especially important in an emergency, when democratic wrangling could waste precious time. But the leader obviously needs to be as sensitive as he or she is competent, and of course every member of the group should have no-resentment-guaranteed veto power over questions of whether to paddle in marginal conditions.

Finally, although it requires an exponentially greater degree of commitment and responsibility, consider going alone.

The difference in experience between having four companions and having only one is considerable, but the difference between having one and having none is profound. With other humans near, you draw a circle around yourself and your companions—a small human universe that you must deal with on many social levels, and outside of which is the world through which you are traveling. Alone, there are no circles. The world around you is your only universe, and you must either embrace it or live in terror of it.

MEDICAL KITS FOR EXTENDED EXPEDITIONS

As you read in Chapter 3 (page 39), I believe in comprehensive medical kits. But for long-term first-aid self-sufficiency, you'll need to fortify even a well-stocked kit.

First, add extra quantities of the basic medicines, cold packs, and bandages already in your kit. In addition, you should consider including prescription antibiotics and other medications designed to handle ailments of extended duration. Build this part of your kit in close cooperation with your doctor, because the longer you are on any medication, the greater the likelihood of side effects.

Diarrhea and vomiting, a combination caused by a variety of pathogens, can be life-threatening in a remote situation, due to dehydration. Prescription-strength antidiarrheals and oral rehydration salt packs are vital.

A final component to consider is an emergency dental kit, which contains material for temporarily covering or filling a cracked tooth or cavity, plus topical anesthetics to ease pain. These kits are available from commercial first-aid kit suppliers and some outdoor retailers.

If you are with a group, you will probably carry a large kit to serve everyone. But don't put all your first-aid eggs in one basket. Each participant should have a personal kit, and you should have backup for the essential items in the group kit, carried in a different kayak.

See Appendix A, beginning on page 203, for resources such as contacts for manufacturers and suppliers, further reading in books and magazines, and sources for hard-to-find trip-planning items such as charts and coastal guides.

PROVISIONING FOR AN EXTENDED EXPEDITION

You'll need the most compact and spoilage-resistant foods possible to sustain you for a long period away from the possibility of replenishment. Modern dehydrated and freeze-dried foods fit the bill—but only if you're paddling where you have regular access to fresh water. It's pointless to carry dehydrated food if you also have to carry the water to rehydrate it.

Even when packing for a very long voyage, it is likely you'll run out of space before you exceed the recommended weight limit for your kayak. When you've bought the food for the trip, repackage it (see sidebar, page 144), to both eliminate the excess packaging common to almost all commercial foods, and to organize it by meals. Some people keep separate bags for all the breakfasts, all lunches, and all dinners; others layer the meals by order—breakfast, lunch, dinner, breakfast, lunch, dinner—in bags designated week #1, week #2, and so on. The former system works better if you like to vary your menu spontaneously, because it's easier to rummage through a bag containing only dinners if you're not feeling like the turkey tetrazzini scheduled for evening meal number 24.

I like organizing complete meals in one large zip-top bag—a main course, a side dish or dessert, and some crackers or Melba toast. Every few meals I hide some sort of treat, such as a small can of fruit, or a tin of smoked oysters or salmon. It makes diving for meals a lot more fun.

11

C A M P I N G

Roughing It in Style

When you construct a home in the wilderness—whether it's for one night or 10—efficiency equals comfort, and comfort equals more rest and better performance on the water. If you take a little extra time to set up a proper camp, that time will be returned when you don't have to fiddle with things or look for misplaced gear or find a new spot for the tent.

Choosing a Campsite

This is going to sound a bit peculiar, but bear with me. The first rule of kayak camping is to choose a campsite that is not in the ocean.

See, I told you. But believe me, it happens more often than you'd think. A group of paddlers scouts a nice beach, and identifies what appears to be the high-tide line. They pitch their tents a good 20 feet behind it—for safety, you understand. And that night the tide, on a rising full moon, comes in 30 feet beyond its previous mark. There are shouts, cries of chagrin, flashlight beams bouncing wildly, general chaos.

Still don't believe this could happen? Check out the article in the October 1996 issue of *Sea Kayaker* magazine, the author of which had the good humor to share her experience as a lesson to the rest of us. It's one of at least a half-dozen such incidents of which I'm personally aware.

The process of choosing a campsite begins well before you have stopped for the night. Assuming you are unfamiliar with the area, a morning perusal of the chart is in order, to identify likely spots. These include coves, inlets, the mouths of streams, or the sheltered sides of islands or peninsulas. Take into account prevailing winds and wave patterns you have noticed or

that the chart indicates. Cross-reference the chart with your tide table—if you're in an area of major tides, avoid shallow bays where the shore might recede 200 yards between landing and launching, unless you can time both your arrival and departure for high tide.

It's easy to get too goal oriented. If you've picked a spot 15 miles down the coast, and a perfect little unmarked bay appears at mile 13, STOP! Sea kayaking should be a spontaneous experience. If you need to cover a lot of mileage in the next few days, just tell yourself that by stopping early you can get an even earlier start tomorrow. Which is of course a flat-out lie, but you'll buy it.

Once you've arrived at a promising spot—say, a cozy inlet sheltered from surf and wind—find the highest high-tide line you can identify. I mean the storm-tide line, the hurricane-tide line, the highest

After finding a site far from the highest possible water, select a flat spot for your tent, preferably in sand; avoid trampling or removing vegetation, disturbing nesting birds, or camping in biologically delicate desert or tundra areas.

point where any flotsam has blown. Put several unquestionably terrestrial plants—pine trees, saguaro cactus, baobabs—between you and the water. *Then* look for a nice flat spot to pitch your tent.

Securing Gear

Several years ago, four guys were camped on an island in the Sea of Cortez, with two double folding kayaks. One night as they slept, an infamous Baja katabatic wind known as an *elefante* came howling down from

Always make sure your gear is well-secured and as far from high water as possible. Place spray skirts, PFDs and other light gear in the cockpits and secure the cockpit covers, which also keep blowing sand out of your gear. Some paddlers turn their boats over, to minimize sun exposure on their decks if they're staying in one place for an extended period. Note the paddles tucked well under the hulls; it's also a good idea to tie down the paddles, as well as the boats, if winds are strong.

the mainland peninsula. From the direction of the beach the four heard a *thump*, then a *thump . . . thump, thumpthumpthumpsplash.*

The wind had picked up one of the boats and cartwheeled it into the sea, never to be seen again. After several days without any sign of possible assistance, the four paddled 10 miles back to the peninsula in, and on, the remaining boat.

It's unusual to lose a whole kayak, but paddles, spray skirts, and PFDs disappear all the time. So before you do anything else in camp, make sure your gear is secured.

When you first land, make sure your spray skirt and PFD are stowed under the deck bungees before you wander off to scout for a site. Tuck your paddle under the curve of the hull. When you've found a good spot, move the kayaks above the storm-tide line, in a hollow in the beach if possible, and place them all side by side and nearly touching. I run a line through all the bow toggles to a tree or shrub; if there is nothing to tie to, for example on Arctic tundra, I still tie all the boats together. It's much more difficult for a gust to pick up two or more boats than one.

Some people turn their boats over on the beach, which protects the deck gelcoat from the sun. Where I kayak the beaches are usually so rough that the deck would be more abused upside down; also, I'm in the habit of storing food and certain other things in the boat to keep them away from rodents, so I like easy access to the hatches.

If the spray skirts and PFDs need drying, make sure they are well secured by bungees; afterward, I put them in the cockpit and secure the nylon cockpit cover I always carry. The paddles go between the boats, tied in a bundle if it is really windy. Once you've unloaded what you need for the night, secure the hatch covers in place.

Organizing Camp

Trust me on this: an organized camp will make you a happier and better kayaker.

After a full day on the water, the last thing you need is to have to rummage around finding stuff. Gear that is scattered all over is just itching to get lost or blown away, and you probably won't miss it until you're 20 miles down the coast.

I pitch the tent first, because it is the core of the camp, and more or less determines where I'll arrange everything else. The orientation of the tent depends on where I am—I might want it to catch the night breezes, or avoid them; same with the morning sun. I make sure the tent is well staked, with guylines out as well if the weather has been ornery. I don't want to be up at two in the morning having to nail it back down.

If it is at all possible, make sure the spot is *level*— short of permanently altering the landscape. The slightest bit of slope makes itself uncomfortably apparent at night. If it's not possible to get a completely level pitch, orient the tent so your head will be uphill. This is at least tolerable.

Inside the tent I lay out my sleeping bag, to let it fluff, and stand my "personals" dry bag near the door. This has my books, a reading light, journal, a little shortwave radio/clock, and other things I'll want while I'm in the tent. I also put the first-aid kit inside near the door, just so I always know where it is (if you're with a group, make sure everyone knows). My clothes bag or bags go under the vestibule, and the stuff sacks for the tent and sleeping bag store in one of the hanging mesh pockets inside.

Then I set up the kitchen. I clear an area for the stove, and arrange the dry bags containing pots and so

Set up a central kitchen/socializing center that is out of the weather but easily accessible to everyone. Drinking water and snacks can be set out handily.

Kayak Fishing

Augmenting your trip diet with fresh-caught fish is delicious and fun, too. You can fish from your kayak or from shore, using either a simple handline or a multipiece rod and spinning reel.

A handline can be as simple as a hundred yards of 10-pound-test fishing line wrapped around a Coke bottle, with a hook and bait on the end, or a jig—a lure designed to be jiggled up and down in the water near rocks and other likely spots for fish. I use 10-pound line because I figure I don't want to be attached to anything while in my kayak that would require stronger line; however, I know of kayakers who have landed fish such as halibut that weighed more than 100 pounds.

(continued on page 165)

forth as a wind block. I set out drinking-water and the snack bag. If it's sunny and hot, or threatening rain, I'll set up the Moss Parawing for a cooking and socializing shelter. I make sure nothing can be blown away by a sudden wind, and nothing can be ruined by a sudden rain. If I'm in bear country I find a tree for the food bag; if I'm in rodent or coyote territory the food stays in the boat.

When I'm finished, the entire setup is pretty much immune to natural disaster, and I can get out some snacks and the Thermalounger and go enjoy the evening.

I also have a four-piece spinning rod with a Penn reel that I use from the boat and from shore. It has 10-pound line as well, but I often put a short leader of 20- or 25-pound test line on the end, because inshore fish dive for rocks when caught, and cut right through lighter line.

Shiny lures, such as the polished Kastmaster, seem to work best for me, but consult local fishermen to find out what they prefer.

If you're disinclined to fish, and you're paddling near commercial fishing grounds, you can buy fresh fish directly from the fishermen (wait until they're not working to approach the boats). These two salmon provided a group of four with three days of sumptuous meals.

If you're going to be camped for several days, and the tent is exposed to the sun, either take it down each day, which is a pain, or leave the fly attached. Sunlight degrades nylon, but the coating on the fly makes it more resistant than the uncoated canopy underneath—and a fly is much cheaper to replace than a canopy.

Cooking

The biggest downside to kayak cooking is having to do it on the ground—sand blowing around, companions walking by kicking dirt, large bugs checking out the ingredients. It's a savage existence.

If you're camped on a beach blessed with lots of rocks or logs, get creative to construct your kitchen up high. In the Pacific Northwest, for instance, you can often find big logs lodged above the tide line that have enough flat surfaces to set up a nice counter at waist level, just like home. If all you have are some flat rocks, just raising everything by a few inches makes a big difference. Pay close attention to stability, however—it's no good getting your pots and stove off the ground if there's a good chance you'll knock them off.

If you're camped on a sandy beach and have to use the substrate, organize your stove, pots, utensils, and ingredients first so you can sit down once and reach everything you'll need. Getting up and down repeatedly is the best way to wind up with crunchy meals. Use your Thermalounger (you did buy one after reading Chapter 9, didn't you?) to ensconce yourself comfortably, and then have the camp underlings—that is, anyone who isn't cooking—bring you anything you've forgotten, and keep you supplied with cocktails.

In areas with a lot of driftwood, such as British Columbia (a heartbreaking benefit of massive forest clearcutting throughout the region), camp kitchens approach the convenience of home, with waist-level "countertops."

If you camp in sandy coves with no large rocks or drift-wood, situate your camp chair, stove, utensils, and food bags so that you don't have to move around once you start cooking.

If you've brought an Outback Oven and are planning to bake a dessert, you can get it set up and cooking on a second stove while the main meal is being prepared. Just don't forget it and scorch the brownies.

Hors d'oeurves may be fashionable at home, but on a kayak trip they are nearly mandatory. Appetites are ravenous by the end of the day, so a cutting board arranged with crackers and cheese will fend off those circling hyenas while the cook prepares the main meal.

If you're part of a group, make sure you arrange in advance how the cooking chores will be divided. Sometimes you'll have one person who is happy to be the designated cook; sometimes you'll switch off;

sometimes you'll have a kitchen crew of several people. No matter what, however, the cook *never* has to do the dishes.

Some acquaintances of mine who do a lot of group trips devised a good system to ensure properly cleaned and sterilized cooking gear. They use three collapsible wash basins, in the first of which is very hot soapy water. The second is a hot rinse with a tiny bit of bleach in it, and the third is a freshwater rinse. The bleach dip and sometimes the last rinse water can be reused several times. The dishes are immediately dried afterward. This system produces more pollutants than a simple seawater scrub (see Low-Impact Camping, page 174), but might be essential to maintain hygiene in a big group.

When traveling in a group, you can take more gear for the kitchen. A multi-burner stove with stand and a roll-up table are nearly mandatory for groups of eight or more.

167

Camp Luxuries (and Oddities)

Never underestimate the value of a few luxuries while exploring the wilds. One well-timed hot shower, or a shave, can be a great reviver when you're feeling gritty and tired.

Here are some great—and a few odd—camp luxuries I've come across over the years:

- SunShower. These collapsible showers can be filled with cold water and left in the sun for a few hours to heat up, or you can fill them with water warmed on the stove. Accessories include a nifty privacy enclosure.

(continued on page 169)

- Espresso maker and coffee-bean grinder. Single-shot aluminum espresso steamers and tiny hand grinders (available at larger specialty outdoor retailers) just might be considered necessities by some serious kayakers. Especially if they're from you-know-where.
- Portable hand-operated blender. Yup. A few years back I saw a small 12-ounce plastic one at an outdoor retailer show—you worked the blades by yanking on a string like a ripcord. It was a riot. Margaritas anyone? First you'd need a portable icemaker—maybe someone will invent a foot-operated model.
- Hammock. Backpacker's hammocks are small and light, and are pure heaven strung between a couple of trees at the beach.

Never underestimate the value of a pick-me-up, such as a shave after five days out (there's no rule that says wilderness travelers need look like refugees).

Hiking and Beachcombing

I read a book once about a couple who kayaked completely around Baja California. I expected it to be an inspirational account; instead, it was the most depressing tale I could imagine. The only thing the two could think of was to complete the journey. Any delay whatsoever chafed at them, and the book dwelt on little but the daily struggle for mileage and their fears that they wouldn't make it to the Colorado River by the date they had set all the way back in San Diego. No, *thanks*. I was reminded of one of critic Dorothy Parker's gems: "This is not a book to be tossed aside lightly. It should be thrown with great force."

I love kayaks, and I love paddling, but to me the sea kayak is still just an elegant and efficient means to a different goal: the appreciation of the world through which I am moving. Whether I choose to paddle deserted coastlines and hike unspoiled wilderness, or explore seafront pubs along an ancient sailing route, my eye is on the journey, not the finish line.

A small fanny pack stored somewhere in the boat is all you need to open up a world of hiking and beach-combing. Some manufacturers make fanny packs that double as cockpit packs by attaching behind the seat-back. Some of these are even waterproof, providing secure storage for cameras (see Appendix A for sources).

Treat inland hiking the same way you do pad-dling—go well prepared, then relax and enjoy yourself. Your chart compass, signal mirror, and meteor flares will fit easily in the pack, along with first-aid essentials.

Take snacks and at least 1 liter of water. A container of matches and a tube of fire-starting paste take up lit-tle room, and would allow you to keep warm and dry if you're stuck out for the night.

I am passionate about books, and I especially enjoy reading natural-history books covering the area I'm visiting. Usually I'll bring several field guides for hik-ing, plus a book or two of regional essays for camp reading. If you're interested, but not quite so impas-sioned, you can usually buy a single guide covering the major plants, mammals, and birds you're likely to see. I've found it's better to wait until you get to the area you're visiting to look for local guides. In fact, one of the finest bookstores I've ever found was a tiny but carefully stocked shop called Boreal Books in Inuvik, Northwest Territories—200 miles north of the Arctic Circle.

Inland hiking is one of the many pleasures of exploring by kayak. These hikers are high above Johnstone Strait off Vancouver Island.

Binocular Astronomy

One of the most awe-inspiring rewards of kayak touring comes at night, away from the overpowering glare of city lights. We get to see the heavens as they were meant to be, with thousands of stars twinkling crisply against a velvet backdrop. Often the best approach is just to lie on the beach and take it all in. But sometimes it's fun to look a little closer.

Many people don't realize how much a simple pair of binoculars can enhance celestial viewing. For example, an ordinary 7 × 35 instrument will easily show you the four Galilean moons of Jupiter, the greenish glow of the Orion Nebula, or the fuzzy blob of the Andromeda Galaxy.

Several books are available that deal strictly with binocular astronomy, including *Exploring the Night Sky with Binoculars,* by Patrick Moore (Cambridge University Press, 1986); and *Touring the Universe Through Binoculars,* by Philip Harrington (John Wiley and Sons, 1990). Bookstores carry yearly star charts that also give the locations of the planets and any passing comets.

A pair of small but good binoculars, around 8 × 30 or 7 × 35, could be considered essential gear. Use them for scouting coasts for landings, checking out approaching shipping hazards, birding, and even binocular astronomy. These Swarovski 8 × 30s are very lightweight, rubber armored, and waterproof.

If you're in an area with a good tidal range and stretches of flat, rocky shore, the receding tide will leave a universe of discovery waiting for you.

Twice each day, intertidal organisms must switch from a submerged existence in salt water to an exposed, often sun-scorched (or freezing) perch in the open air. In between, they might be battered by huge waves or drenched by freshwater rain showers. They can be preyed upon by animals from either environment. It's wondrous that anything at all can survive

A Kayak Naturalist's Kit

In addition to your binoculars and field guides, there are a few neat tools that are great for exploring and recording the closer details of nature.

Take a moment each day to record your experiences and inspirations in a journal.

- Journal. Keep one. It doesn't have to be eloquent or beautifully illustrated. Just jot down the day's events and impressions. You will be glad you have it in years to come, when you reminisce about your adventures.
- Pocket microscope. I have one made by Pentax that fits into a little case about 3 inches long. It doubles as a passable telescope.
- Hand lens. For larger things than will fit under the microscope. I *assume* all you guys out there are mature enough not to try to do the death ray thing on ants with it.
- Hand net. For gently scooping up mobile tidepool animals to examine.

(continued on page 173)

- Small plant press. Used, with discretion and within local rules, to preserve flowers or parts of plants.
- 4″ × 6″ sheet of clear acrylic. Lay this over interesting tracks you find, using small pebbles to hold it off the surface. Then use an erasable marker to carefully trace the outline of the track from above. Transfer the tracing to your field notebook for later perusal or identification. Note: this size sheet will cover approximately one-quarter of a grizzly bear track.

While exploring around your camp, you never know what you'll find. This huge wolf track was found near one of the author's Arctic camps.

in this no-man's-land—but the diversity of the intertidal zone is stupendous. Remember, however, that many of the creatures here have evolved defenses suitable to their existence—spines, spicules, and the like—and that, while they may be adapted to a harsh environment, they are not adapted to being stomped on.

When setting up camp, take care to locate it well away from nests or freshwater sources for wildlife. The author had to move camp when this Arctic tern let them know in uncertain terms they were trespassing near her nest.

Buy a guide to the intertidal life of the area, wear your rubber boots or water shoes (sandals if you're careful of scrapes), and just poke around a bit. Remember to put everything you move back in its place; this especially applies if you turn over any rocks. The organisms under rocks are there because they can't survive in the open. And in tropical areas, don't walk on coral formations.

An interesting extension of tidepooling is snorkeling, which requires only a mask, snorkel, and fins (and you can get along without the fins). You don't have to dive to 75 feet to appreciate the underwater world; you can have a blast in water you can stand up in.

Low-Impact Camping

As sea kayaking becomes more popular, it is increasingly vital that we pay attention to our impact on the places we visit. Some bad behavior is obvious—don't leave trash, don't cut down saplings for lean-tos, that sort of thing. But good stewardship of our coasts goes beyond this. Our goal must be to leave each campsite as pristine as we found it, or more so.

One of the best ways to practice low-impact camping is to camp in spots that have already been impacted. If you see a site that shows obvious signs of use, reuse it rather than finding a virgin spot 100 feet away. Avoid and help restore spots that are just beginning to show wear—fill in holes, scatter rocks.

If you are using an apparently untouched site, keep in mind that you want it to still look untouched when you leave. Pitch the tent on sand or

Scrub your dishes in clean sand in the intertidal zone, then rinse with a little hot water. This saves your freshwater and obviates the need for toxic detergents, which can enter the marine ecosystem.

lowed by a hot-water rinse (unless you have Teflon-coated pots, which sand would annihilate). At the least this will serve as a good precleaning, and reduce the need for soap. If you use soap, buy a biodegradable brand and use a collapsible wash basin to keep the dishwater away from freshwater sources.

Fires are problematic. It's easy to simply say don't build one—but most of us enjoy a cheerful beachside fire every now and then. So just keep its impact as small as possible. Use driftwood for fuel if any is available, to avoid depleting the supply of downed wood in the forest (which is a necessary part of the nutrient cycle). Don't use up any natural wood in desert areas. If there is a well-established fire ring, use it; if not, don't build one. Dig a depression in the beach sand or bare dirt and light a modest fire. When it is out, drown and crush the coals and bury the ashes.

Opinion varies widely on the proper method of disposing of solid human waste. Good arguments have been made for depositing it in the intertidal area, to be swept out with the incoming tide. I don't take this approach, but it's for a very personal reason. I have an abhorrence of the way humans have used the oceans as sewers and dumps for hundreds of years, and indeed still do on a massive scale. I consider it my moral responsibility as a land animal to keep my waste on land. So I use shallow "catholes" for toilets, no more than a few inches deep, because this is where the most soil microorganisms live. I carefully burn toilet paper.

gravel if possible, not on top of vegetation. Don't camp within a few hundred feet of streams, to avoid trampling fragile streamside vegetation. Don't dig a drainage trench around the tent—if you bought a good tent you won't need one.

Instead of using detergent on pots and dishes, try scrubbing them with sand in the intertidal zone, fol-

Tips for Watching Marine Wildlife

A sea kayaker enjoys an immense advantage, both practically and morally, over a powerboater for enjoying the life of the oceans. A sea kayak is quiet, leaves no pollution, and has no propeller to injure or even kill. And its relative slowness essentially eliminates the possibility of seriously harassing most sea creatures.

There's a matter of philosophy, too. Let's face it: a sea kayaker, by the very fact that he or she has chosen an engineless craft with which to travel, is less likely than a powerboater to be impatient to see everything *right now,* an attitude that often leads to carelessness.

Nevertheless, even sea kayakers can adversely affect the creatures we want to watch. If we paddle close enough to a group of seals sunning on rocks that they dive into the water, we have made them expend energy to avoid us, and have exposed them to a greater possibility of predation. The same can happen with any other animal that alters its activity because of our presence.

The best method for watching wildlife from a kayak is to be passive. If you see a group of dolphins or orcas headed toward you, stop paddling and drift, letting them come as close as they wish. Don't worry—they *do* know right where you are. One time when my wife used the quiet drift technique, a group of orcas came so close she could hear their clicks and squeals through the hull of her kayak. I was a hundred feet away from her, watching as the enormous, straight fin of a male orca came directly at my kayak. It slowly submerged, and I looked down to see 30 feet of orca pass under my keel, the tip of the fin so close I could have reached down and touched it. Then the fin rose smoothly out of the water on the other side, and continued on its way.

If you want to decrease your distance to an animal or group of animals, paddle quietly on a tangent course, not right at them. If the animals show signs of agitation, back off immediately. Many times marine mammals such as seals and dolphins will swim right up and inspect you, curious rather than afraid. In that case either drift while watching them, or continue paddling just as you were when they approached.

Camping Hazards

INSECTS

I have experienced many of the nasty insects you hear about—clouds of Arctic mosquitoes, stealthy northwestern blackflies, no-see-ums, you name it. But I am here to tell you, with considerable regional pride, that *nothing* compares to a little Sea of Cortez beast called a *jejene* (heh-HEH-nay). These tiny blood-sucking gnats, which live near mangrove estuaries and are active from April though December, arrive in coordinated squadrons and attack through any defenses. Pour a pool of pure chromosome-warping DEET in the palm of your hand; they will land in it and do a few backstroke laps to cool off before renewing their assault. Their bites leave tiny red marks, which every night at exactly 2 A.M. turn to welts that itch like nothing you have ever experienced. The only saving grace is that they are mostly restricted to the estuaries, and are dormant during the best paddling months in Mexico.

There are many more dramatic camping hazards, but none causes more consistent annoyance than insects. However, thwarting the worst of them is not too difficult, and you can at least indulge in revenge now and then by squashing a few dozen.

Insect repellent is effective against most species, but beware products that contain more than 50 percent DEET. DEET (N, N-diethyl-meta-toluamide) is genuinely evil stuff, and has actually caused a couple of deaths in children from prolonged overuse. Products with 20 to 30 percent DEET have been shown to be as effective as more potent formulas, although they might need to be applied more often. Try applying the repellent to your collar and sleeves instead of directly on yourself—but only if you're wearing natural fibers. DEET damages synthetic fibers. Some newer DEET products incorporate a nonabsorbent agent that might slow absorption into your body.

Sawyer Products has introduced a new composite repellent called Sawyer Gold, consisting of 16 percent DEET, plus a compound known as R326, said to be effective against blackflies, gnats, and jejenes, too! If the sample I just received works, Sawyer will have my business for life. Actually they already do, thanks to a product called Itch-Balm, which is the only thing I've used that relieves the itch of jejene bites.

If you're worried about being in contact with a substance that melts polyester and rearranges DNA sequences, try Permethrin, a chemical designed to be applied to your clothing and tent (*not* on your skin). And if you'd like to skip the Better Living Through Chemistry approach altogether, try a headnet instead. We've used them to good effect in Canada, on one stretch that was particularly blessed with mosquitoes. The protection was nearly perfect, although the cross-eyed view of several hundred bloodthirsty insects clinging to the mesh and poking their proboscises through it was kind of creepy.

If you are camping in insect country, pick a site exposed to a breeze, instead of a sheltered nook. It doesn't take much of a wind to put down mosquitoes, but be ready—if the breeze dies even for a moment they'll be back quickly. *Jejenes,* as near as I can measure, are capable of sustained hovering in winds greater than 70 miles per hour.

For a group trip through heavy insect company, consider bringing a screen tent big enough to shelter everyone, for eating and socializing.

BEARS

The only bears that will regularly, purposefully hunt humans are polar bears. Attacks by grizzly and black bears are nearly always the result of surprise, a perceived threat to cubs, or the aggressive defense of a food source. So the best way to avoid trouble with grizzly and black bears is to avoid surprising, threatening, or feeding them.

If you camp in bear country, keep your food away from you, tied high in a tree (at least 12 feet). Set up your kitchen 50 to 100 feet away from the rest of the camp, so you can abandon it if a bear approaches, and never take snacks or any other food into the tent (in fact, you shouldn't store anything that smells—lotion, toothpaste, etc.—in your tent in bear country). Eat in one place, sleep in another. Don't camp near streams, along which bears forage, and when you fetch water or go hiking, go in pairs if possible and make plenty of noise. If you're in a group, keep the sleeping tents close together rather than scattered all over the landscape.

Bear-proof plastic food containers are available that will fit through most rear kayak hatches, and although they're expensive (from Garcia Machine, around $80; see Appendix A) they really work. I watched a demonstration video at a trade show once, in which they threw a container full of food into various bear enclosures at a zoo. The canister resisted brutal pounding by a grizzly bear—but watching the polar bear was really spooky. He tried the blunt-force approach for a couple of minutes; when that didn't work, he sat down and *thought* about it. Then he picked up the container by bracing it between one paw and his chest, climbed to the top of his little simulated iceberg, and threw it off the cliff to the rocks below. The canister held, but the cunning that went into the plan made me hope no polar bear ever views my kayak as a food container.

Defense against an actual bear attack is a last resort, but must be considered. Capsicum-based bear spray (pepper spray) has been proved effective in numerous real-world incidents (including a couple involving polar bears), and is easily carried by every member of the group. It's not perfect, but at least results in no permanent harm to the animal. The biggest drawback is the limited range—you must wait until the bear is *really* close before spraying. Remind me to tell you sometime about how my wife and I and a couple of naturalists at a camp in the Northwest Territories decided to test our bear spray, without noticing a slight breeze blowing our way from the direction of the bush that served as our faux bear.

Fortunately, many charges by bears are simply bluff, and will be brought up short before they are even in range of pepper spray. Whether you have a defense or not, do not run from a charging bear. Stand your ground and look down. If actually attacked, your only possible strategy is to curl up tightly and play dead. Many times an attacking bear will leave when it decides you are no longer a threat.

Firearms require considerably more commitment from the user. On one trip where polar bears were a slight, but real, possibility, I carried, in addition to capsicum spray, a bolt-action .458 Winchester magnum rifle. The .458 is a massively powerful cartridge originally designed for elephant hunting, and would instantly drop any bear on earth with a well-placed shot. But a rifle requires a good deal of experience to aim effectively in a life-or-death situation. A 12-gauge shotgun, loaded with buckshot or slugs, is a little easier to handle, but even so, only those familiar with shooting should consider such a weapon. And you must be prepared to make an instantaneous decision to end an animal's life if you feel your own is in the balance. Far too many bears and other animals have been killed by trigger-happy outdoorspeople who mistook bluff or even normal behavior for aggression.

Some people carry handguns in bear country, usually a .44 magnum or something similar. But, Dirty Harry movies notwithstanding, *any* handgun cartridge is marginal at best for quickly stopping a charging bear. Even a perfectly placed shot will likely not kill the animal in time to prevent it from reaching its target. It's been done, but the participants were lucky.

Take extreme care with firearms in a marine environment, lest they corrode. They should be cleaned and oiled every night, and stored in a waterproof case with desiccant packets, if possible. Shotguns are commonly available in stainless steel, which minimizes such problems.

Obviously, if you plan to carry firearms or capsicum spray you must check the federal or state regulations at your destination, and every step in between.

An option for travel in serious bear country is a trip-wire or infrared perimeter alarm, which are compact and reliable. I'll have one along for a far-north solo journey I'm planning. If you deploy one for a group, make sure everyone remembers where it's set, or you'll wind up with a very tense scene when someone gets up to pee in the middle of the night.

Remember that avoidance is by far the best method of dealing with bears. If you stay out of their way, and don't do anything to attract them into your camp, the chances of trouble are minute.

My favorite story of a bear-related injury involved two guys sleeping next to each other in the open in Yellowstone. One of them, who hadn't washed his face after dinner, awoke to find a black bear *licking* it. He screamed, which startled the poor bear so much that it fell back on its haunches trying to escape, landing on and breaking the guy's leg.

COUGARS

Cougars, or mountain lions, have been responsible for a very small number of attacks on humans in wilderness areas (attacks in developed areas, where the animals are losing their natural habitat, are an entirely different situation). The wilderness attacks are nearly always the result of mistaken identity. They often involve someone crouching near a stream or in a similar attitude, so the animal does not recognize the victim as a human. In most of these cases, the attack is broken off as soon as the mistake is realized.

Cougars are normally extremely shy animals, and will vanish at the scent or sight of a human. The best defense against an unlikely incident is to visit streams and toilet sites in pairs, and make lots of human noises.

OTHER CAMP MARAUDERS

Forget bears and cougars. The most common and troublesome camp raiders found everywhere in the world are rodents, followed closely (in North America) by coyotes and raccoons. Rodents will gladly gnaw their way through dry bags to sample your camp fare, and pack rats will not only raid and sample, they will haul off stuff. We lost several Lexan kitchen utensils to a pack rat in Baja; somewhere down by Punta San Francisquito is a pack rat with a very well-stocked nest.

To fend off rodent and other mammalian parties, store your gear in your kayak with the hatches well secured. Hanging them is not a guarantee, especially from raccoons. One night we woke up to a strange thumping sound coming from the kayaks. Inspection revealed a coyote standing on one of the kayaks, trying various methods to pry off the hatch cover under which resided our food (this was in Mexico—not bear

Rodents are nuisances all over the world; apparently displeased with finding all the food stashed securely inside the boat, a rodent made quick work of the bowline.

country). We've had a few problems with rodents gnawing through line on the boats; the only thing you can do about that is carry lots of spare line.

All kayaker tourers should have basic first-aid training, and wilderness first-aid training is even better. In the wilderness, help could be hours or even days away. See Appendix A for listings of wilderness first-aid schools and books on first aid in the wilderness and for mariners.

VENOMOUS ANIMALS

Scorpions are present in many areas, but they are very common in Baja California and other desert areas. They hide under rocks and wood during the day, and come out to hunt at night, retreating again at dawn. Thus you'll often find them under your tent in the morning. But scorpions are nothing to be afraid of. Don't walk around barefoot, and don't put your hands (or butt) where you can't see, especially when collecting firewood.

There are many species of scorpion. The smallest ones, the bark scorpions of the genus *Centruroides,* pack the biggest punch, but even they pose no danger to a healthy adult (barring an allergic reaction—see stinging insects, below). If stung, you'll be in a great deal of pain for several hours, but that's about it. A cold pack will help; do not under any circumstances apply a tourniquet or immerse the affected limb in ice.

Rattlesnakes are another oversensationalized threat. First of all, the current mortality rate in the United States from rattlesnake bite is less than one-tenth of 1 percent; that is, fewer than 1 in 1,000 who are bitten die. Second, most bites happen to people who are handling the snakes—in fact, an astonishing percentage involve young men who have been drinking. And in up to one-quarter of all bites no venom is injected. The primary purpose of the venom is for procuring

The scorpion packing the biggest punch is one of the smallest, the bark scorpion (in the genus Centruroides).

food, not self-defense, so in some snakes a defensive bite doesn't trigger the mechanism.

That said, when you are far from medical help you should obviously be alert. Take the same precautions you do for scorpions. Rattlesnakes are most active from spring through fall, but they can be out any time. I have found them in December and January, and below the high-tide line as well as back in the desertscrub. If you see one, just admire it from a safe distance. Its only reaction if it sees you will be to get away.

I recommend carrying a first-aid suction device called the Extractor, made by Sawyer. It is the only such device proven to remove a significant amount of venom (the tiny, old-fashioned rubber suction-cup kits are worthless). But, to be effective, the Extractor must be applied to the wound within a *very* short time—within a couple of minutes if possible. See Appendix A for sources.

If one of your party is bitten, keep the victim calm. Exertion is bad; the pulse rate should be kept as low as possible. Immediately apply the Extractor, using the supplied instructions. Then quickly get the victim to a hospital.

Do not apply a tourniquet, do not incise the bite, do not immerse the affected limb in ice, and do not administer codeine derivatives, which are vasodilators and will hasten the spread of venom. Do not kill the snake for identification. Modern antivenin is *polyvalent;* that is, it is effective on the venom of many species, and the hospital staff will recognize from symptoms the nature of the venom. One book recommends killing the snake with your *heel.* Yikes. That's a great way to wind up with two victims to treat.

STINGING INSECTS

Statistically, you are in far more danger from bees than bears or rattlesnakes, because of the danger of an allergic reaction to the sting. In severe cases, anaphylaxis can occur and result in death from suffocation, as the victim's throat swells massively enough to prevent breathing. More people die from bee stings in the United States each year than all other from animal attacks combined.

Consider including in your first-aid kit an EpiPen, an auto-injector that delivers a dose of epinephrine to a victim of anaphylaxis. The EpiPen is easy to use; you simply pull off a safety cap and press the syringe against the victim's thigh. However, it is a prescription-only device, and can be harmful or even fatal if used in the wrong circumstances, so consult your doctor carefully before carrying one.

If you watch where you walk and put your hands, you are unlikely to run into trouble with rattlesnakes (this is a Mojave rattlesnake, in the Sonoran Desert near the Sea of Cortez).

PART

FOUR

TRANSPORT, MAINTENANCE, AND REPAIR

12
TRAVELING WITH A KAYAK

I know someone who commutes to work by sea kayak. He lives near the waterfront in a large seaport (I won't say which one, but it's the only place I've ever seen a Midas Muffler shop advertising espresso), and simply plops his boat in the water and paddles across a nearly landlocked bay and up a channel to his shop. If he decides to take a week-long kayak tour, he just keeps going.

Consider, at the opposite end of the scale, the commute I had when I was leading sea kayaking tours in the Sea of Cortez from my home in Tucson, Arizona. With a trailer full of five to seven kayaks behind my old Land Cruiser, I headed south on 60 miles of good interstate highway, followed by 200 miles of rough paved road, followed by 60 miles of *very* rough paved road. Then I traveled anywhere from 15 to 40 miles, depending on the trip, on world-class dirt washboard to reach a picturesque put-in site in a Seri Indian village. And those were the short trips—my other regular tours were in Bahía de los Angeles, in Baja, a two-day drive. On one private trip to the Canadian Arctic, we put more than 7,000 miles on a new Toyota truck, all with two kayaks on top.

Rugged country means rugged racks to take the abuse.

Roof Racks

Over the years, I went through several permutations of mounts on the trailer, from quickie homemade to the latest commercial cradles. At the same time, on the trips my wife and I took we experimented with many different commercial roof racks, and I performed some side-by-side comparisons for magazine articles.

One thing I learned was that racks such as the Yakima and Thule can put up with far more abuse than one would think. On one trip to Baja I was guiding a couple, and we traveled in their Toyota 4-Runner, with a Yakima rack and saddles. I was a bit leery of the gutterless mounts on the 4-Runner, typical of most modern vehicles, and the fact that the bars could be mounted only about 3 feet apart. In addition to my single we had a 20-foot double that stuck out over 8 feet on each end of the rack.

Coming over the notoriously windy Tecate Divide out of San Diego, many semis were pulled off the road to wait out a howling crosswind. We persevered, getting punched around by the gusts while I anxiously peered up at the boats. Suddenly an almighty blast flung the vehicle clear out of its lane and into the emergency strip. We braked to a stop and, shaken, got out to assess the damage. Incredibly, the entire rack system with the boats on it had shifted rearward about an inch, despite the broad clamps securing the towers to the door frame. Yet everything was still solid and attached. We continued at a drastically reduced pace.

My only misgiving with Yakima racks involved the round crossbars. No matter how tightly I cinched the saddle clamps, the saddles would try to rotate on the bar on a rough road, canting at an angle under the boat's hull, even when I pulled the securing straps as tight as I could around the boat. It wasn't a terrible problem, but it meant I had to get out every 10 to 20 miles on a dirt road and readjust everything. On paved roads there was no such tendency.

The Yakima TLC saddles worked very well on a number of different hull shapes. I didn't like the two-piece straps, which were connected to the saddle with pins and push-on castle nuts. I replaced the pins with stainless steel bolts and nylock nuts from a marine hardware store.

My favorite roof rack for kayaks for many years has been the Thule. I like the rectangular bars—no saddle-rotating here—and the one-piece strap that threads through the saddle and all the way around the boat. The largely metal saddles inspire confidence, and, unlike Yakima, the towers clamp on the roof without a wrench.

The only problem I ever had with the Thule was a rather bizarre one. We had the rack mounted on a camper shell on the back of our Toyota pickup, on a trip through Canada. On one windy stretch we heard a peculiar buzzing coming from the roof. At the next gas stop I checked, and was horrified to find both front securing straps for the boats nearly frayed through, where they extend from saddle to saddle underneath the hulls of the kayaks. Apparently some strange turbulence had set up a high-frequency vibration in the straps, and almost worn them through. Fortunately we had spare straps along (lesson one for this chapter), and I duct-taped the new straps to the crossbar under the boats. I've never heard of this before, and have concluded that the combination of truck, camper, and airflow created a very unusual situation. It's something to remember, however.

Recently, Yakima has fired a new salvo in the roof-rack wars with their Hully-Rollers, a combination saddle/roller system that permits you to roll the kayak up onto the roof rack on the rollers, which then lock and act as saddles. This solves a major problem of putting sea kayaks on

roof racks, particularly with tall sport-utility vehicles, and even more particularly for people loading boats by themselves. I am testing a set as I write this, and so far I'm impressed.

Several other companies make nice rack systems, but none I've seen so far produce purpose-made kayak saddles. If you have such a rack and don't want to invest in another whole system, try the saddles from South Shore Kayaks, which are designed to fit most racks with either round or rectangular bars (see Appendix A for contact information).

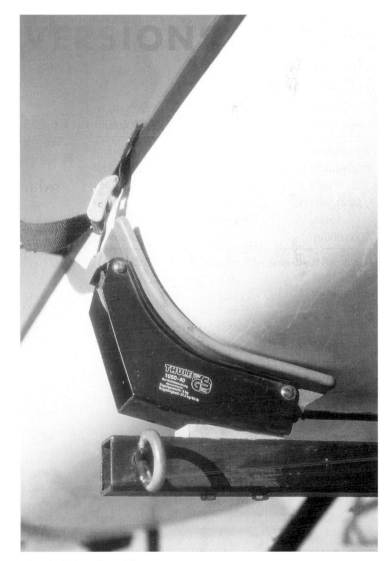

The Thule kayak saddle.

SECURING KAYAKS ON ROOF RACKS

Once you've decided on a roof-rack system, and are ready to install it on your vehicle, space the crossbars as far apart as possible. Crosswinds will be your biggest enemy, and the less of a lever they have to push against on the bow or stern of the kayak, the less stress will be placed on the system.

Take your time setting up the saddles. Make sure the boats are parallel to each other and pointing straight down the road, to reduce wind resistance. Shift the kayaks forward and back a bit, to find the right place for the straps to cross the deck. The boat should be nearly centered on the rack, but you also don't want the straps to chafe against deck hardware.

On rotomolded kayaks, try to place the saddles as nearly as possible under the bulkheads; in fact I would do this even if it meant moving the crossbars slightly closer together. Cinching down a plastic boat on an unsupported part of the hull could cause a "set"—a bend or warpage in the hull that can take days to slowly return to normal, and will screw up the handling in the meantime. No matter what your boat material, don't crank down too hard on the straps. On decent roads, good and snug is tight enough (for you engineers, "good and snug" translates to a torque rendering of 12 Newton/meters multiplied by the square root of strap length).

Always tie a line from the bow of the kayak to your vehicle somewhere near the front bumper. This line should be just taut, without putting significant downward pressure on the bow. If something happens—a broken strap, a loose mount—the bow line will not only help keep the boat on the vehicle, but might alert

When securing your boat on a roof rack, it should be nearly centered on the rack, but you also don't want the straps to chafe against deck hardware. Make sure the saddle hardware is tightened firmly to the rack, and when you cinch down the boat, do so snugly but not too tightly.

you to the danger if it starts jerking back and forth. Stern lines are a good idea as well, but it's at the bow where the wind would most likely snatch the boat and rip it off the roof if something gave.

An aside here: sometime in your kayaking career, I'm not sure when, but sometime, you *will* forget to untie the bow line and will attempt to pull the kayak off the roof, cursing and yanking when it seems to hang up on an invisible obstacle.

Use a cockpit cover, if you have one, to keep debris and rain out of the cockpit while on the road. Make sure there are no loose strap ends or other lines to flail about; tuck them under the deck bungees or tie them together. If you have a rudder that flips up over the deck, it's usually better to lower it to its deployed position, or the wind will yank it out of its slot and force it over to the side, stressing the mount and cables (although I recently saw a Dagger kayak with a built-in bungee to secure the blade in its slot—bravo). *Watch your head* on the blade. Finally, once on the road, check the boats at each gas stop by giving them a good shaking by the bow or stern, and check all the hardware connections on the rack and saddles.

SPECIAL MOUNTS

Rack makers produce mounts to fit nearly any vehicle roof. But you can run into problems if you try to do something different, such as mounting the rack on a truck camper. What you need are "artificial raingutters," short brackets that duplicate the lip of an old-fashioned car raingutter. These can be bolted to a camper shell to provide a rigid mounting platform. They are sold by most rack manufacturers.

The nice thing about mounting a rack to a camper shell is that you can space the bars as far apart as you like. On one shell I had, I installed mounts to space the bars about 7 feet apart for kayaks, and put in an extra pair of mounts so I could put the bars closer together for carrying bicycles. Most gutter kits come with backing plates; if not, make sure you use large backing washers on the bolts, and always seal the heck out of the holes with butyl rubber or silicone sealant.

Sometimes even the artificial raingutters won't work. I recently fabricated a set of aluminum mounts to attach bars to the flat roof of our pop-up camper. I

used square tubing to form the base, cut so I could drill through the roof framework to mount them, and used angle iron to form the "gutter." I pop-riveted the assembly together, then took them to a welder who welded them permanently. The mounts spread the load over a wide area and are immensely strong, but corrosion-resistant.

What if you have a pickup, but no camper? No problem—several companies manufacture racks that form a frame over the bed of the truck. One, the Bedrack, from Canyon Sports Racks (see Appendix B) consists of a single bar that extends vertically from the center of the bed to roof height, with a crossbar that takes standard kayak saddles. The assembly is held rigidly in place by four straps that connect to each corner of the bed. You use a standard rack crossbar on the cab to support the front of the boats. Other available bed-mounted rack systems use a square frame structure like a contractor's rack.

Trailers

Most vehicles can't carry more than two kayaks abreast on the roof (I don't like the mounts that carry them on edge—not enough support and too much side windage). If you need to carry three or four or more kayaks, a trailer is the best solution.

For light duty, sport trailers such as the TerraPac by Trailerlite work well. The TerraPac is a convertible trailer that can carry several kayaks at once on a frame structure, or two kayaks atop an enclosed cargo box. The latter would be a nice setup for a couple with a compact car, or a small family if you mounted double kayaks on the trailer.

For my touring business in Mexico, I needed something quite a bit stronger. So I designed and, with the help of my father-in-law, welded a trailer using heavy box-section frame rails and 1½-inch square tubing for the superstructure. For the axle I used an old mobile-home axle and wheels. I mounted Thule saddles on the crossmembers. The trailer could carry up to nine kayaks, properly supported, plus several hundred pounds of gear and water in a plywood-lined cargo box the size of a compact pickup bed. The entire cost—not counting all those expensive saddles—was less than $500.

Traveling by Air

Make no mistake, traveling by air with a hard-shell kayak will be expensive. Airlines view hard-shell kayaks as freight, not luggage, and charge accordingly. Even sectional hard-shell boats are targeted for a premium, although it is less than for a full-length boat. The only really reasonable way to fly with a kayak is to take a folding model, which, depending on the carrier and your other luggage, can sometimes be classified as excess baggage.

If you want to transport a hard-shell boat by air, try every approach and every company you can. Rates vary tremendously, depending on the carrier, route, the person you're talking to, the day of the week—the vagaries are endless. In one afternoon, researching an Arctic trip, I had rates for return fares for my 17-foot hard-shell vary by more than $1,000. Sometimes it's cheaper to ship the boat on the same plane you're traveling in; sometimes it's cheaper to hire an air-freight company and send it separately. The farther out on the frontier you go, the more expensive flying is—but the less perturbed the companies are when you ask about "unusual" luggage.

In really far-flung areas, where independent bush pilots still operate with small floatplanes, normal rate schedules go out the window. How much you pay to get yourself and your boats somewhere will depend on whether or not the pilot was headed there anyway, or if you can hop on a return flight from another delivery, or catch a pilot who's been idle for a while. Don't be afraid to bargain, as long as you do so politely.

In the far reaches of the world's waterways, float plane travel is common.

Flying with folding kayaks is much simpler. However, don't ignore the possibility of damage to frame parts by careless handlers.

Feathercraft makes much of the fact that its boats fit into one duffel bag. The Klepper uses two, one for the skin and one for the frame. I actually prefer the two-bag system. First, each bag is lighter, and thus less likely to be heaved roughly or dropped. Second, there is room in the Klepper frame bag to add a layer of closed-cell foam padding around the frame members; the Feathercraft duffel is so tightly stuffed nothing else will fit. Unless you have some pressing reason to use one bag to carry your Feathercraft, I would buy two aftermarket duffels and pad the contents. Long Haul Products makes excellent bags for folders, in several sizes.

See Appendix A, beginning on page 201, for lists of boat and accessories manufacturers and suppliers.

Something to keep in mind is that most airlines allow each passenger, as regular luggage, two checked bags of not more than 70 pounds each, plus one carry-on. If you own a Feathercraft, you could send the boat in its single duffel and use another duffel for the rest of your gear, or you could split the boat into two duffels, using the extra space in each to arrange the rest of your gear so that it helps pad the frame members. Sleeping pads, sleeping bags, and tents make excellent fillers for this purpose. The Long Haul bags have plenty of extra room for gear.

Ferries

Catching rides on ferries, such as up the inside passage of Canada and Alaska, has become a popular way for sea kayakers to travel to put-in sites inaccessible by car. It's surprising, then, how often kayakers are still treated as second-class citizens. Frequently, on the larger transport ferries, they are asked to stuff their kayaks under other vehicles, usually semitrucks, to leave more room for other vehicles.

I had heard of this problem cropping up occasionally, but figured there was little use bucking the system, until I read a letter to *Sea Kayaker* magazine from a member of a group that was asked to stash their kayaks under a line of tractor-trailer rigs. The group politely refused—and open deck space was promptly discovered for them. I've since heard of another group getting better service by being assertive. If the ferry is charging you a tariff to carry your kayak, insist on proper treatment. If it's going free, of course, you can't very well be choosy.

It's easier if your kayaks are on a vehicle you are also taking on the ferry, but check the measurement rules closely. Sometimes there are arbitrary length designations for certain vehicles, no matter how long they really are; other times the actual length of the vehicle plus the overhanging kayaks will be measured. In the latter case, if your kayaks do not overhang both ends of the vehicle, you can slide them forward on the racks until the bow is directly above the front bumper, reducing the overall length of the combination. Just don't forget to switch them back to proper position before you drive off down the road at your destination!

Security

The likelihood of having your kayak stolen increases the closer you are to popular sea kayaking areas. For example, I could leave my kayak indefinitely in the front yard of my home in Tucson, confident that few people in this town would recognize it as a *boat,* much less know where to fence it.

On the other hand, in Seattle I recently saw "wanted" posters up in kayak shops, describing a guy who had perfected on-call kayak theft. He would spot a poorly secured kayak somewhere—say, an almost-new red Cadence—and immediately pop an ad in the classifieds: *For sale: almost-new Cadence, red.* If he got any calls (on his digital pager), he would steal the boat and meet the prospective buyer at a dock somewhere. Brilliant.

Preventing kayak theft is just like preventing any other theft—if someone wants it badly enough, and

When traveling with your kayaks, secure them with cable locks, such as the Sure-Lock, made especially for kayaks by Boulter of Earth.

has enough opportunity, he or she *will* get it. The only thing you can do is make it not worth the trouble to get *yours*. Yes, a cheap cable lock can be cut, but if your unlocked boat is sitting next to one locked with a cheap cable, which one do you think will disappear?

At home, store your kayak out of sight of passersby. Keep it in a place that is a pain to get out of, even for you. Then lock it with a chain and substantial padlock.

Three cheers for manufacturers who install security rings in their boats, through which a cable or chain can be threaded. If your kayak has a hanging seat, molded in a single piece of fiberglass with the cockpit coaming, you can thread a chain through that. Otherwise, I suggest glassing-in a security loop on your own (see Chapter 13, page 196).

On the road, with boats on the vehicle, security becomes more difficult. An excellent deterrent against casual theft is the Sure-Lock by Boulter of Earth. It's effective partly because it's easy to install, which means you'll use it more often. Two loops of vinyl-coated steel cable fit over the ends of the kayak, and the end, with an adjustable knob, is passed through the win-

dow of the vehicle. Once you roll up the window, the cable can't be pulled out. In order to steal the boat the thief either needs stout cable cutters, or he needs to break into your car first. It's fast enough that you can pop it on at a lunch stop. Most roof-rack manufacturers also make some sort of security cable.

For night security, I like to lock the boats with chain rather than cable. First, it is a better visual deterrent; second, if anyone tried to cut it and pull the ends out of the boats, it would be more likely to make a racket.

If you stay at hotels while traveling, try to park in front of your room. If that's not possible, park in front of the reception office. One time when the only parking was far away from either, I pulled both kayaks off the roof and stacked them in our room.

Probably the best defense against theft is to simply be alert. That doesn't mean living in a constant state of paranoia; it just means keeping part of your brain open to the situation, and recognizing when it would be smart to take a few precautions.

Incidentally, I'm in the market for a yellow Skerray XL, in nearly new condition, cheap. . . .

13

MAINTENANCE, REPAIR, AND MODIFICATION

Kayak Mechanic 101

A sea kayak is a simple machine. The most sophisticated component on the whole thing is the rudder, which might have, what, maybe six moving parts? So anyone can become a master kayak mechanic.

The first things to learn are field repairs—quick fixes intended to salvage a trip, which might be redone at home later for a more permanent repair. You can also keep up on routine maintenance, the little things that keep your boat looking and functioning like new.

Once you've become comfortable with that, you can start customizing—actually altering features of the kayak to suit your own needs or comfort.

A Comprehensive Repair Kit

The tools needed to repair almost anything that can go wrong on a kayaking trip are so simple there's no excuse not to have a proper set with you on every trip. Everything you'll need will fit in a small dry box.

Buy the best-quality tools you can find. Those 61-piece socket sets that sell for $9.99 aren't worth the pot metal they're made from. The ubiquitous Sears Craftsman brand is excellent; most of the premium brands made for the big chain hardware stores are okay too. Heck, for the amount of stuff you'll need for kayaking, you could afford an order from Snap-On. I guarantee any auto mechanics on your trips will be impressed.

Once you've got your kayaking tools organized, *please* avoid the temptation to use them on the broken lamp or blow-dryer at home. Before you know it, they'll have disappeared forever in that drawer in the kitchen. You know which one. Keep them all in the dry box, ready to go.

Here is a list of what I carry. You can alter this to taste.

A simple repair box.

- Phillips and standard screwdrivers. I found a good one, by ChannelLock, that has four bits contained in the reversible shaft.
- 6-inch adjustable wrench.
- Small ChannelLock pliers. These are much more versatile than ordinary pliers. The new Craftsman Robo-grip pliers are fine too.
- Needlenose pliers.
- Wire cutters. The type I use are called *side cutters.*
- One or two hemostats. Great for manipulating little parts.
- Gerber Multi-Plier. A good backup for all the above, with some nice extra implements. Kershaw has just introduced a multi-tool with locking pliers (similar to Vise-Grips), plus a hacksaw blade. Promising.
- Jeweler's screwdrivers. Useful for many tasks besides tightening jewels.

In addition, my repair kit includes:

- Sharpening stone.
- Duct tape—the cloth type, not the cheaper vinyl stuff. Some kayak companies sell repair tape that is said to adhere to wet surfaces.
- Spare rudder cables and fittings.
- Tent pole repair sleeve.
- Sewing kit (the Black Diamond expedition kit is excellent).
- Electrical tape.
- 30 feet of 3mm kernmantle nylon cord (parachute cord will do in a pinch, but unravels easily).
- A roll of "plumber's tape." This is actually cloth sandpaper with a multitude of uses.
- Single-edge razor blades.
- A tube of Seamstuff or other all-purpose adhesive/sealant.
- Box of dental floss.
- Butane lighter or wood matches.
- For long expeditions, I carry a roll of fiberglass cloth, resin, and disposable latex gloves, for making permanent fiberglass repairs.

Finally, I carry a compartmented polyethylene box for many tiny items: stove and lantern repair parts, swage fittings for cables, spare Fastex buckles, and the like.

If you happen to own a Klepper folding kayak, Mark Eckhart at Long Haul Products has assembled one of the nicest and most comprehensive maintenance and repair kits I've seen, for the Aerius boats (see page 204).

Field Repairs

About 80 percent of field repairs to kayaking gear involve a leaking boat, whether minor or disastrous. Another 10 percent involve rudder and other boat problems, and the remaining fraction is divided among various other gear failures, such as broken paddles.

LEAKS

For hull cracks or splits, or spots where something has rubbed through the hull or actually punctured it, duct tape will provide a secure repair that will last for weeks on either fiberglass or a folder's hull. It might peel off sooner on plastic boats, however.

Here is an effective procedure for taping up a kayak hull.

1. Clean the spot around the hole, and dry it thoroughly.

2. Cut, don't tear, a piece of tape to overlap the hole and apply it carefully to eliminate bubbles under the tape—start at one end and roll the strip on, don't just slap it on flat.

3. Burnish the tape to set the adhesive by rubbing it firmly with something smooth, such as the handle of your Swiss Army knife.

4. Use a razor blade to round the corners of the tape. This will help prevent peeling. (I learned this last trick from Annie Getchell's excellent book, *The Essential Outdoor Gear Manual*. See Appendix A for biblio-

graphic details.) If you want to avoid scoring your gelcoat you can cut the tape before you apply it.

5. If it's a big split, overlap strips of tape to cover all the damage.

6. You're right: duct tape repairs look pretty industrial. Think of it as a badge of courage.

Duct tape also repairs broken frame members on folding kayaks. Find something to use for a splint to support the structure, and tape it to the broken member, wrapping the whole thing in a spiral of tape. A piece of wood

Jonathan fixing rudder. A well-stocked repair kit, housed in a dry box such as this one from Underwater Kinetics, allows the paddler to make just about any repairs in the field.

will work; at last resort a tent pole section, or two side-by-side, works great, at the expense of your tent. For aluminum-framed folders, hose clamps are also useful for splinting, and a small hacksaw for cutting tubing.

The other common place for a leak is the seam where the hull joins the deck on a fiberglass or Kevlar boat. These are harder to locate—often you must dump a few gallons of water inside the boat and tilt it on its side to see where the water comes out. Mark the spot and let it dry completely, then use Seamstuff or a similar adhesive to seal the spot.

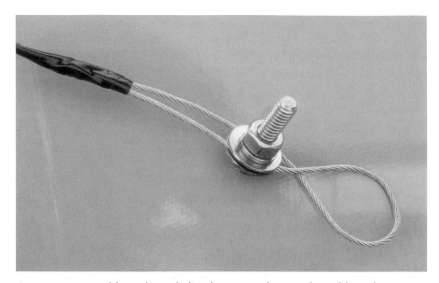

An emergency cable end, made by clamping a loop in the cable with a spare bolt.

RUDDER REPAIRS

Broken cables are the number-one rudder failure. If you've brought a spare cable that's made for your boat, replacement is usually straightforward. But you can make your own cable from a bulk length cut to fit, using crimped-on swages to form loops where needed. The cable and swages are all available from marine hardware stores. The store can also crimp on a loop at the rudder end for you.

If you just cut a rudder cable with wire cutters it tends to fray immediately. Wrap the spot where you'll make the cut with tape first, then use sharp cutters that you haven't been using on coat hangers at home. When you crimp on the swage, don't be afraid to really lean on the pliers you're using to compress the fitting. It's difficult to press too hard.

If, for some reason, you're caught out without a spare cable, and yours breaks at the loop next to the rudder (which is common), you've still got nearly a whole length of cable to work with. Check the pedal assembly where the cable attaches in front. Many times there is enough extra cable so that you can pull out 4 or 5 inches to swage a new loop at the other end. No swages either? You can use a spare bolt and nut to clamp a loop that should hold.

Sometimes, the hole in the rudder arm where the end of the rudder cable attaches can wear through. I once was able to make a new hole in a plastic arm with the awl from a Gerber Multi-Plier.

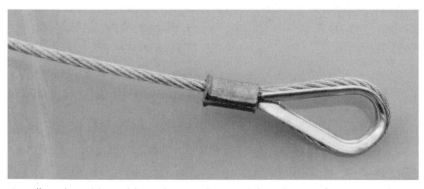

A well-made rudder cable end, securely swaged, with a reinforcing metal eye insert. A fitting like this will far outlast most standard cable ends.

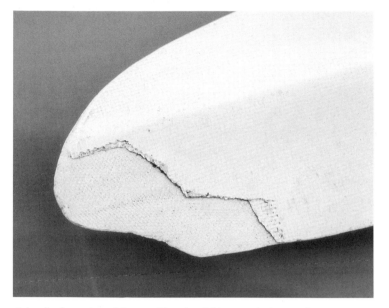

A badly frayed paddle tip. This should be sanded smooth to prevent further splitting.

A good way to prevent being caught shorthanded is to buy a spare for every bolt and fitting on your whole rudder assembly. The entire kit will fit in a little compartmented polyethylene box.

PADDLES

There is little to do to repair a paddle with a completely broken blade; in fact, the only way I would be tempted to try is if it were my last paddle. Then I would rig a splint with tent pole sections and duct tape, making a horribly unbalanced but perhaps usable crutch.

Many times a fiberglass paddle will just begin to split its laminations at the tip of the blade. If you ignore this condition, sand will grind its way in and further split the layers. Use sandpaper to feather the edge back beyond the split. Incidentally, paddle manufacturers can usually replace a broken or split blade for much less than the price of a whole new paddle.

The only other typical problems with paddles involve the joints of two-piece fiberglass paddles. Ironically, I've never had a problem with them loosening—just the opposite. They seem to get tighter and tighter until you can either not get them apart, which isn't too bad, or you cannot put them together, which is bad. I use an 8-inch length of the plumber's-tape sandpaper I mentioned in the tool kit to work on the male end, using a motion that resembles those corny old fat-reducer machines with the rubber belt that wrapped around your middle. Take off a very small amount at a time, and do it evenly all the way around the joint. Once the joint fits again, I use some dry graphite lubricant on it.

DRY BAGS

Most dry-bag repairs involve pinhole leaks, which are easy to spot by holding up the bag to a light source and sticking your head inside. A spot of Seamstuff inside

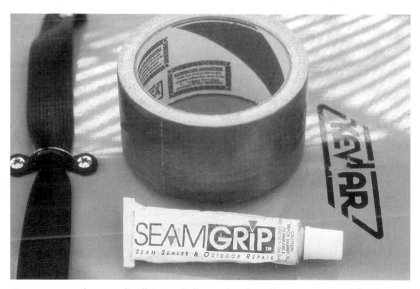

Duct tape and a good adhesive will together handle a majority of field repairs.

and out will seal them forever. Larger tears can be repaired with, yes, duct tape.

Home Repairs and Maintenance

USING FIBERGLASS

For permanent repairs of hull damage, you'll want to put in a fiberglass patch. Likewise, if you want to add a security loop to your boat, or do any number of other customizing jobs, you should learn the basics of fiberglass work. It's very easy.

Fiberglass comprises a woven cloth, and a resin that soaks into the cloth and bonds it when it cures. The materials are hazardous, so work in a ventilated area and use rubber gloves. I like to buy fiberglass cloth in rolls about 4 inches wide. These rolls have bound edges to prevent unraveling. If you have to cut smaller pieces, use care to make sure the edges don't fray too much.

To patch a small hole, say in the bottom of your hull, work from the inside. Sand around the hole to smooth and clean the surface. Wipe it clean with acetone and dry it completely. Put a small piece of waxed paper over the outside of the hole and stick it down with duct tape, to prevent drips coming through the hull.

Mix a small amount of resin according to the instructions. I use a disposable foam paintbrush to apply a layer around and over the hole inside the hull. Cut a piece of cloth about 2 inches square and lay it in the resin over the hole, carefully dabbing it down flat. Use more resin to soak the cloth completely. Then put another piece of cloth about an inch or two bigger each way over the first, and soak it with resin as well. If you want a really smooth finish, you can put a big piece of waxed paper over the patch and use a small squeegee or printer's roller to roll it flat and work out any bubbles (which will show up as a white circle in the clear resin).

Don't overload the cloth with resin, or the patch will lack flexibility. You want the cloth just full enough of resin so the weave is covered smoothly with it.

When the patch has cured, use sandpaper to feather the edges into the existing fiberglass.

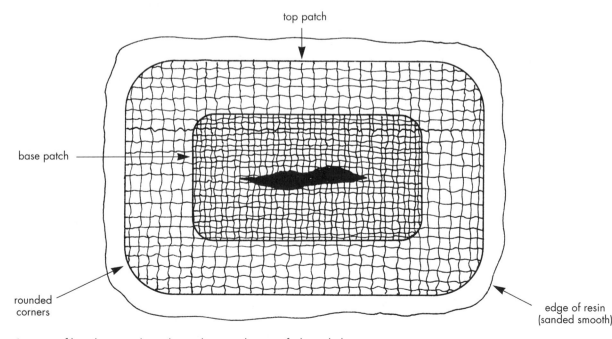

A proper fiberglass patch, with overlapping layers of glass cloth.

GELCOAT PATCHING

Small chips in the gelcoat are common on the bottom curve of the bow, where the boat hits the shore when you are landing. Also, you might want to finish a fiberglass patch by filling in the exterior with new gelcoat.

Usually you can order small amounts of the correct color gelcoat from your boat maker. Otherwise, matching anything but a white hull is difficult.

First, file or sand off any loose flakes of gelcoat in the damaged area. I don't like to overprepare a gouge—the rough surface helps form a mechanical bond with the new gelcoat. Mix a small amount of the patch material according to the instructions, and fill in the gouge (wood Popsicle sticks work great as spatulas). Fill the area to slightly above the surrounding hull profile. When the patch has set, carefully reduce the height with coarse sandpaper, switching to successively finer grades as the patch blends closer to the hull shape. Finally, use wet sandpaper to smooth the patch into the surrounding hull shape, then rubbing compound for final gloss.

For much more on using fiberglass and gelcoat, see *The Essential Outdoor Gear Manual,* by Annie Getchell.

MAINTENANCE

In two words I can tell you most of what you need to know to keep all your kayaking gear in good shape: fresh water. As soon as you get home from each trip use fresh water to *thoroughly* rinse everything that has been in contact with salt water: boat, paddles, spray skirt, PFD, wet suit, dry bags—the works.

Put the boat on a couple of sawhorses, or hang it from slings, and blast every nook and cranny of the cockpit and gear compartments, to flush out trapped sand (if you have a folding boat the flushing process is vital, to keep sand from abrading the hull and frame members).

If need be, use a sponge and mild (nondetergent) soap to clean the hull, rinsing thoroughly. Don't use abrasive cleaners or scrubbing pads. When dry, the hulls of both rigid and folding boats will benefit from an application of 303 Protectant, an ultraviolet inhibitor that helps prevent sun damage. Once or twice

As soon as you get home, clean everything thoroughly with freshwater.

a year a good paste wax job will do wonders for a fiberglass or Kevlar hull, as well as the Hypalon on a folder's hull.

Check the deck bungees and lines, and hatch-cover straps, for signs of aging, and replace them if in doubt. Check rudder fittings for signs of wear or cable fraying. Inspect plastic deck fittings for hairline cracks or a dull, powdery surface appearance, which means the plastic is aging and turning brittle. When this happens the fitting can fail unexpectedly.

For paddles, PFDs, and spray skirts, generally the freshwater rinse is all it takes. Just make sure everything is completely dry before storing. Stains on the neoprene of the spray skirt, as well as on your wet suit, can sometimes be removed with a neoprene shampoo available at dive shops.

Basic Maintenance Rules

- Wash all your gear in fresh water.
- Don't use harsh detergents.
- Dry thoroughly before storing in a cool, dry place.
- Inspect all gear for wear and tear, and repair accordingly.
- Check wood paddles and folding kayak frames for abrasion; revarnish if necessary.

A good way to clean out and repair your boat is to hang it at waist level from webbing loops from a porch roof, or set it on two sawhorses.

Customizing

I bought my second sea kayak sight unseen, strictly swayed by looks and design features gleaned from a catalog. The first time I sat in it I was launching on a three-day trip.

Big mistake. Fifteen minutes into the paddle my posterior was completely numb. No amount of squirming would alleviate the discomfort, and I spent the rest of the trip stuffing various combinations of clothing between me and the torture device the company had cheerfully referred to as a "seat."

The same boat had a peculiar rudder-control system consisting of a flexible fiberglass assembly that bolted to a track on the floor of the cockpit and operated the rudder through Dacron lines instead of stainless steel cable. It was easy to adjust, and centered the rudder blade automatically, but I experienced far too much flex in the system for my tastes, especially in the heavy following sea we experienced on the second day.

So, when I got home, out came the saber saw and a big, sharp chisel. I cut away the mount for the seat, which was integral with the cockpit rim. Then I slid the chisel under the rudder-pedal mount and beat on it with an enormous hammer until it split free from the floor (a nerve-racking process). I drilled through the sides of the cockpit and installed standard sliding rudder pedals, and replaced the Dacron lines with stout stainless cables. Then I installed a replacement seat from a

Borrowing Ideas

Tip: One of the best ways to get ideas for customizing your boat is to see what others have done. Don't be afraid to ask a fellow kayaker you meet on a lunch stop to look over her boat's great custom underdeck compartment, or someone's custom seat cover with foam padding and thigh braces. No doubt they'll be proud of their boat, and love to tell you all about how they customized it.

different kayak company, one I knew was comfortable for me and that used fiberglass loops bonded to the floor to secure it—easily done at home.

The result? Well, the result was a comfortable kayak that lived up to its promises in every other respect—in fact, it become my main craft for expeditions and guiding for almost 10 years.

The moral of the story is, *paddle the dang kayak before you buy it*. But the sub-moral is, don't be afraid to change things that might be weak points on an otherwise excellent boat.

Once you've purchased a kayak, take it on at least one trip before doing anything drastic. Some things that seem wrong might just be idiosyncratic. Then, when you've decided something needs changing, make sure the change is compatible with the boat—don't cut out the seat unless you have another one you *know* will fit and won't change the center of gravity.

Sometimes you can just modify what's there. One of the kayaks in my touring business fleet had a fiberglass seat that hung from the cockpit rim. It offered no thigh support at all, and when I looked under it I was horrified to find a full inch between the bottom of the seat and the hull. An inch in seat height makes a considerable difference in the center of gravity on a kayak. So I removed the rear mounting bolts and drilled new holes ¾ of an inch lower. This rotated the

back of the seat down, lowering the center of gravity and increasing thigh support. It worked perfectly—comfort was increased and the boat was noticeably more stable.

If you decide to do any sawing and drilling on your kayak, remember the old carpenter's rule: Measure twice, cut once. I usually measure about five times before I do anything irreversible. Get used to the idea of drilling your boat by installing a few simple accessories, such as a Kayak Safe spray-skirt release, or the hardware for a Driftstopper sea anchor. The first time you put drill bit to gelcoat it will sound like fingernails on a blackboard, but you'll become accustomed to it.

While we're on the subject of seats—the fiberglass seats that are molded in a yoke hanging from the cockpit rim make excellent mounts for flares and other emergency gear. There is usually room between the seat and the side of the hull for a tube made of PVC pipe, which can hold a parachute flare or other signaling devices. Another good spot is on the back of a hinged seat.

One of the best modifications you can perform on a kayak is to increase the strength of the rudder system. The rather thin cable that comes on most of them can be replaced with thicker gauge, and many fittings can be replaced with stronger items from a chandlery

Repair Kits: The Cardinal Rule

If you use something out of the kit put it back in the kit; if you use up something in the kit, write it down on a pad of paper you keep in the kit for that purpose, and replace it as soon as you return home.

(ship's store). This isn't to say that what comes from the factory is inadequate; you're just building in an extra margin of strength.

Proper Gear Storage

BOATS

Fiberglass kayaks are easy to store. As long as they're out of the sun, anything additional is just pampering.

If you do have to store the boat where it gets sun, don't wrap it in anything such as a plastic tarp, which seems to create some sort of a greenhouse effect and hasten gelcoat oxidation. Instead rig the tarp as an awning a couple of feet above the boat.

I store my kayaks hull up. If they sit for a time and collect a layer of dust, it's easier to clean off the bottom, and sponging doesn't create the swirl marks it would in the shiny deck gelcoat. At various times I've used wood cradles to support the boats, or nylon slings hanging from the carport beams. I store my boat with a cockpit cover and the cargo hatches installed to keep out dust—but I live in a dry climate. In damp areas you should allow air to circulate to prevent mildew.

Polyethylene kayaks require more care. They must *definitely* be kept out of the sun, and also must be supported evenly to prevent the hull from warping or sagging at the ends ("hogging" as it's known in ships). Support the boat, either in slings or on cradles, at the bulkheads for maximum stiffness, on edge if possible. If you have a garage with an 18-foot ceiling, you can also stand the boat on end, which is how the factory probably stored it before they shipped it.

Folding kayaks should, if possible, be stored *un*folded. The ideal situation is with the hull laid out flat on a ventilated shelf in a cool, dark place. If you don't have the space for this—after all, that's why many of us buy folding kayaks—at least try to keep the hull loosely rolled, and reroll it a different way every few months to prevent permanent creases. Mark Eckhart at Long Haul Products recommends folding it in half under a bed. Sprinkling the hull with a little talcum powder inside and out will help to absorb moisture and reduce the chance of mildew.

For information about caring for all types of outdoor gear, I highly recommend *The Essential Outdoor Gear Manual,* by Annie Getchell. This book is just loaded with good information.

ACCESSORIES

It's a bit of an indulgence, but I like to keep my paddles in a soft case made for them (mine is from Werner). It keeps them together, grit-free, and easy to transport, plus it's stylish as heck.

For storing other gear, I use those inexpensive plastic bins with the flip-top lids. They keep everything organized and clean, and make packing for each trip a breeze. I throw a packet of desiccant in each to ensure dryness; these are available at some hardware stores. Pack stuff loosely enough so that air can circulate.

Keep track of your dated items: flares, pepper spray, lithium batteries, and so forth. I don't know anyone except small-aircraft pilots who actually replace things right when they're supposed to, so use your own judgment. Expired flares make great New Year's toys, but you didn't read it here.

Well, I think this is it. You own a beautiful, seaworthy kayak and accessories, you've practiced in it and provisioned it, have packed it and explored in it and repaired it and treated it properly at the end of the trip. It's time to start planning for the next journey. Be safe and have fun!

APPENDIX A

RESOURCES

This list is not a complete catalog of all the excellent equipment and information resources available for kayakers; for the most part it includes items mentioned in the text, as well as other useful resources. Any omissions were simply due to lack of space and are not intended as a comment on the quality of any gear or resources not listed. If you contact any of these manufacturers, please tell them you read about them in this book so they'll send me free stuff.

Boat Manufacturers

Aire Inflatables
 P.O. Box 3412
 Boise, ID 83703
 (208) 344-7506

Current Designs
 U.S. Office: Wenonah Canoe, Inc.
 Box 247
 Winona, MN 55987
 (507) 454-5430

Dagger Kayaks
 P.O. Box 1500
 Harriman, TN 37748
 (423) 882-0404

Easy Rider Kayaks
 P.O. Box 88108
 Seattle, WA 98138
 (206) 228-3633

Eddyline Kayaks
 1344 Ashten Rd
 Burlington, WA 98233
 (360) 757-2300

Feathercraft Folding Kayaks
 4-1244 Cartwright St.
 Vancouver, BC V6H 3R8 Canada
 (604) 681-8437

Klepper Folding Kayaks
 100 Cadillac Dr., Suite 117
 Sacramento, CA 95825
 (800) 323-3525

Mariner Kayaks
 2134 Westlake Ave. North
 Seattle, WA 98109
 (206) 284-8404

Necky Kayaks
 1100 Riverside Rd.
 Abbotsford, BC V2S 7P1 Canada
 (604) 850-1206

Northwest Kayaks
  15145 NE 90th St.
  Redmond, WA 98052
  (206) 869-1107

Ocean Kayak (sit-on-tops)
  2460 Salashan Loop
  Ferndale, WA 98248
  (800) 8-KAYAKS

P & H Designs
  1107 Station Rd., Unit 1
  Bellport, NY 11713
  (516) 286-1988

Pacific Water Sports
  16055 Pacific Highway South
  Seattle, WA 98188
  (206) 246-9385

Perception
  P.O. Box 8002
  Easley, SC 29641
  (803) 859-7518

Pygmy Boats (kits)
  P.O. Box 1529
  Pt. Townsend, WA 98368
  (360) 385-6143

Rainforest Designs/Nimbus
  6-9903 240 St.
  Albion, BC V0M 1B0 Canada
  (604) 467-9932

Southern Exposure Sea Kayaks
  P.O. Box 4530
  Location 18487 U.S. 1
  Tequesta, FL 33469
  (561) 575-4530

Valley Canoe Products/Great River Outfitters
  4180 Elizabeth Lake Rd.
  Waterford, MI 48328
  (810) 683-4770
  grokayak@ix.netcom.com

Wilderness Systems
  1110 Surrett Dr.
  High Point, NC 27260
  (910) 883-7410

Paddling Equipment

PFDS

Extrasport
  5305 NW 35th Ct.
  Miami, FL 33142
  (305) 633-2945

Lotus Designs
  1060 Old Mars Mill Highway
  Weaverville, NC 28787
  (704) 689-2470

Palm Equipment
  Great River Outfitters
  4180 Elizabeth Lake Rd.
  Waterford, MI 48328
  (810) 683-4770

Seda
  926 Coolidge Ave.
  National City, CA 91950
  (619) 336-2444

Stohlquist
  P.O. Box 3059
  Buena Vista, CA 81211
  (719) 395-2422

PADDLES

Aqua-Bound
  1-9520 192nd St.
  Surrey, BC V4N 3R8 Canada
  (604) 882-2052

Cricket
  17530 W Highway 50
  Maysville, Salida, CO 81201
  (719) 539-5010

Eddyline/Swift Paddles
  1344 Ashten Rd.
  Burlington, WA 98233
  (360) 757-2300

Lightning Paddles
  22800 S. Unger Rd.
  Colton, OR 97017
  (503) 824-2938
  www.paddles.com

Nimbus Paddles
4915 Chisholm St.
Delta, BC V4K 2K6 Canada
(604) 940-1957

Sawyer Paddles
299 Rogue River Parkway
Talent, OR 97540
(541) 535-3606

Werner Paddles
P.O. Box 1139
Sultan, WA 98294
(800) 275-3311

SPRAY SKIRTS

Kokatat
5350 Ericson Way
Arcata, CA 95521
(800) 225-9749

Palm/Rapidstyle Equipment
Great River Outfitters
4180 Elizabeth Lake Rd.
Waterford, MI 48328
(810) 683-4770

Perception
P.O. Box 8002
Easley, SC 29641
(803) 859-7518

Snap Dragon Design
14320 N.E. 21st St., #15
Bellevue, WA 98007
(206) 957-3575

Safety Equipment

ACR Electronics (strobes, EPIRBS, lights)
5757 Ravenswood Rd.
Fort Lauderdale, FL 33312
(800) 432-0227

Adventure Medical Kits
P.O. Box 43309
Oakland, CA 94624
(800) 324-3517

Atwater Carey (medical kits)
1 Repel Rd.
Jackson, WI 53037
(414) 677-4121

Boulter of Earth (Driftstopper sea anchor)
46 Sussex Rd.
Washington Township, NJ 07675
(201) 722-0033

Gerber (multi-tool, knives)
14200 S.W. 72nd Ave.
Portland, OR 97223
(503) 777-6905

Great River Outfitters (towing systems, deck
   pumps)
4180 Elizabeth Lake Rd.
Waterford, MI 48328
(810) 683-4770

Kayak Safe (spray-skirt release)
P.O. Box 1508
Mill Valley, CA 94941
(415) 381-1421

Motorola Sports Radios
1301 E. Algonquin Rd.
Schaumburg, IL 60196
(800) 448-6686

Sea Wings (sponsons)
Georgian Bay Kayak
231 Gordon Dr.
Penetanguishene, ON L9M 1Y2 Canada
(705) 549-3722
http://www.bconnex.net/~timkayak

See/Rescue (distress banners)
219 Koko Isle Circle, Suite 602
Honolulu, HI 96825
(800) 224-1123
seerescue@aol.com

Spyderco (knives)
4565 Highway 93
Golden, CO 80402
(303) 279-8383

West Marine (radios, Pains–Wessex flares,
distress flags)
P.O. Box 50070
Watsonville, CA 95077
(800) 538-0775

Clothing, Outerwear, and Footwear

ExOfficio (clothing)
1419 Elliot Ave. West
Seattle, WA 98119
(800) 833-0831

Five-Ten (water shoes)
P.O. Box 1185
Redlands, CA 92373
(909) 798-4222

Kokatat (outerwear, dry suits)
5350 Ericson Way
Arcata, CA 95521
(707) 822-7621

Patagonia (clothing, outerwear, water shoes)
259 W. Santa Clara St.
Ventura, CA 93001
(805) 643-8616

RailRiders (clothing)
40 Smith Place
Cambridge, MA 02138
(617) 864-5969

Tarponwear (clothing)
P.O. Box 2272
Jackson, WY 83301
(307) 739-9755

Teva (sandals and water shoes)
1132 Mark Ave.
Carpinteria, CA 93013
(805) 684-1252

Vasque (water shoes)
314 Main St.
Red Wing, MN 55066
(612) 388-8211

Accessories for Sea Kayaking

BDH (Safe Pack dry container)
Available through Great River Outfitters
4180 Elizabeth Lake Rd.
Waterford, MI 48328
(810) 683-4770

Boulter of Earth (Driftstopper sea anchor,
Sure-lock cable lock)
46 Sussex Rd.
Washington Township, NJ 07675
(201) 722-0033

Cascade Designs (dry bags, waterproof fanny packs)
4000 1st Ave. South
Seattle, WA 98134
(206) 583-0583

Compac 50 (built-in bilge pump)
Henderson (Chimp bilge pump)
Available through Great River Outfitters
4180 Elizabeth Lake Rd.
Waterford, MI 48328
(810) 683-4770

Dagger Canoe/Headwaters (accessories)
P.O. Box 1500
Harriman, TN 37748
(423) 882-0404

Kayak Safe (spray-skirt release)
P.O. Box 1508
Mill Valley, CA 94941
(415) 381-1421

Long Haul Products (Klepper, other folding
kayak accessories)
2526 S. Adams St.
Denver, CO 80210
(303) 782-9743

Mark Pack Works (deck bags, sails, paddle floats)
230 Madison St.
Oakland, CA 94607
(510) 452-0243

Oregon Scientific (electronic weather station)
Available from Speedtech Instruments
10413 Deerfoot Dr.
Great Falls, VA 22066
(800) 760-0004
http://www.speedtech.com

Ortlieb (map cases, dry bags)
Available from NewSport
17650 140th Ave. S.E.
Renton, WA 98058
(800) 649-1763

Pelican Products (dry boxes, flashlights)
23215 Early Ave.
Torrance, CA 90505
(310) 326-4700

Primex (boat cart, sails, deck bags)
P.O. Box 505
Benicia, CA 94510
(800) 422-2482
primex@worldnet.att.net

Voyageur (dry bags, waterproof deck bags,
accessories)
P.O. Box 610
Watsfield, VT 05673
(802) 496-6247

Racks and Trailers

Bedrack (pickup rack)
Canyon Sports Racks
P.O. Box 502175
San Diego, CA 92150
(800) 414-9019

South Shore Kayaks (kayak saddles)
245 Main St.
Farmingdale, NY 11735
(516) 249-3537

Trailerlite (TerraPac trailer)
850A Calle Plano
Camarillo, CA 93012
(800) 854-8366

Thule
42 Silvermine Rd.
Seymour, CT 06483
(203) 881-4832

Yakima
P.O. Box 4899
Arcata, CA 95518
(800) 468-9000

Camping Equipment Manufacturers

Adventure Foods
481 Banjo Lane
Whittier, NC 28789
(704) 497-7529

Basic Designs/Stearns (SunShower, accessories)
P.O. Box 1498
St. Cloud, MN 56302
(612) 252-1642

Bibler Tents/Black Diamond (single-wall tents)
2084 E. 3900 South
Salt Lake City, UT 84124
(801) 278-5552

Black Diamond (expedition sewing kit)
2084 E. 3900 South
Salt Lake City, UT 84124
(801) 278-5552

Camping Gaz/Bleuet (stoves, lanterns)
Suunto USA
2151 F Las Palmas Dr., Suite G
Carlsbad, CA 92009
(619) 931-9875

Cascade Designs (Therm-a-Rest, foam mattresses,
Outback Oven, accessories)
4000 1st Ave. South
Seattle, WA 98134
(206) 583-0583

Coleman (stoves, lanterns, sleeping bags, tents, accessories)
P.O. Box 2931
Wichita, KS 67201
(316) 832-2778

Crazy Creek (Thermalounger, camp chairs)
P.O. Box 1050
Red Lodge, MT 59068
(406) 446-3446

Garcia Machine (bear-proof food containers)
14097 Ave. 272
Visalia, CA 93292
(209) 732-3785

Katadyn USA (water filters)
3019 N. Scottsdale Ave.
Scottsdale, AZ 85251
(602) 990-3131

Marmot Mountain International (tents,
sleeping bags, clothing)
2321 Circadian Way
Santa Rosa, CA 95407
(707) 544-4590

Moss Tents (tents, Parawing)
P.O. Box 577
Camden, ME 04843
(207) 236-0505

Mountain Hardwear (tents, sleeping bags, outerwear)
950A Gilman St.
Berkeley, CA 94710
(510) 559-6700

MSR (stoves, cookware, water filters)
4225 2nd Ave. South
Seattle, WA 98134
(206) 624-8573

Outdoor Research (pouches, first aid, accessories)
2203 1st Ave. South
Seattle, WA 98134
(206) 467-8197

Pelican (waterproof flashlights, boxes)
23215 Early Ave.
Torrance, CA 90505
(310) 326-4700

Petzl (headlamps)
PMI/Petzl Distribution
P.O. Box 803
Lafayette, GA 30728
(706) 764-1437

Primus (lanterns, stoves)
1462 U.S. Route 20
Cherry Valley, IL 61016
(815) 332-4951

Princeton Tec (waterproof flashlights, accessories)
P.O. Box 8057
Trenton, NJ 08650
(609) 298-9331

PÜR (water filters)
9300 N. 75th Ave.
Minneapolis, MN 55428
(800) 8457873

Sierra Designs (tents, bags, outerwear)
1255 Powell St.
Emeryville, CA 94608
(510) 450-9555

Sweetwater (water filters)
2505 Trade Center Ave.
Longmont, CO 80503
(303) 678-0447

Boat, Accessories, and Resource Retailers by Mail and Internet

Always patronize your local kayaking, outdoor, and book stores first—it's good for your town's economy, good for making friends, good for you, too (saves shipping and all the ancillary environmental costs associated therein). Use these resources if your local store cannot help you locate something.

Adventurous Traveler Bookstore
(800) 282-3963
books@atbook.com
www.AdventurousTraveler.com

Great River Outfitters
4180 Elizabeth Lake Rd.
Waterford, MI 48328
(810) 683-4770
grokayak@ix.netcom.com

Nantahala Outdoor Center
Outfitter's Store Mail Order
13077 Highway 19 West
Bryson City, NC 28713
(800) 367-3521
www.nocweb.com

Northwest Outdoor Center
2100 Westlake Ave. North
Seattle, WA 98109
(206) 281-9694

West Marine
P.O. Box 50070
Watsonville, CA 95077
(800) 538-0775

Schools for Sea Kayaking and Wilderness Skills

Leave No Trace, Inc.
P.O. Box 997
Boulder, CO 80306
(303) 442-8222 or (800) 332-4100

Monterey Bay Kayaks
693 Del Monte Ave.
Monterey, CA 93940
(408) 373-5397
http://mntereykayaks.com/tour

Nantahala Outdoor Center
13077 Highway 19 West
Bryson City, NC 28713
(888) 662-1662, ex. 600

National Outdoor Leadership School (NOLS)
288 Main Street
Lander, WY 82520
(800) 332-4100

Outward Bound
945 Pennsylvania St
Denver, CO 80203
(307) 837-0880

Princeton University Outdoor Action Program
http://www.princeton.edu/~rcurtis/oa.html

Southwest Sea Kayaks
2590 Ingraham St.
San Diego, CA 92109
(619) 222-3616
kayaked@aol.com

Southwind Kayak Center
17855 Sky Park Circle #A
Irvine, CA 92714
(800) 768-8494

Wilderness Medical Associates
RFD 2 Box 890
Bryant Pond, ME 04219
(800) 742-2931

Wilderness Medicine Institute
P.O. Box 9
Pitkin, CO 81241
This is only a partial listing of hundreds of good schools. Contact the Trade Association for Sea Kayaking or the North American Paddlesports Association for more contacts (see page 209).

In Print

MAGAZINES
Atlantic Coastal Kayaker
P.O. Box 520
Ipswich, MA 01938

Canoe and Kayak
P.O. Box 7011
Red Oak, IA 51591
(206) 827-6363

Outside
400 Market Street
Santa Fe, NM 87501
(505) 989-7100
annual buyer's guide, spring issue

Paddler
P.O. Box 697
Fallbrook, CA 92028
(619) 630-2293

Paddle Sports Magazine
(619) 630-2293

Sea Kayaker magazine
7001 Seaview Ave. N.W.
Seattle, WA 98117
(206) 789-1326

Wave~Length
Gabriola Island, BC
(604) 247-9789
http://www.wie.com/~wavenet/.

BOOKS

Some of these books might be out of print; visit your
library or secondhand bookseller.

PADDLING AND SEAMANSHIP

(*Including sources for charts and maps*)

Ashley Book of Knots (New York: Doubleday, 1993).

The Complete Book of Sea Kayaking, by Derek
Hutchinson (Old Saybrook, CT: The Globe
Pequot Press, 1995).

Complete Folding Kayaker, by Ralph Díaz (Camden,
ME: Ragged Mountain Press, 1994).

Eskimo Rolling, by Derek Hutchinson (Camden, ME:
Ragged Mountain Press, 1994, 2d edition).

*The Essential Sea Kayaker: A Complete Course for the
Open Water Paddler,* by David Seidman (Camden,
ME: Ragged Mountain Press, 1992).

Fundamentals of Kayak Navigation, by David Burch
(Old Saybrook, CT: The Globe Pequot Press,1993).

*The Map Catalog: Every Kind of Map and Chart on the
Earth and Even Some Above It,* by Joel Makower
(New York: Tilden Press, 1992).

*The Whole Paddler's Catalog: Views, Reviews, and
Resources,* edited by Zip Kellogg (Camden, ME:
Ragged Mountain Press, 1997).

KAYAKING ADVENTURE AND TRAVEL

A Boat in Our Baggage, by Maria Coffey (Camden,
ME: Ragged Mountain Press, 1995).

Alone At Sea, by Dr. Hannes Lindemann (Germany:
Polner Verlag, 1992).

A Thousand Miles in a Rob Roy Canoe, by John
MacGregor (London: British Canoe Union, 1963).

Commitments and Open Crossings, by Bill Taylor
(London: Diadem Books, 1990).

The Happy Isles of Oceania, by Paul Theroux (New
York: Ballantine Books, 1993).

The Hidden Coast, by Joel W. Rogers (Bothell, WA:
Alaska Northwest Books, 1991).

Seekers of the Horizon, edited by Will Nordby (Old
Saybrook, CT: The Globe Pequot Press, 1989).

GENERAL OUTDOOR

(*With sections of interest to sea kayakers*)

*Backwoods Ethics: Environmental Issues for Hikers and
Campers* and *Wilderness Ethics: Preserving the Spirit
of Wildness,* by Laura and Guy Waterman
(Woodstock, VT: Countryman Press, 1993).

*The Essential Outdoor Gear Manual: Equipment Care
& Repair for Outdoorspeople,* by Annie Getchell
(Camden, ME: Ragged Mountain Press, 1995).

*How to Shit in the Woods: An Environmentally Sound
Approach to a Lost Art,* by Kathleen Meyer
(Berkeley, CA: Ten Speed Press, 1989).

The New Wilderness Handbook, by Paul Petzoldt
(New York: W. W. Norton, 1984).

*The Outdoor Athlete: Total Training for Outdoor Per-
formance,* by Steve Ilg (Evergreen, CO: Cordillera
Press, 1989).

Ragged Mountain Press Guide to Outdoor Sports, by
Jonathan Hanson and Roseann Beggy Hanson
(Camden, ME: Ragged Mountain Press, 1997).

*Soft Paths: How to Enjoy the Wilderness Without
Harming It,* by Bruce Hampton and David Cole
(Mechanicsburg, PA: Stackpole Books, 1995).

*The Ultimate Adventure Sourcebook: The Complete
Resource for Adventure Sports and Travel,* by Paul
McMenamin, et al. (Atlanta: Turner Publishing,
1992).

FIRST AID AND SPORTS MEDICINE

Commonsense Outdoor Medicine and Emergency Companion, 3d edition, by Newell Breyfogle (Camden, ME: Ragged Mountain Press, 1994).

Hypothermia: Death by Exposure, by William W. Forgey, M.D. (Merrillville, IN: ICS Books, 1985).

Medicine for the Outdoors: A Guide to Emergency Medical Procedures and First Aid, by Paul S. Auerbach, M.D. (Boston: Little, Brown, 1991).

The Onboard Medical Handbook: First Aid and Emergency Medicine Afloat, by Paul Gill, Jr., M.D. (Camden, ME: International Marine, 1997).

Sports Health: The Complete Book of Athletic Injuries, by William Southmayd, M.D., and Marshall Hoffman (New York: Perigee Books, 1984).

COOKING

Good Food for Camp and Trail: All-Natural Recipes for Delicious Meals Outdoors, by Dorcas Miller (Boulder: Pruett Publishing Company, 1993).

Kayak Cookery, by Linda Daniel (Old Saybrook, CT: The Globe Pequot Press, 1988).

Trail Food: Drying and Cooking Food for Backpackers and Paddlers, by Alan S. Kesselheim (Camden, ME: Ragged Mountain Press, 1997).

The One Pan Gourmet: Fresh Food on the Trail, by Don Jacobson (Camden, ME: Ragged Mountain Press, 1993).

The Portable Baker: Baking on Boat and Trail, by Jean and Samuel Spangenberg (Camden, ME: Ragged Mountain Press, 1997).

VIDEOS

Performance Sea Kayaking: The Basics . . . and Beyond (Performance Video and Instruction, Inc., Durango, CO; 970-259-1361)

Weather

NOAA (National Oceanic and Atmospheric Administration), Network Information Center Weather Page, www.nnic.noaa.gov

Weathering the Wilderness: The Sierra Club Guide to Practical Meteorology, by William E. Reifsnyder (San Francisco: Sierra Club Books, 1980).

Events and Symposia

Cape Breton Seakayak Symposium, sponsored by Island Scafari Seakayaking, Louisbourg, Nova Scotia; (902) 733-2309 (July)

Trade Association of Sea Kayaking (TASK), Mequon, WI; (414) 242-5228; sponsors the following symposia:

- East Coast Canoe and Kayak Symposium, (April)
- Chesapeake PaddleFest (May)
- Alaska Sea Kayak Symposium (May)
- West Coast Sea Kayak Symposium (September)

Organizations

SEA KAYAKING

Trade Association of Sea Kayaking, 12455 N. Wauwatosa Rd., Mequon, WI 53097; (414) 242-5228; http://www.halcyon.com/wtr/TASK.html.

North American Paddlesports Association, 12455 N. Wauwatosa Rd., Mequon, WI 53097; (414) 242-5228; http://www.halcyon.com/wtr/watersports_resources.html.

CONSERVATION

(*Organizations that have ocean-related conservation campaigns*)

Cousteau Society
Chesapeake, VA
(804) 523-9335
http://www.sky.net/~emily/cousteau.soc/

National Audubon Society
700 Broadway
New York, NY 10003
(212) 979-3000

Sea Shepherd Conservation Society
Marina del Rey, CA
(310) 301-7325

Sierra Club
85 Second St., 2nd Floor
San Francisco, CA 94105
(415) 977-5500

On the Web

Please be aware that World Wide Web page addresses (URLs, or Uniform Resource Locators) change frequently. If you cannot find a page listed below, try searching for the subject in a global search engine, such as Lycos, Infoseek, or Magellan.

GORP (Great Outdoor Recreation Pages), http://www.gorp.com/

General Paddling Information News Group (includes whitewater), news:rec.paddle

Outside Online, http://outside.starwave.com

Yahoo Outdoor Pages, http://www.yahoo.com/entertainment/outdoors

and

Yahoo Outdoor Magazines Reference Page, http://www.yahoo.com/entertainment/outdoors/magazines/

APPENDIX B

PROVISIONING LISTS

Master List

PADDLING GEAR

Boat	Paddles	Spray skirt
PFD	Bilge pump	Bailer
Sponge	Security cable	Cockpit cover
Compass	Deck bag	Dry bags and boxes

SAFETY EQUIPMENT

Meteor flares	Parachute flares	Paddle float
Signal mirror	Whistle	Strobe
VHF radio	Sea anchor	Smoke flares
Handheld flares	EPIRB	See/Rescue banner
Tow line	Sea Wings	Barometer
Knife	Anemometer	

NAVIGATION

Charts	Compass	Tide tables
Dividers	Map measurer	Straightedge
GPS	Pilot guide	Pencil
Chart case		

KITCHEN

Fuel bottle(s)	Potscrubber	Cooking knife
Stove	Dish soap	Spatula
Stove repair kit	Cooking oil	Spices
Heat diffuser	Pots	Potgripper
Fry pan	Griddle	Outback Oven
Utensils	Spatula	Large spoon

Whisk	Matches	Measuring cup
Plates	Bowls	Cups
Trash bags	Paper towels	Aluminum foil
Can opener	Grater	Bottle opener
zip-top bags	Containers	Grill
Filter holder	Coffee filters	Thermos
Egg holder	Spice kit	Water bottles
Water filter		

BEDROOM

Tent	Ground cloth	Stakes
Tarp	Parawing	Therm-a-Rest
Thermalounger	Sleeping bag	Bag liner
Pillow	Guylines	Awning poles

BATHROOM

Soap/Sea soap	Shampoo	Towel
Toothbrush	Toothpaste	Mirror
Comb	Brush	Deodorant
Razor	Lotion	SunShower
Toilet paper	Matches	Trowel

MEDICAL KIT

Sunscreen	Insect repellent	Hydrocortisone
Band-Aids	Chapstick	cream
SAM splint	Bandage shears	Dressings
Thermometer	Sawyer Extractor	Sting-eze swabs
Forceps	Moleskin	Hemostats
Ace bandage	Elbow support	Spenco 2nd Skin
		Needle

Eye pads   Adhesive tape   Cold packs

Knuckle   Irrigation syringe   Butterfly closures
  bandages

Antiseptic swabs Dental kit   10% iodine solution

Dramamine   Aspirin   Acetaminophen

Antihistamine   Ibuprofen   Pepto-Bismol
                                          tablets

Mylanta   Immodium   Aloe vera gel

Prescription drugs   EpiPen

Eyedrops

CLOTHING

Pants   Shirts   Underwear

Hats   Socks   Fleece jacket

Paddling jacket   Wet suit   Dry suit

Thermalstretch   Gloves   Booties
  suit

Water shoes   Sandals   Hiking shoes

Shorts   Sweater   Thermal underwear

Bandannas   Pogies   Rubber boots

Belt   Sunglasses

MISCELLANEOUS

Flashlight   Spare flashlight   Batteries

Spare bulbs   Lantern   Spare mantles

Fanny pack   Binoculars   Camera equipment

Fishing gear   Field guides   Naturalist gear

Journal   Snorkeling gear   Bear repellent

TOOLS AND SPARE PARTS

See Chapter 13, page 192.

APPENDIX C

ENGLISH AND METRIC CONVERSIONS

Here's a simple and easy way to convert from English to metric measurements, or vice versa. Just grab your calculator.

- Multiply English units by the given factor to get metric units.
- Divide metric units by the given factor to get English units.

English Units	Factor	Metric Units
inches	2.54	centimeters
feet	30.48	centimeters
yards	0.9144	meters
pounds	0.454	kilograms
ounces	28.34	grams
fluid ounces	28.41	milliliters

(Compiled by Nick Schade, *The Strip-Built Sea Kayak*, International Marine, 1998)

I N D E X